A Feast Of

FLOWERS

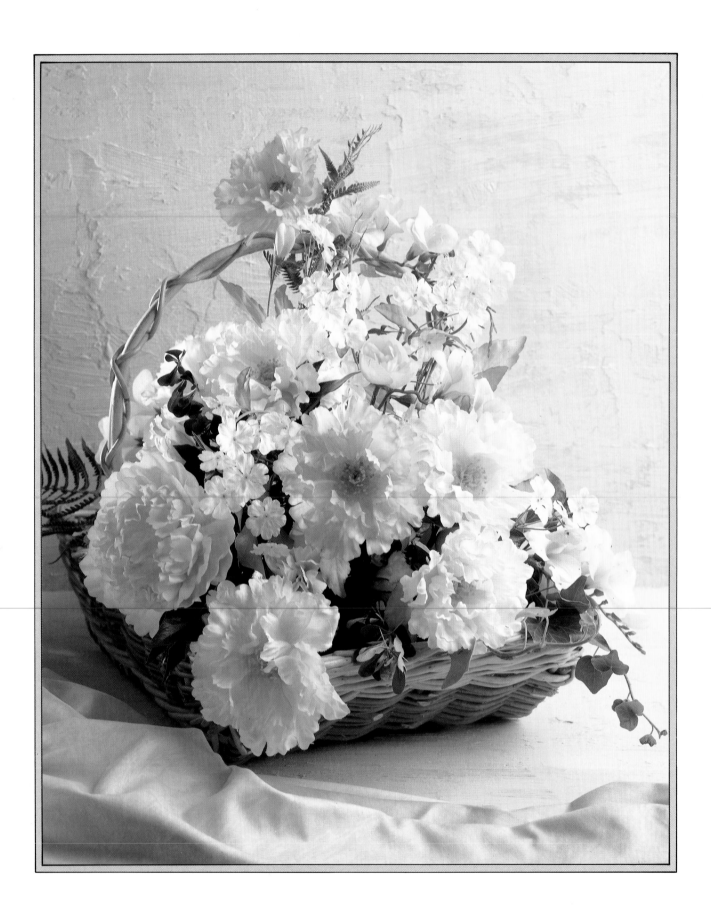

A Feast Of

FLOWERS

Arranged · Dried · Artificial

PAMELA WESTLAND

MARSHALL CAVENDISH

Published by Marshall Cavendish Books Limited
119 Wardour Street
London W1V 3TD

© Marshall Cavendish Limited 1987, 1991

Earlier editions of this book were
published under the title *Creative
Flowercraft*.
This edition published 1991

ISBN 1 85435 394 2

Printed and bound in Singapore.

CONTENTS

INTRODUCTION
Page 7

Chapter 1
ARRANGING FRESH FLOWERS
Page 8

Chapter 2
DRIED FLOWER CRAFT
Page 66

Chapter 3
ARTIFICIAL FLOWERS
Page 100

Chapter 4
HEALTH AND BEAUTY
Page 130

Chapter 5
FOOD AND FLOWERS
Page 148

INDEX
Page 165

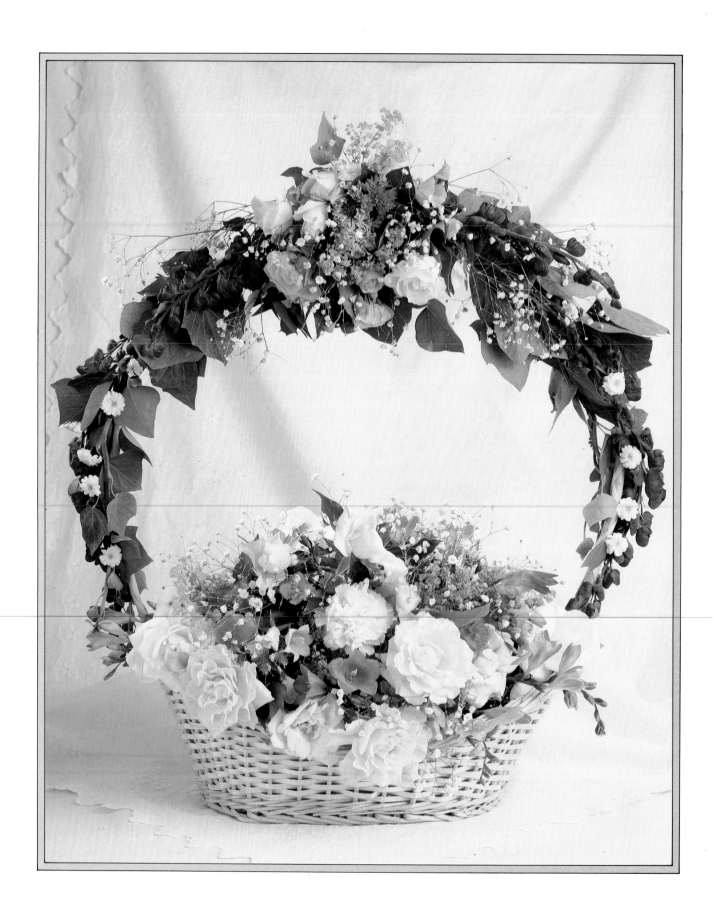

INTRODUCTION

Flowers are an important and wonderful part of our lives and our heritage. When we walk round a garden, the beauty of the flower borders, the medley of colours and the mingling scents have an effect which is both calming and exciting. When we pass a flower stall or florist's shop on a busy or gloomy day, the glimpse of buckets and bunches of brilliant blooms gives the heart – and the imagination – a lift.

For natural materials to decorate our homes and set the scene for memorable family and public occasions, we choose flowers – as we do when we want to express our deepest feelings, of joy, congratulations or sympathy. Flowers have a special role as a fashion accessory, at the most joyous of occasions such as weddings, or festivals or during blissful midsummer days when wearing flowers in our hats, our hair and on our clothes expresses most strongly what we feel.

Flowers have a special role on our tables too, not only as decorations but as delicious ingredients. In generations past flowers were food and drink to people who did not consider that vegetables and flowers had distinct uses; many people were as likely to toss marigolds in salads and make a dessert from roses as they were to put these flowers in a vase.

Catching sight of flowers growing in all their majesty and simplicity, it is tempting to wish the season could go on for ever, and that flowers would never fade. Here is a wish that is easily granted, as we discover that more and more plant materials can be dried in the air or in powder – some even in microwave ovens – and will retain their colour, shape and form almost indefinitely.

Designing with dried blooms is a branch of flower craft which has lasting satisfaction. A basket of dried rosebuds, marjoram, lady's mantle and larkspur can be pure nostalgia – summer captured and held as a beautiful and tangible memory. Our instructions show you how easily this dream can come true.

The fragrance of flowers accounts for a significant part of their charm. Centuries ago people scented their rooms with dried flower pot pourri, and enhanced their own personal appeal with floral scents and cosmetics. Today when natural products are finding renewed favour, this is a therapeutic aspect of flower craft that is both topical and relevant. Many of our recipes for skin care, hair care and other beauty products draw on medieval herbals for their authenticity, many of our ideas show you how to turn these pure, homemade products into the most delightful and acceptable of gifts.

Since flowers from the palest rose to the boldest sunflower are so beautiful, it would be surprising indeed if they had not inspired the flattery of imitation. Here is a pastime which requires little artistic talent, yet offers an exhilarating challenge. How, with crepe paper, silk or satin can you hope to emulate nature itself? Our design instructions show you simply and clearly the various techniques needed to create paper, fabric, sugar and even bread flowers, and our photographs demonstrate just how delightful they can be.

This book is a celebration of the beauty of flowers. It covers every aspect of the craft from the moment you bring flowers into the home, to the time when you use them in designs, cosmetics, food and drinks, and when with a little leisure time to spare, you decide to create everlasting blooms of your own.

A handful of flowers and leaves picked from the garden, combined with a few purchased blooms can make a rich, and generous display.

Chapter 1
ARRANGING FRESH FLOWERS

Arranging flowers is very much a matter of creating a feeling, a look, a mood, an impression; and, as an art form, it is a wonderful way of expressing your own personality. No two people would cut an identical bunch of flowers if they had the freedom of a lovely garden, or make a precisely similar selection of blooms if they were given *carte blanche* in a flower market.

One person might seek out the most striking shapes of flowers in one particular colour and then select others to complement them in terms of tone and texture; another might gather up a modest posy of tiny blooms in pale and insignificant tints; a third person, perhaps without being aware of it, might instinctively select bold, showy blooms in widely contrasting colours; and yet another would concentrate on foliage with well-defined colours and shapes, adding a few eye-catching flowers as highlights.

No two people would arrange a bunch of flowers in precisely the same way either – designing with flowers makes such a personal statement that there are no hard and fast rules to follow. There are, however, certain general guidelines which make it easier to create, with complete assurance, the effect you seek, whether it is casual or classically formal.

Colour has a profound effect not only on the flower design itself but – taking into account the background

Before visiting your local florist see what plants are to hand. Potted herbs, a garden rose bush heavy with blooms, or an evergreen shrub that needs pruning could all provide good display materials.

and lighting – the way it is perceived. You would set yourself an uphill task if you tried to brighten a shadowy room corner with a bunch of deep crimson anemones, or a vase of dark green foliage, but put red and green together and you will find that each colour brings out the best in the other.

Mixing and matching the colours of plant materials has all the fascination of creating colours on an artist's palette; and to achieve pleasing designs with flowers a similar appreciation of colour is useful. In several of the following pages we explore the intriguing theory of colour as it relates to flower craft, and show how to translate that knowledge into floral designs which, however simple, make maximum impact.

CONTAINERS AND HOLDERS

The hunt for the ideal container, whether you are arranging flowers just because it is a lovely day or to set the scene for a celebration party, can take you into every part of the home. Jugs, teapots, wine glasses, trays, boxes, baking trays, cooking pans, flower pots, nothing escapes the attention of the floral art enthusiast. We examine the design possibilities of various types of container – those with especially narrow or wide apertures, ones with a built-in pedestal and others which are completely flat – and the materials you need, in each case, to hold the stems in place.

Crumpled wire mesh, marbles, blocks of soaked foam and heavy metal pin-holders are sometimes associated only with the most complicated and formal of designs, but even the most carefree of flower groups may be easier to arrange and prettier to look at if the stems are held with a scrap of crushed wire. Using such materials does not make the arranger's task more difficult, as is sometimes supposed, but considerably easier. Not only that, the materials allow you to shape your designs. A group of tulips gently inclined in just the way they grow, a ring of fragrant leaves and flowers as a wall decoration or a stone jar spilling over with purple foliage will invariably need holding materials to help you formulate the designs.

Our ideas for flowers to carry and wear range from a totally uninhibited head-dress, digging deep into centuries of pastoral tradition for its origins, to romantically pretty and frankly feminine posies, headband and lapel flowers to wear for a wedding. With a certain amount of practice, a little help from a roll of fine wire and our step-by-step diagrams, these wedding-day designs are easy and very rewarding to create.

BEFORE YOU BEGIN

Whether you have a brilliantly coloured bunch of hothouse flowers bought on impulse, or a cluster of pretty blooms cut from the garden you naturally want to keep looking their best for as long as possible.

Take market flowers first. They have probably had a long journey, and will often have to adjust to a drastic change of temperature. Make the transition as easy as possible. Cut all flower stems as soon as you get them home, preferably under water. This prevents the formation of an air lock (which would inhibit the stems from taking up water) and is especially worthwhile for all sappy specimens.

Fill a wide-necked bowl with tepid water – making sure that it is not ice-cold, as that would be too much of a shock for the plants. Then, with a sharp-bladed craft-knife or secateurs, cut the stems diagonally, at a wide angle. This action exposes the maximum surface area to their only source of nourishment, the water. Give all flowers a good long drink in a bucket of tepid water, all day or even overnight.

Gathering flowers from the garden puts you in control at every stage. In the summer, cut them at the coolest time of the day, in the morning or evening, never in the full glare of the sun. And on a really hot day take a bucket of tepid water around the garden and plunge the stems into it immediately they are cut.

Cut is the operative word. Never snap, twist, tear or wrench stems from the plant. This not only risks damaging the parent plant but at worst, can wrest it from the ground. In addition, jagged stems are open to infection which can shorten significantly the vase life of the flowers. If you are given to rushing out and gathering a few flowers on the spur of the moment, keep a pair of secateurs at the ready. Once indoors, recut the stem ends, preferably under water.

Ideally, cut flowers at their 'full bud' stage. For long spikes like larkspur and clarkia this means capturing them when a few lower blooms are fully open and the rest taper to a thin point of tight buds.

VARYING THE TREATMENT

Different plant types need different kinds of treatment. The flowers of spring bulbs (the poet Wordsworth's 'host of golden daffodils' for example) are the ones to buy or cut on impulse, but to arrange on the following day. Be sure to cut off the lower, white fleshy part of the stems, even if it means lowering your sights from the tall arrangement you had in mind – the base of this type of stem is a lazy drinker. Leave bulb flowers in their pre-arrangement water for several hours, to allow the sap to drain off. This is an offensive substance that sours the water.

Other plants with sappy stems, including poppies, zinnias, euphorbias (spurge) and poinsettias, need a drastic approach in order to seal in the sap. Cut the stems (under water again) and seal the wound (for that is what a cut is) by burning it with a match or candle flame. It is not necessarily the chore it sounds. You can achieve a steady rhythm by keeping two candles burning, and picking up and searing two stems at a time.

Tulips can pose a special problem as they tend to twist and turn in all directions. To keep them on the straight and narrow, wrap the stems closely in newspaper or thick wrapping paper before putting them in water.

The tall stately flowers with long, hollow stems – delphiniums and lupins are examples – crave individual attention, too. Cut the stems at an angle and, using a syringe or small funnel, fill the stems with water, before plugging them with tight little wads of cotton wool. This seals in their own private water reservoir.

One more major category to consider is plants with woody stems, such as roses, hydrangeas and many other shrubs. Strip 5-7.5 cm (2-3 inches) off the bark from the stem end and lightly crush the base with a hammer, or split it criss-cross with a sharp blade.

Both methods achieve the desired result, encouraging the stem to take up water more readily. An initial aperitif of warm water in a deep container works wonders, especially with wilting roses.

PRESERVING LIFE

Now all the flowers are suitably prepared and ready to be arranged. Later in this book we look at the choice of container, stem-holding material, and the design and shape of arrangements. Let us jump that stage for the moment and assume the design is complete. What can you do to keep it in all its glory?

First of all, if the flowers are arranged in water, make sure that it is constantly as fresh as possible. Scrupulously clean containers go without saying, so stripping off all leaves that would be immersed in water helps. A few pieces of charcoal, or a sachet of commercially prepared 'preserving solution' or simply an aspirin and 2.5 ml (½ tsp) of bleach in the water will increase the life of the flowers. Top up the water daily, and keep the holding foam evenly moist.

Be as vigilant about cut flowers as you might about those growing in the garden. Cut off leaves as they discolour, snip off dead and faded flowers and from time to time re-cut stems to encourage new buds.

Place your arrangement where it will win the most compliments, but resist the magnetism of a sunny windowsill or a cosy corner near a radiator. Cut flowers like it cool. If the room is hot and stuffy at night, transfer the flowers to a cool spot, even if this is the garage floor: they will reward you handsomely.

COLOUR SENSE

Think about flowers. Think about colour. Put the two together, and you create the most amazing living permutation in the world – a floral kaleidoscope. Think of a bowl of red tulips silhouetted against a shadowy white wall. Each flower is so sharply defined it seems almost one dimensional, like a naive, primitive painting. Not only that, but because of the starkness of the colour contrast, the red flowers will be visually intensified in colour. They will appear almost black, losing much of their detail, and be highlighted only in terms of their shape.

Replace those red flowers with white ones and, white on white, the mood changes dramatically. You no longer see the sculptured shape of the flowers so clearly. Instead, you become more aware of the velvety softness of the petals and their waxlike sheen. The wall and the flowers may share a common neutral colour, but they will never share a natural texture.

Fill that bowl for a third time, with flowers in every colour of the rainbow, and you swing into an entirely different mood. The flowers may be of a similar size and shape – say they are tulips again – but some will shout out to be noticed, while others will almost defy definition at even a second or third glance. And that takes a bit of explaining.

The reasons are many and various, and we would have to study the group carefully to see exactly which colours meet in the arrangement, how pale or dark those colours are, whether the design is seen in natural or artificial light, and from which direction the main light source comes. All that theory apart – and we come to its significance later – one thing is certain. That bowl of jazzy, colour-saturated tulips will be a happy sight indeed.

PRIMARIES AND SECONDARIES

Look at a garden or across a sweep of countryside and you will find that there's no point in trying to count the number of hues you see in nature. There are only three primary colours and three secondary colours, but there is a breathtaking, infinitesimal number of hues which appear in all kinds of plant material, and are yours for the choosing.

No-one suggests that it is essential to go deeply into the engrossing theory of colour before you can arrange a bowl of summer flowers or select a suitable container for them. But there's no denying that a little knowledge, absorbed and then almost forgotten, is a great help in achieving just the natural, carefree effect you want.

The three primary colours are red, yellow and blue. These are the ones that, as pigments, cannot be made by mixing other colours together. Imagine those three colours in segments of a wheel – or slices of a cake – with spaces between each of them. Those alternating spaces are taken up by the secondary colours, the ones made by mixing two of the primaries. Mix primary red and yellow together and you get secondary orange, to fill in the gap between them. In flower terms that means marigolds, zinnias, dahlias, chrysanthemums, for instance.

Mix primary yellow and blue and you get green, and the basis for every conceivable green from the sharpest lime of frothy alchemilla mollis to the deep, blue-green of spiky evergreen leaves such as yew and cupressus.

Stir up the remaining pair of primary colours, blue and red, for the whole range of deep, mysterious purples – violets, lavender, saintpaulias and anemones – the last of the three secondary colours.

That gives you the six principal colours, positioned around the imaginary wheel in the sequence they are seen in the rainbow. But it doesn't end there. Study any petal or leaf and you will see, almost without exception, that the depth of the colour is anything but constant. A vibrant red poppy petal will appear much darker at the base where it is thicker, but shade to a

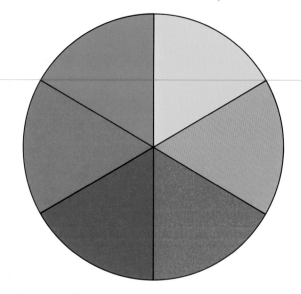

As these casually placed containers show, striking arrangements need not necessarily include unusual hues or closely harmonized colours.

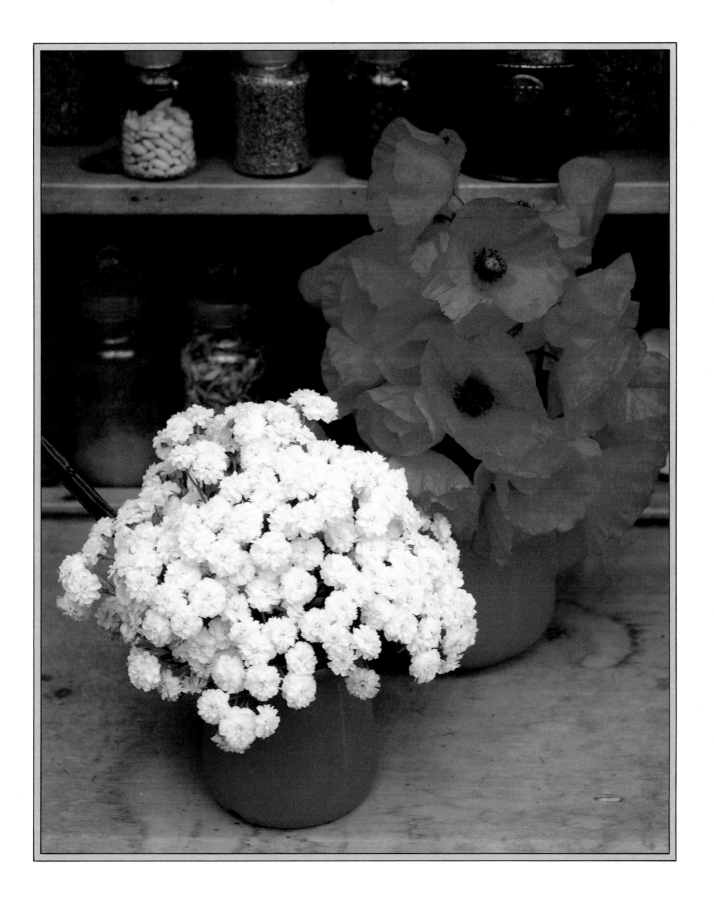

paler tint at the tip. If the petal is translucent, and light is shining through it, the colour will be significantly weakened and appear much paler. This light factor fundamentally alters the character of the colour.

ACROSS THE RANGE

Shades, tones and tints are familiar words which have specific meanings in relation to colour, meanings which are sometimes obscured in everyday usage. Shades are the deepest hues of any colour, created by mixing the raw colour with black. To reproduce the colour of the very deepest, velvety-ermine, old fashioned roses an artist would mix red and black; to capture the strongest hue of a purple iris or hyacinth would need red, blue and black, and so on.

Tones are inbetweens, achieved by mixing the basic colour with grey. Red and grey in varying proportions would portray the zingy, vibrant pinks of, for example, carnations, fuchsias and paeonies. And at the palest end of the scale are the tints, made by blending the base colour with white; red with a dash of white for a red slightly on the pale side of scarlet; white with a dash of red for sweet peas in the most delicate tints of sugar-almond colours.

And there you have it, six colours, a never ending range of shades, tones and tints of each of them, and a dazzling choice when it comes to the moment of decision; what to put with what in order to make the very best of your plant materials.

Back to the artist's colour wheel again. The sequence of the colours in the six segments is the key to the effect each flower and leaf will have on its neighbours in any group you arrange.

COLOUR PARTNERSHIPS

To bring the phrase 'the attraction of opposites' to life in your designs, try linking flowers and leaves in each of the three pairs of colours opposite each other on the imaginary wheel. Red and green, orange and blue, and yellow and purple are the pairings considered to be most flattering to each other, and are termed 'complementary colours'.

Suppose you have a single red flower that you would like to use, to become the focus of attention in a design. Help it on its way by surrounding it with green flowers, bracts or leaves. A brilliant deep red carnation nestling in a bowl of that lovely pale green variety of nicotiana; a cluster of flame-red roses tumbling over a spire of misty Bells of Ireland; even a single specimen

rose placed so that it is viewed against a background of leaves on the stem, or that joyful natural gift of winter, jazzy red berries glowing among the evergreens. No other colour but green will pay reds of whatever hue such a perfect compliment. No other neighbouring colour, and certainly not neutral white, will make the red appear so vibrant, yet allow the eye to take in every detail of the line, form and texture of the flower or fruit.

At first glance, the orange and blue partnership may seem to offer less spontaneous possibilities. But the theory holds good. Gather together a handful of orange and blue pansies, orange marigolds and blue cornflowers, or a single sunshine gold alstroemeria amidst a bunch of midnight blue lilies and you will find that they sit in perfect harmony.

For the third 'colour marriage', yellow and purple, there can be no more delightful examples than a child's Mother's Day posy of dainty primroses and

Above: *This predominately yellow and white arrangement, using garden-grown wild flowers, comes to life with the addition of flowers in the complementary colour of purple.*
Opposite: *Simple but novel, this design, with anemone and spray chrysanthemum heads on a cake cooling tray, uses a similar colour combination.*

violets, or the showier springtime alternative of daffodils and anemones.

If a single precious flower has survived a bunch which was an extravagant fling at the florist's, turn on the spotlight by mingling it with yellow blooms. The purple will glow like a flower bathed in sunlight.

Just as an experiment, and to prove the point, hold a flower of a similar colour against blues and reds. These are the colours placed on each side of purple on the colour roundabout and, being so closely related, want a share of its limelight. Now you will scarcely notice your purple flower at all. It has become a 'shy violet'.

GOOD NEIGHBOURS

Colour mixtures chosen from hues which are neighbours on the colour wheel are termed 'adjacent'. A bunch of anemones is a perfect example, all the blue, purple and red flowers attracting equal attention and forming a unified group. Another would be orange and yellow spray chrysanthemums arranged with green foliage of a more or less equal hue (dark green with strong shades, light green with pale tints). Don't expect there to be any obvious stars of the show, just a uniformly good looking chorus.

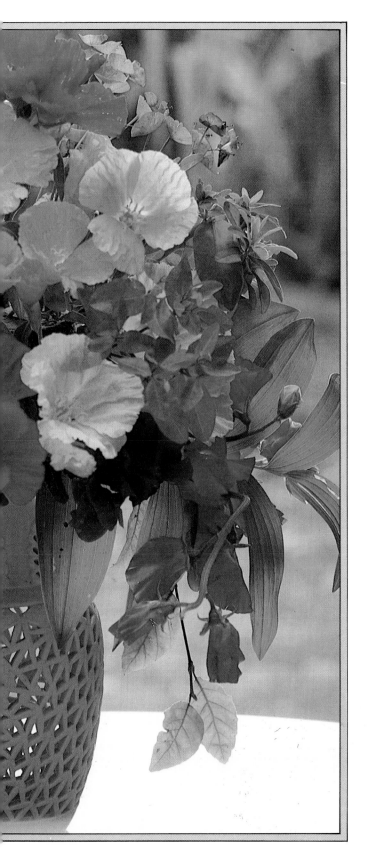

Far left: *A single red chrysanthemum in the midst of muted green foliage provides a strong focal point for this arrangement.*
Left: *By contrast, red flowers scattered amongst salmon and pink coloured blooms lose their dramatic impact, but add depth to this vase arrangement.*

In many flower designs green, the colour of such a high proportion of foliage, joins grey, brown and white as a neutral colour. This is because, in the context of plant materials, we expect to see green leaves (brown ones, too) and so tend to discount their colour as a contributory element.

MATCHING MOODS

So much for the effect that various colours have on each other. What about the effect they have on you, and on your home? You can match your mood, set the background to a party or other special occasion, emphasise good architectural points such as an arch or window or even disguise less agreeable features simply with the colours of the flowers you choose.

Red flowers have a number of connotations. First and foremost, perhaps, the romantic one. Red roses signify true love; red rosebuds a young, tender, unfolding love. A heart shaped posy of red roses offered on St Valentine's day or on a special anniversary speaks volumes, and does so more charmingly than words. (Other examples of the enchanting – and largely Victorian inspired – language of flowers are given on pages 98-9).

There is no problem if you wish to create a romantic mood, then. Red flowers of other species can convey a bold, devil-may-care spirit. A pitcher of bright scarlet chrysanthemums might seem to suggest an uncompromising attitude, almost a challenge, and a jug of field poppies a relaxed, informal mood. Casually blended with a clutch of grasses or cereals, poppies look delightfully at home in a farmhouse-style kitchen, setting the scene for a harvest buffet or a simple soup and salad meal.

If reds span every mood from high romance to happy-go-lucky, pink flowers are without exception in a softer mould. Pink roses, carnations and pinks

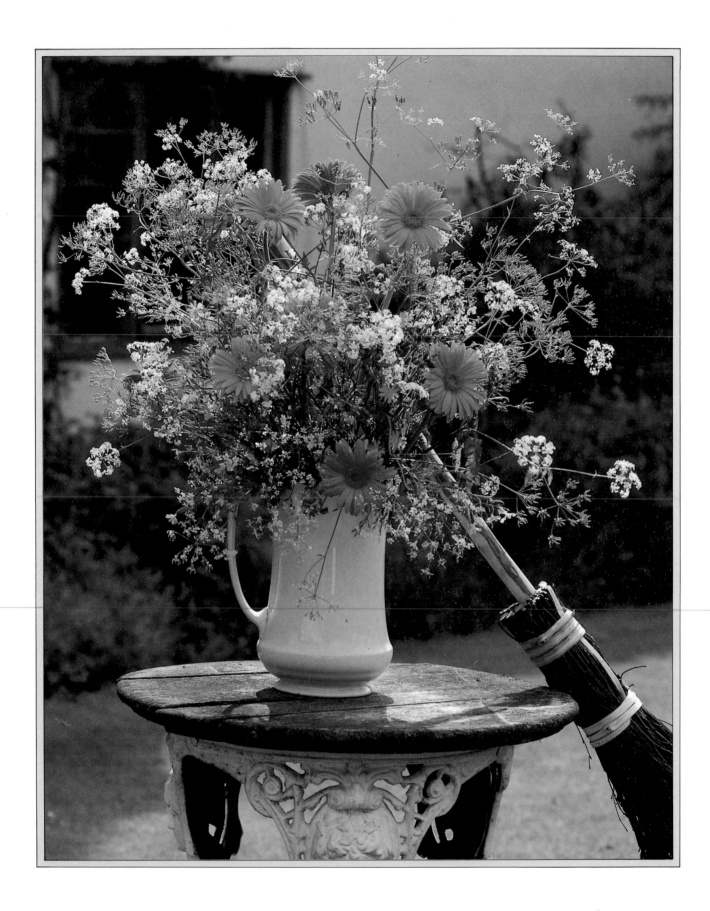

are the number one choice of young brides for flowers to carry and wear, and set a nostalgic scene in formal arrangements in church or the reception hall. A basket of pink daisies to greet the birth of a baby, a cascade of pink lilies as a gift for an honoured guest – somehow pink spells achievement and glamour.

Orange flowers positively glow. Arrange a basket of orange gaillardias, or gerberas in the hearth when it is not quite cold enough to light a fire, and you can almost toast your hands on the comforting effect. Fill an earthenware pot with pale tangerine-orange wallflowers or marigolds and they will gleam beside a patio barbecue long after the last embers have died away. To bring out every last flicker of warmth, arrange orange flowers from elegant lilies to innocent daisy types, in copper pots and pans.

SUN POWER

There is no doubt about it, yellow is a happy, 'open the windows and let the sun stream in' colour. You have only to introduce yellow flowers of any kind and you create rays of imaginary sunshine in the home. It is, I suspect, impossible to arrange yellow flowers of any kind and yet create a sombre design. From the first citrus yellow daffodils of spring through to the rich, golden tones of falling leaves and, timed to coincide with them, glowing dahlias and chrysanthemums, yellow flowers gladden the heart. Between times there are dazzling buttercups and yellow-centred daisies, so tempting that creative fingers itch to twine them round a hatband, or link them to form a bracelet. Fingers trailing over the side of the boat, a picnic on the river bank, that's the kind of mood that the yellow flowers of summer seem to suggest.

Think of green flowers, of green foliage, and you can almost hear the tinkling of a waterfall, the swish of a stream, the curving upwards spray of a fountain. Green has a cooling effect. As a neutral colour in the plant context it separates vibrant colours and dilutes

Partly smothered by a veil of sheep's parsley, the showy, vibrant pink gerberas in this display become more pleasing to the eye.

exuberant mixtures. In this way the addition of green foliage or other plant materials renders sharp colour combinations attractive and acceptable.

Blue is for beauty, it is said. It is also a 'cool' colour but – unlike green – not considered a neutral hue which merges into the background. From the palest tints of dainty wild flowers such as speedwell to the deep, resonant shades of grape hyacinths and iris, blue spans almost every mood.

Reminiscent of a brilliant cloudless sky, blue flowers evoke a countrified air; perpetual cornflowers, forget-me-nots, periwinkle, even thistles look bright and beautiful against a glowing orange or yellow wall or curtain. Tall spires of midnight blue delphinium, larkspur and clarkia, and their less stately cousins, lilac, flag irises and lilies lend an air of unmistakable elegance. These are a grand choice for formal occasions and large areas.

Purple, perhaps the most impressive and formal colour of all, is not all that easy to use. Clusters of purple flowers in a group composed largely of yellow, blue and white can be the most rewarding. But having said that, a shallow bowl filled to overflowing with a single variety of deep, shadowy purple iris can look positively regal.

WHITE LIGHTS

The mention of white as neutral in terms of plant colour may be misleading, and worthy of comment. Some keen floral artists can scarcely conceive of a design without highlights of white – and that is just the element it does provide. Do not blend white flowers with others which you want to emphasize – they will surely steal the show – and never dot white flowers here, there and everywhere in a design. Unless, that is, you crave a polka dot creation. For almost without exception the white material will glow out of the design like a beacon and, no matter how much it is in fact recessed, it will appear dominant.

It takes exceptions to prove a rule, or disprove a statement. In the case of white plant materials the exceptions are all the misty, frothy flowers. Tiny gypsophila and the alternatives of snow-flaky sheep's parsley or cow parsley can draw a soft, flattering veil over powerful colours and strong outlines, and create the illusion of a soft tint in place of a vibrant hue. If ever someone gives you a bunch of, shall we say, carnations or pinks that are a deal too bright for your liking, curtain them with see-through whites – the floral equivalent to curtain 'sheers' – and give the showy creatures a new and more modest personality.

Juggling successfully with flower colours, shaking the floral kaleidoscope, is almost like having a new source of light at your fingertips. Use white, yellow and the palest tints of pink, orange, green and blue flowers and foliage to advantage.

These are the colours to brighten a dark corner, draw attention to a shadowy arch or other design feature, silhouette against a dark piece of furniture – a polished dark oak chest maybe – or use outdoors for an evening party. As twilight falls and trees and shrubs fade into gentle obscurity, a tub of pastel coloured flowers will glow far into the night.

EXTRA REFLECTIONS

By contrast, strong, bold colours will catch the eye only if the design is adequately lighted. In shadowy situations even the most brazen reds and oranges can go quite gloomy on you, and deep blues and purples will completely disappear.

It follows, naturally, that light has a visual make-or-break part to play in floral craft. Most flattering of all, and difficult to imitate precisely, are shafts of streaming sunlight. Yet even this can prove to be too much of a good thing. For the sake of longevity, place fresh and dried flowers, for preference, in diffused light, or where light is reflected, but not in the full glare of hot sun. Delightful as it is to see a jug of flowers on a sunny windowsill, the pleasure can be short lived. Sun and strong light draw out colour from natural plant materials and, of course, from synthetic materials too.

You might try turning a spotlight on a flower group. Experiment by twisting the light source so that it strikes the flowers from different angles; you will find that you can completely change the mood of the design. Shine a light from behind, through a glass bowl filled perhaps with glass marbles and holding delicate foliage, and you create the illusion of cool, running water. Throw a light on to a well defined flower arrangement against a pale wall, and the shadows it casts will add a new dimension. Light a bowl of flowers from above and you look into a sea of upturned faces, like pansies basking in the sunshine. Light a group from one side and you create an apparently wider range of tints and shades in the plant materials.

Colour and light. Light and dark. A single flower colour – a monotone design that is anything but monotonous – or a group composed of all the colours of the rainbow. Which is it to be? It's an exciting, exhilarating, never ending choice.

GETTING INTO SHAPE

The long and the short of it is that you can arrange flowers in any shape or form that pleases you. For what is flower craft except an art form, a way of expressing personal taste and individual interpretation of colour and balance? When all is said and done the only judgment to be made is whether the casual cluster of flowers in a jug or the towering arrangement on a concert platform is pleasing. For beauty, as everyone knows, is in the eye of the beholder.

Inspiration for flower designs is all around us, in gardens and many other kinds of landscape, in the work of artists, designers and photographers, in glimpses of colour, tricks of the light, in anything, in fact, that captures our imagination.

NATURAL BEAUTY

Nature itself is, of course, the greatest inspiration of all. If we can arrange flowers so that they seem as 'natural' as possible, and appear as close as can be to the way they grow, then our designs cannot fail to be attractive and pleasing.

As we have seen, a close observation of the countryside and the town garden gives a valuable insight into the infinitesimal range of colours that are all around us. Such observation also opens our eyes to the shapes formed by plants as they grow. We notice the ramrod straightness of some strong stems like gladioli and bulrushes; the severely angular twists of others, a gnarled old apple tree, for example; the gentle curves of delicate grasses gradually bent in the path of the wind; the way the branches of a sturdy oak tree radiate from the tree trunk like water cascading from a single source – and all these factors contribute to the ways we choose to arrange flowers.

Like slender, long-necked birds scanning the horizon, these freesias attract attention with their simple forms and clear-cut lines.

EXPLORING THE ARTS

We can draw our inspiration from the work of artists, observing with what simplicity Van Gogh treated a pot of sunflowers, and the glorious profusion of the flower collections of the works of the Dutch Old Masters. The latter, painted spring, summer, autumn and winter flowers as they bloomed and gathered them together later, in multi-seasonal bouquets on canvas. Today we can use dried or artificial flowers in the same way.

Visiting art galleries to see how painters over the centuries have portrayed flowers, museums to study floral motifs on pottery, jewellery, drapes and tapestries, and exhibitions of photography for a through-the-lens interpretation of plant materials, allows anyone who loves flowers to build up a bank of artistic impressions to interpret, however freely, for their own designs.

Armchair explorers, with no time for gallery browsing, can build up an inspirational collection of postcards, greetings cards, magazine cuttings and scraps of material. A Greek holiday postcard showing an earthenware pot brimming over with sweet basil set on a flight of sun drenched white stone steps does not necessarily make you want to rush out and buy a packet of basil seeds, though it well might. The soft, cushiony shape of the plant sets the mind racing. Could you achieve a similar effect with a bowl of pale green nicotiana flowers veiled with misty alchemilla mollis and displayed against a dazzling white wall? The answer is probably. But you don't quite know. Until you try.

The natural twist and flow of stems and the rounded and angular shapes of flowers and leaves are infallible clues to the mood and feeling of the arrangement you can create; evoking the bouncy soft characteristics of basil would be impossible with hard-edged mahonia or holly leaves, or with angular flowers like lilies and strelitzias.

THE TRADITIONAL SHAPES

Whether you plan your designs along traditional lines – to produce arrangements that could lead eventually to show and competition work – or decline to follow any guidelines at all is purely a matter of choice. But it is always worth learning a little of the recognised floral art code in order to create arrangements with 'formal' outlines.

Traditional floral art has its roots firmly planted in the close relationship between the shape of the plant

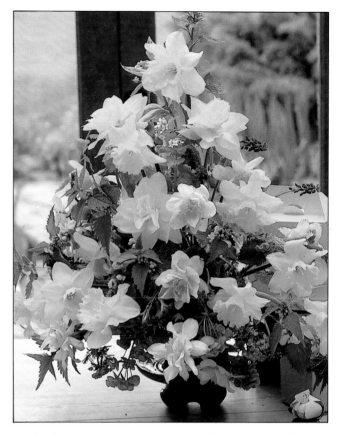

A plastic saucer holding a cylinder of foam supports this pyramid of daffodils.

material and the shape of the arrangement – a tip well worth taking, however much freedom you like to give yourself. Traditional design shapes may remind you of a geometry lesson – there are equal triangles, asymmetrical triangles, L shapes, curves, verticals, horizontals, and crescents – but interpreted in flowers and flowing leaves these shapes are far removed indeed from mathematical models.

The classroom and slide rule do come to mind, however, when calculating proportion and balance. In formalized designs the length of the longest stem is carefully calculated to be in a pre-determined ratio to the height or width of the container, or in some cases the base on which the container stands.

In a horizontal design, the long low kind that looks so much at home on a dining table, the main side stems are generally thought to be in perfect visual balance when they are each one and a half times the length of the container. Similarly for a vertical arrangement – the type that so eye-catchingly fills a niche or alcove – it is recommended that the tallest stem should extend to a height one and a half times that of the container. It is not a question of taking a rule to every arrangement, but of judging the

proportions by eye. Time and again you will find that what looks most easy and natural in this type of design, turns out to be within these guidelines.

It must be emphasized that we are dealing only with traditional designs which verge on the formal. Outside these limits, it is perfectly possible to place a bunch of white marguerites in a tall cylindrical vase, with no stems showing at all, and achieve a design which will have an agreeable vertical shape.

One of the simplest 'geometric' shapes is the equal triangle, which can be created on a flat dish, atop a tall container or, most formal of all, and often referred to as the 'English' design, on a pedestal. Draw an imaginary line through the centre of the container and the planned design, and that is where you place the tallest stem. The height of this stem should relate to the size of the container – it would look awkward and gangly to have a very long upright stem 'growing' out of a small compact container.

CARDINAL POINTS

The central or main stem is the key to all traditional floral art, and should be chosen most carefully. If you are aiming for crisp, straight lines, select a strong stem that will retain its military bearing and not wilt under the strain after a day or two. For a softer look, choose a stem with a very gentle curve.

Depending upon what effect you wish to create, the three points of the triangle may be defined either with bare twigs for a stark silhouette; or with flowering shrub branches such as forsythia and winter jasmine; or with spires of flowers such as delphinium, larkspur, clarkia or Bells of Ireland. For large pedestals, slender branches of foliage of lime, beech, copper beech or oak look good, and will bring the woodlands gracefully into your work.

If your triangular arrangement is raised in any way – if you are creating a table arrangement on a pedestal cake stand, or using a floor-standing pedestal – it is important to select lower side stems which have natural curves, some bearing to the right and some to the left. Be careful about snipping indiscriminately with the secateurs since the ultimate choice will be between trying to twist some stems almost to breaking point, or placing half of them the reverse way round, revealing the back of the leaves. No matter how attractive that view is, of one point you can be certain – the two sides will not match.

Once the central stem is positioned, the base of that stem becomes the 'growing source' of much of the material to follow. So be sure that there is plenty

Above: *Under this arc of flowers lies a foam block kept in position by a coffee jar lid.*
Right: *For an alternative display in restricted space, try an L-shaped composition keeping the plants free-flowing, and not too severely geometrical.*
Opposite: *A plastic ring filled with foam supports this brilliant, multi-coloured flower ring.*

of stem-pushing space around it. When you have just a few more vital stems to place, it is frustrating to discover that the pinholder is crammed to capacity or the block of foam is overcrowded to splitting point. (We go into more detail about these technicalities and how to avoid such frustrations in the following chapter.)

In a well balanced design, the eye should travel from the tip of the central stem down to the base of the stem, and then out to each side. It is usually best to 'strengthen' the central stem visually by placing another one slightly shorter and just to one side of it, partially overlapping, and another stem, shorter still, slightly to the other side. This avoids a spindly look near the centre.

FOCUSING ATTENTION

Since all other stems are placed as if they spring from the same source – like the branches of a tree radiating from the central trunk – this area becomes the centre of attention. In floral art terms, that is to say that it becomes the focal point. This is where you place your choicest flower, a single bloom of contrasting colour, a cluster of brilliantly light catching berries, or a posy of tiny blooms nestling among long-stemmed flowers, whatever you choose to make a visual statement.

From the central 'growing point', place the two main side stems, which in an equal triangle must naturally be of equal length, and then strengthen them with other stems that are slightly shorter. Now you can begin to fill in the design, recessing some flowers close against the container, and thrusting others forward to avoid a flat one-dimensional arrangement.

As you fill in the outlines keep the visual balance equal. This does not mean placing identical blooms in an identical spot on each side, or creating mirror images. It simply means having an equal 'weight' of material. To achieve this end, it can be helpful to divide the main flowers and stems into two groups; then you will be sure not to end up with a lop-sided look.

For an asymmetrical triangle (which might, in strictly nonmathematical terms, be described as a cross between an equal triangle and an L shape), follow the same guidelines but place the main upright stem off-centre and make one side point markedly shorter and a little higher than the other.

An L-shaped arrangement is a perfect example of just how well-balanced an asymmetrical design can be. The vertical stem should be about one and a half times the length of the container. The horizontal stem, placed almost parallel to the table or window ledge, will have more visual emphasis than the upright one, and appear longer than it really is. Compensate for this optical illusion by cutting the horizontal stem to between a half and three-quarters of the length of the upright stem. For instance, if the container is a dish, 20 cm (8 in) long, then the vertical stem should measure 30 cm (12 in) and the horizontal one, 15-22.5 cm (6-9 in).

Do not feel compelled to take the capital 'L' shape too literally in the interpretation of this design. A harsh right angle looks most ungainly. Place two or more shorter stems behind the main upright and leaning slightly backwards and, still behind the vertical, at least two of the largest flowers, leaves or pieces of fruit to balance others enclosed within the angle. Without these the design not only looks too angular, but also seems in danger of toppling over.

BEAUTY RULES

Traditional flower arrangements are not all sharp angles and rule measurements, of course – there is plenty of scope for gentle curves, smooth arcs, natural swoops and swirls forming crescents and even S shapes. One of the most classic shapes of all is the Hogarth curve (also known as the 'lazy S'), named after the 18th century English painter, William Hogarth, who called all flowing curves 'the line of beauty'. The elongated S, created with naturally curving stems, sits gracefully on a raised container such as a candlestick, the plant material curving gently upwards on one side and downwards on the other – though it is not an easy balance for beginners to achieve.

A similar container, one with a built-in pedestal, can be used to create a formal crescent shape, an arc of stems forming a dome effect in the centre and splashing down on each side like spouts from a fountain. An informal no-rules-to-follow version could simply be a bunch of tulips dipping in all directions over the rim of a tall vase.

An alternative is to invert the design. This scheme with the sides curving upwards in a continuous gentle

arc, can be balanced on a raised container. It will also look coolly elegant in a shallow glass bowl with icy blue and green material. You could use spiky stems of broom to outline the shape, and fill in with green hellebores and shafts of blue anemones and forget-me-nots.

Above: *Lily-flowered tulips held securely in a cylinder of foam within a shallow container create a sculptural, diagonal line.*

Opposite: *More loosely defined, the shape of this bunch of pinks, veering off-centre from the vase, provides an unusual feature.*

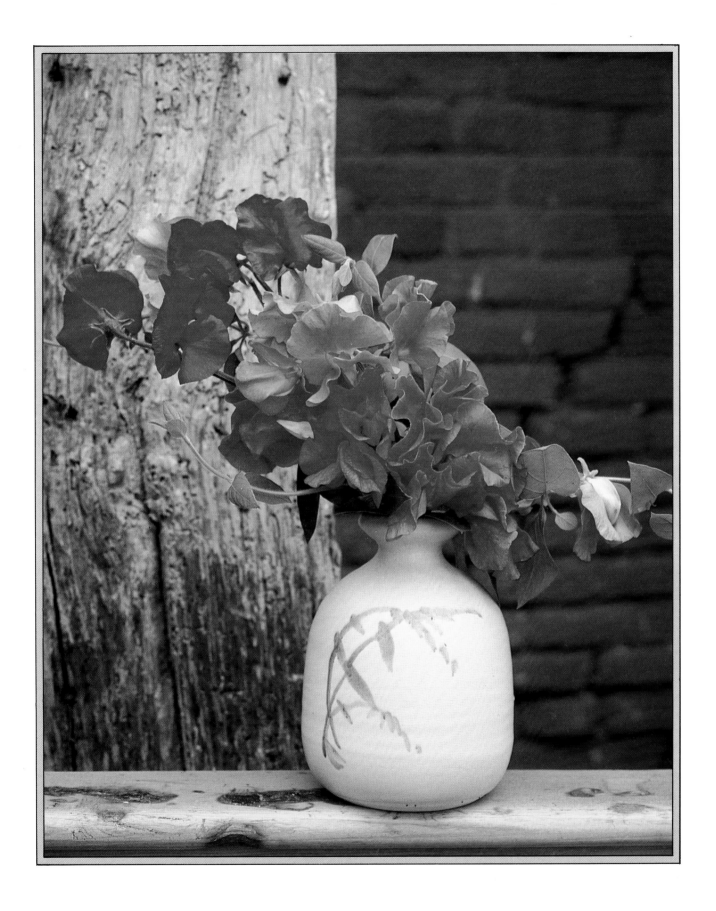

NATURAL DESIGNS

In all types of floral art, the size and shape of the flowers, leaves and other plant materials used, is just as important as what might be called the mathematical proportions of the design. The main central stem of an equal triangle may well be in correct proportion to the size of the container, but it would look uncomfortably top heavy if it had a giant dahlia perched on top of it.

In general, to achieve an easy-on-the-eye balance in traditional arrangements, flowers and foliage should be placed in graded formation. For the points of a triangle, the tips of an S shape or the limits of a crescent, use the thinnest, finest stems, or flowers in tight bud. In the centre of the design, place sprays of medium sized leaves and moderate sized flowers or those in half-open bud. For the base of the design you can achieve visual weight with large leaves such as those of hostas, bergenias, geraniums, nasturtiums – depending on the scale of the group – and the largest of the flowers, with fully opened blooms.

This sequence is entirely logical, as it follows the natural growing pattern. Consider a stately stem of delphinium just coming into flower. The buds at the top are still tightly closed, forming a point like that of a sword. Those towards the centre of the stem are beginning to open, and the shape is fuller and more rounded. And those at the base of the stem reveal the promise of things to come, the open flowers in all their glory.

GARDEN EXERCISE

It is an interesting exercise, relaxing, too, to walk around a garden or garden centre putting the flowers and foliage mentally into pigeonholes, into the three categories of pointed, midway and rounded – for the tips, centre and base of stylized designs.

A clump of purple foxgloves just coming into flower invites transition into the three points of a triangle. Hollyhocks, too large to use on the stem, make pretty fillers at the base, each flower used separately. Trails of variegated periwinkle and lamium leaves make pretty green and cream cascades while honeysuckle and clematis stems offer interesting foliage. Euphorbias bridge the gap between flowers and foliage with their brilliant green heads.

In the following section we go into the intriguing hunt for unusual containers, for formal and fun designs, and explore the many ways of keeping stems firmly in line.

CHOOSING CONTAINERS

No dictionary definition could possibly do justice to the description of a container for flowers. That fascinating article can be anything you can imagine or use to put flowers in, on, on top of, behind, beside, through, around or under. And, no matter if it is for fresh flowers, it does not even need to hold water. That's where an inner container comes in. So when it comes to choosing something to complement and contain fresh, dried or artificial flowers, one thing is certain. Absolutely anything goes.

Just to get the feel of the dazzling choice around us, let's have a look at the possibilities. You can arrange flowers in a lustre jug; inside a plaited bread ring as the centrepiece for a harvest supper; on a woven cane tray; balanced elegantly, pedestal fashion, on top of a tall wine carafe; behind a twisty, twirling piece of beach driftwood; tucked beside a frilled and scalloped piece of blue coral; pushed through the criss-crossed wires of a cake cooling tray; perhaps ringed around the rim of a silver candle-stick; or even recalling a Victorian bell jar, under an upturned glass tumbler.

There is obviously a close link between the container and the shape of the arrangement you plan. Traditional designs usually demand containers that facilitate building the triangles, horizontals and crescents we discussed in the previous chapter. But fun and even fantasy enter into the proceedings when you are creating free-style designs. Often a startlingly unusual container will call for the simplest adornment. A single white lily in a piece of steel piping might be enough to say it all.

Baking trays, teapots, jelly moulds, storage jars and measuring flasks are just a few of the potential containers you may find about your home.

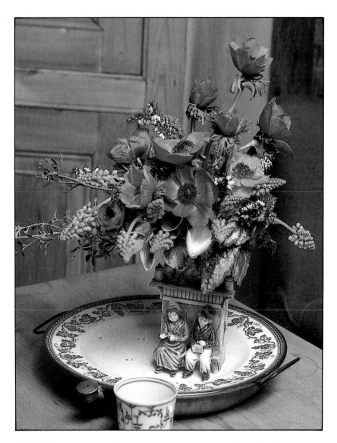

A Delftware container complements the blues of the anemones and grape hyacinths.

The container and the plant materials naturally forge a strong visual link. And in many flower designs there is another link that is anything but visual – the holding material that keeps the stems firmly in place and, according to its type, allows you to create any shape you wish.

STAGING THE PROPS

Take a tall, wide-necked cylindrical vase. Using no hidden persuaders (known in the floral art world as 'mechanics') at all, you might arrange a handful of flowers gracefully, but find you have little control over the stems. Some may decide to flop obstinately this way and that. By securing a pinholder in the base of the container, you can be sure that even the heaviest stems – such as branches of apple blossom – will stand obediently in line. If you fill the neck of the vase with a piece of crumpled wire mesh, creating a jagged dome full of uneven holes, you can push stems in at a variety of angles – confident that you know who is the boss.

By filling the aperture with a piece of stem-holding foam – pre-soaked in water for fresh materials – extending a little above the rim, you can angle stems horizontally and almost vertically downwards. They will all be held firmly and (if it applies) be able to take up water from the foam.

A neater way by far, however, is to fix another container to the top of the vase, and fill this with foam. Keep it topped up with water as required. An ideal solution for a cylindrical vase might be a plastic 'foam saucer' which has an indentation just the right size for holding a cylindrical block of foam. Stick the saucer firmly to the vase with extra tacky florist's clay or water-resistant tape, wobble it relentlessly to make sure it is secure and then go ahead with your arrangement, on a simple, improvised pedestal.

For flower displays on a large scale, such as a true, floor standing pedestal, stem holding precautions have to be more rigorous. As the container will never show, it does not matter how mundane and utilitarian it is. A large, deep vessel such as a pâté or baking dish will do. Fit it with one or two rectangular blocks of soaked foam standing on end and extending well above the rim. This will be your passport to downward sloping stems. Then, to make sure that a concentration of thick stems does not destroy it, cover the foam with crushed wire netting. Secure the dish to the pedestal top by the surest means you know – wrapping it round and round, like a parcel, with fine twine, wiring it to the pedestal rim or the upright.

THE CONTAINER HUNT

One of the most elating aspects of flower craft is the search for 'the right container'. Indeed, the continuing hunt for classic or unusual items can be an absorbing pastime in itself. Once you are really smitten by the bug it is almost impossible to let a car boot sale, a jumble sale, charity shop or auction go unheeded. You never know what you might find.

A lovely rose spattered coffee pot which is chipped or cracked may be unable to take its place on the after-dinner tray. But that does not stop it looking absolutely stunning, spilling over with clusters of old-fashioned roses, any one of which will discreetly cover the flaw. A two-handled blue and white china soup tureen may have outlived its lid, but be ready for a new lease of life as an elegant container for a symmetrical arrangement. A Victorian oil lamp base may cease to cast a romantic glow on life, but that base, as shapely a pedestal as you will ever find, can gleam anew with a profusion of softly trailing flowers and leaves. A wine glass with a barley-sugar twist stem may be somewhat depreciated in value if it is the sole survivor of a set, but it can look enchanting with a posy of wild flowers on a dressing table.

If your inclination in floral art is towards classic and historical designs, contemporary, in-period containers can be costly. Blue and white Wedgwood urns, alabaster cupid vases, Venetian glass epergnes and hand-painted porcelain bowls are, very often, expensive. But florist's shops and floral art clubs have a wide selection of passable reproductions at ball-park prices, and it is well worthwhile starting to build the foundation of your 'flower room' shelf from here, and then go bargain-hunting.

JUG ARRANGEMENTS

Jugs of all kinds are natural containers for flowers, and offer boundless opportunities for expressive arrangements. If you can find one of those beautiful two-handled jugs – there are some glorious ones in both black and white – you can create a whole medley of symmetrical designs from equal triangles to groupings that are perfectly balanced. Forget all about symmetry if you are using any vessel with only one handle, such as jugs, drinking mugs, cups, coffee pots and tea pots, the handle will throw any carefully contrived design out of balance.

For a lovely rough and tumble effect, you can leave all the holding materials on the shelf and just let the stems have their own way. A yellow jug brimming over with white ranunculus, their yellow centres perfectly echoing the golden container; a blue and white jug amassed with white and blue anemones or a deep green jug filled to overflowing with dainty lilies of the valley and their leaves, such combinations can create some delightful effects.

Think of the container and the flowers as two partners in design, and try to relate the colours in some way. A plain whiter-than-white container holding only brilliant red, blue or orange flowers, can be quite distracting, the blooms appearing to float on nothingness. Add a clutch of white flowers, at least one tipping the rim, and the whole group comes together.

Study patterned containers carefully before you make your flower selection, and give at least a passing

A china teapot with just a hint of decoration is the perfect container for this showy bunch of sweet peas.

nod to a recognizable visual link. A blue Oriental porcelain jug spattered with cherry blossom and chirping birds, for instance, does not demand a slavish copy; you don't have to wait for blossom time to come around. Most blue flowers will look in their element, though a very deep shade – some hyacinths, for example – might be top heavy. A mixture of pink and blue anemones would spring no surprises, but could look messy atop a busy decoration. Pink with a single splash of blue, or blue with a dash of pink could be more restful.

There is something about the rustly-papery quality of helichrysum that marries particularly well with the Oriental image. Thick, full white *Helichrysum bracteatum* curving this way and that way on their gawky stems could steal the show. And for fun and frivolity add a lone highlight, such as one pink freesia.

GROUPING FOR DESIGN

Anyone who loves to have flowers in the home is almost bound to build up a collection of jugs. You find a lovely old stone jar one time, a tiny creamer the next, add another, and another, and suddenly you are faced with a choice. Which one to use as a container today? It is a choice that need never be made. You can create a fascinating still life by grouping three or four jugs together and linking them visually with flower types and colours. It is a mix and match situation with endless permutations. Stagger a group of jugs in echelon along a dining table and they are great for a casual party. Range them against a wall that sets off the colours to perfection. Cluster them in the centre of a side table. Or create a miniature vision of small jugs filled with tiny wild flowers – lawn daisies, forget-me-nots, speedwell, primroses – to attract a bird's-eye-view on a low coffee table.

From the minute to the magnificent, you can have floral fun with one of those massive water jug and hand basin sets that crops up frequently on sales stalls. You can play it straight, fill the neck of the jug with crumpled wire mesh and go to town on a striking display. A jug with pinky overtones would look pretty with a profusion of pink and green hydrangea flowers – at their best when they are just beginning to open – paeonies, roses and (a personal favourite) alchemilla mollis.

Stand the jug of flowers in its matching bowl and you can add a jokey extra. Tape a piece of soaked foam just inside the bowl, close to the rim, and fashion a complementary design of smaller blooms – side shoots and buds – and trailing leaves, some dipping low on to the table, some climbing like tendrils to link the jug and bowl.

Arrangements for the lunch or dinner table look comfortably at home in one or two pieces of the matching tableware. A cup and saucer with a trailing design in the cup and a few flower heads floating in the saucer; a similar treatment for a gravy boat or stand; individual floral tributes at each place setting, in egg cups or ramekin dishes from the set, guarantee a look of complete harmony throughout the meal.

GLASS AND MARBLES

Glinting, glittering, glowing glasses make fabulous containers for mealtimes, at their best when they can bask in the gleam of candle-light. A single glass holding a few flowers might not make much impression in the centre of a large table. But you could set one beside each place. Have a linking theme but a slightly different colour emphasis in each arrangement, and the notion can become a conversation ice-breaker at the start of a meal.

Trumpet-shaped wine glasses can pose a problem for the arranger, the wide V neck offering the stems too much freedom. A small piece of crumpled wire would hold the stems and be lost, visually, amongst them. But this is a solution only for junk-shop items. Never risk scratching valuable glass in this way. A handful of tiny smooth pebbles or marbles is one answer. Another is to insert a criss-cross mat of short, clean stems to get to grips with those in the arrangement.

There is a certain coolness and tranquillity about glass containers that suggest special effects, reminiscent of tinkling streams and leaping fountains. Partly fill a goldfish bowl or a rectangular glass bowl with marbles and go for a casual look with a bunch or two of head-drooping tulips. The waxy sheen of their petals perfectly picks up the cool cue.

Polish up a heavy glass dish – even an ash tray would do – and be sure it is absolutely dry before you fix a pinholder slightly to one side. Arrange a few stems in graded heights – let's choose lemon alstroemeria for their ice-maiden looks – cover the metal holder with concealing leaves and trail a few flowers and leaves, letting some dip into the water.

MAKING FLOWER FLOATS

Floating flowers, a tradition borrowed from the East, are another choice. Select a shallow glass or china bowl, fill it with water and cut off the flower heads with a minimum of stem, just enough to leave them with a drinking straw. At its simplest you can float a single perfect flower – a cream spider chrysanthemum, a pale pink paeony or a scarlet camellia, maybe.

Dog roses team well with this metallic creamer.

It is fun to be more adventurous and create a flower patchwork. Make rings – concentric circles – of yellow doronicum and white marguerites with a single yellow rose in the centre. Pick off the lower blooms from a stem of blue delphinium and ring them around pink and white campanula flowers – the possibilities are endless.

On a similar theme, set a wire cake-cooking tray over a shallow glass baking dish of water and arrange short-cut flower heads in a geometric or abstract pattern, just pushing them through the holes. It is like painting a canvas with living colour, and this device ensures the flowers do not float out of alignment.

You may unearth in the kitchen a surprising galaxy of unusual containers. A muffin pan could take single flowers or tiny nosegays in each of the six holes; you could use a metal coffee-filter cup with an inner container, a fluted brioche mould or ice cream bombe, as decorative as many a custom-made vase; a brightly coloured enamel colander (lined with polythene to hold a block of foam); a cane cutlery basket for a harvest festival theme of cereals and fruits; a cast iron skillet (protected against the moisture) spilling over with gazania, marigolds, geum and nasturtiums in sunny-side-up breakfast egg colours – you can turn your *batterie de cuisine* into a versatile battery of flower containers.

FRUIT OF THE WOOD

Wood is a splendid background for flowers. On your treasure hunt in the kitchen do not discount bread boards, chopping boards, cheese boards, rattan trays and wooden cheese box lids just because they are flat. A spot of tacky clay will hold a dish or saucer in place. In goes a pinholder or cylinder of foam, and you are away. The tempting combination of flowers and fruit is particularly effective when you use a wooden container, whether it is a board, an olive pestle and mortar, an old dairy butter container or a polished mahogany tea box.

Fruit offers you a whole new range of shape and texture contrasts – no flower is quite as round, quite as shiny as a well polished apple. Fruit also poses different fixing problems, because of its weight, and in most cases needs to be wired in place. You will need a packet of florist's stub wires or a reel of medium-gauge wire. Twist a wire firmly around each short stem of small russet coloured apples and pears, or push a wire through the fruit at the stalk end and twist the two ends together to make a false stalk. That is how to cope with satsumas, tangerines and the other

small 'oranges', limes and lemons. Wire clusters of cherries together into a voluptuous bunch. And weave a long piece of doubled wire around the stalk through a bunch of grapes, twisting it into a firm-gripping loop at the end.

You may find it helps to prepare a container with soaked foam and then cover it with a high-peaked dome of crumpled wire mesh. Wire or tie the netting to the container so that even the heaviest fruits cannot dislodge it, and then twist the fruit wires around the dome. Tuck in soft and pretty flowers and leaves in a design to admire now and eat later.

Perhaps it is stating the obvious, that vases come in all shapes and sizes, to suit all moods and occasions, in all materials and textures. But there is a wealth to choose from – for instance, a 30's-style pink shell shaped wall vase to fill to overflowing with sugar-almond coloured ranunculus, a rough glazed pottery cube section – a splendid foil for bleached seedheads; a porcelain specimen vase to hold a single rosebud or camellia; or a green glass urn in which to create a masterpiece of foliage, fruit and flowers. The dictionary would have a hard time of it, embracing all of these under one definition.

Under a lavish display of fruit, flowers and foliage, soaked foam covered with a cage of wire mesh ensures that all wired stems will stay firmly in place.

USING AROMATIC PLANTS

The heady fragrance of night-scented stock and nicotiana at evening time, the beckoning waft of deep perfume from damask and moss rose bushes, the sweet, almost moist aroma given off by a carpet of thyme as it is crushed underfoot, and the culinary-inspiring spiciness of fennel, marjoram, mints and dill as you brush past them in the herb patch are delights of a summer's garden that linger long in the memory. Delights that you can transport into the home, combining the pleasure of the colour and texture of flowers and foliage with their heavenly scents.

There is nothing new, of course, in the notion of scenting rooms with aromatic plants. In the Middle Ages fragrant plants were strewn on floors and even in the streets to mask offensive odours. Herbs were hung in bunches to discourage insects from making their home in kitchens and living rooms – in wardrobes and linen chests, too – and in sickrooms as a gentle antiseptic. Churches and public halls that may not be in constant daily use can be transformed by a scented arrangement. It is a strange thing, but all human senses are so closely linked that a pleasing aroma in a room can make it seem lighter, brighter and an altogether more agreeable place to be.

PLANNING AHEAD

If you are arranging flowers for a big occasion, and if the timetable allows, complete the designs the evening before the event. Make sure that the containers are well topped up with water, spray all the flowers and leaves with a fine mist of water and move the arrangements to the coolest part of the room. When you open the door on the big day, the welcoming fragrance will have reached every corner.

Throughout the seasons such a glorious selection of aromatic flowers comes into bloom that it is tempting to gather armfuls of them together, like a fresh flower pot pourri, and enjoy their heady fragrance all at once, lilac, mock orange blossom, hyacinths, carnations and roses tumbling over each other in perfumed profusion.

But this is one temptation that should be resisted. The widely differing scents of fresh flowers, once they are cut, do not blend together with anything like the subtleness of a bowl of dried flower petals. When you think of it, this is not surprising, for in a pot pourri the dried petals are mingled together with spices, aromatic oils and a fixative, their various perfumes linked and left to mature, like ingredients in a composite dish brought together with a sauce.

The perfume of each fresh flower, however, is competing with its neighbours, and it is all too easy to create a head-on clash of personalities. The result is an overpowering, cloying scent, the kind you would never want to buy in a bottle. Better by far to limit your choice to only two scented flower types – roses and carnations are perfect partners, for example – and then add complementary aromatic leaves if you wish.

A MEDLEY OF PERFUMES

One of the headiest floral scents belongs to the hyacinth, which is much under-rated as a cut flower. Here is one that, for perfume, is head and shoulders above its competitors when you are decorating a large room. The huge, densely packed blooms look magnificent in a shallow bowl, the flower heads radiating outwards to form a wide-topped cone. They are also useful filler material for pedestals, giving good visual weight at the base of the design.

All bulb flowers, with their fleshy stems, need a little cosseting before being arranged, and are happier in water than soaked foam. Hyacinths, because of the weight ratio of flower to stem, are an extra-special case. Follow the usual procedure of cutting the stems under water and giving them a good long drink overnight. If the heads do threaten to overpower the stems, push a piece of thick wire up from the base to the tip. This will keep the stems straight or, indeed, if your design requires it, enable you to coax them into gentle, but controlled, curves.

Beautiful cut plants, that smell delightful too, add a charming touch to a celebratory event. Here three white, china jugs hold a loose arrangement of roses, pinks, chamomile, carnations, mint, lemon balm and wild grasses.

Laurel leaves form an attractive, dark background for this herb ring which includes sprigs of rosemary, curry plant, lavender, sage, bay and pelargoniums.

There is a delightfully high perfume count among flowering shrubs. With their graceful curves, branches of Mexican orange *(Choisya ternata)*, mock orange blossom (philadelphus) and lilac rise to great heights for designs on a large scale. The first two, with their gentle clusters of pure white and sweetly scented flowers, are a popular choice for bridal arrangements. They are also a good choice for groups that have to be seen literally in a poor light. Not so lilac; because these flowers are so much more densely packed they need the assistance of good, clear lighting. Without this the flower heads can 'burn out' and look almost sombre.

As with all woody, flowering shrubs, it is best to sacrifice the leaves at the outset, as they wilt long before the flowers fade, and include other sprays of foliage which have been specially treated according to type (more details on pages 10 and 11). Strip off the leaves, strip back a little of the bark and split or lightly crush the stem ends, and then leave them deep in tepid water overnight.

BALANCING THE SCENTS

Lilies of all kinds grace any occasion with their majestic good looks and exotic scent. Whether you mingle them with other blooms or accentuate their positive outlines by featuring them alone, plan an uncrowded, open design and allow plenty of space for buds to open freely. The waxy petals are deceptively delicate and bruise easily. And, incidentally, the pollen permanently dyes anything it comes into contact with.

Roses are probably the number one favourite among scented flowers, and if you are planning a garden it is worth selecting them as much for their scent as for their colour. We have to go back a few generations, to the old-fashioned types, for the sweetest perfume among the damasks, Provence and moss roses that evoke pot pourri in the making.

They are such a charming feature of the garden that it seems almost a shame to cut them. To make the very most of roses indoors, strip off the thorns and lower leaves and treat the stems as for all woody material. Gather the roses into a bunch, wrap a wad of paper under the flower heads to protect them from steam, stand the stems deep in warm water, and leave them overnight. An aspirin in the water when you arrange them will help the flowers and their perfume to linger longer.

Can you think of anything more welcoming than to open the door of a guest bedroom and sense –

even before you see it – a group of sweetly scented flowers? A china teapot spilling over with pale pink and crimson old roses, a specimen vase holding a few elegant stems of freesia, a cup and saucer filled to the brim with tiny garden pinks and aromatic leaves, would all extend the most gracious of welcomes.

A little flower scent goes a long way in bedrooms – where heavily perfumed blooms can be cloying – and on dining tables where strong floral scents compete unfavourably with any subtle blend of flavours you may serve. Not only that, they can be off- putting to anyone who likes to savour the bouquet of the wine. So in these situations, hyacinths are out.

HERBAL ROOMS

Culinary herbs complement scented flowers of all kinds, and naturally bring their own aroma to an unscented group. A casual display of herbs – thyme, mint, chamomile, sage, broad-leaved parsley – all tumbling over each other just as they grow, softens the functional appearance of a kitchen. Don't spend too much time on the arrangement, though, as it is sure to be depleted as one stem after another finds its way into the salad.

The evergreen herbs like bay, rosemary and sage and the seedheads of others such as fennel, caraway, and dill are good keepers, and have their aromatic part to play in long lasting arrangements. Long spikes of rosemary look lovely in winter with holly and ivy, and sage with its furry grey-green or purple leaves is a good 'base filler' to cover holding materials. The bright yellow clusters of fennel seedheads add a hint of spice to a golden arrangement, and a 'see-through' feature that is a good contrast to heavy blooms.

ENJOYING THE SCENT

Most herbs – lovage, marjoram, mint and savory, to mention only a few – are 'medium keepers' and will last a few days in water. Others can be disappointing unless you single them out for special treatment. So, if you want to enjoy the sharp citrus odour and variegated colours of lemon balm, the long slender spikes of tarragon and the furry softness – to say nothing of the bright blue flowers – of borage, burn the stem ends in a candle flame before putting them in water. Scent, like colour, is an intensely personal choice. My own memento of a summer's garden would be a nosegay of pink clove carnations, wild roses, feverfew, thyme, marjoram, purple sage, apple mint and a spray of clove or cinnamon.

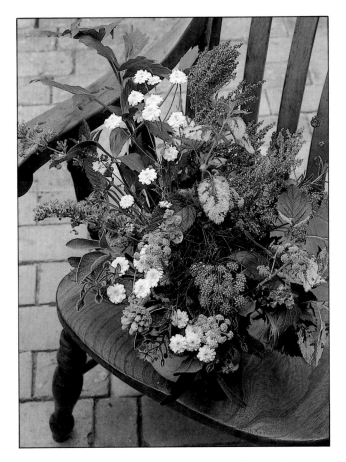

In a casually arrayed bunch of herbs and flowers that includes dock, lavender, sage, borage and feverfew, variegated lemon balm and marjoram add visual interest.

CULTIVATING THE WILD LOOK

Cycling home with sheaves of bluebells trailing over the panier, filling willow baskets with wild primroses gathered from the banks of a stream, and picking buttercups to hold under someone's chin while you chant, 'Do you like butter?' are childhood memories that are destined to fade into obscurity, never to be precisely repeated. For, wherever you live and whatever the current regulations about picking wild flowers, there is now a moral issue at stake. Wild flowers, whether they are shy violets or showy orchids, are part of our nation's heritage, there for all to enjoy and not for just a few to plunder.

The law in Britain forbids the digging up of any wild plant without the specific permission of the owner of the land, and the picking of any protected plants, all those species considered in danger of extinction. It is within the law to pick rampant weeds; but species that are prolific in one region may well be on the verge of extinction in another, and you have to know which are which. Many people take the issue further, and for instance claim that broken twigs and rotting wood on the ground may be home to certain species of insects or beetles so that, in effect, all natural materials should be left for their wildlife value.

In the United States the laws vary from one state to another. In some it is permissible to pick wild flowers growing more than a few minutes' walk away from the highway; in others regulations are more specific and less relaxed.

Whatever the current state of the law, this is an issue on which public opinion seems to be one jump ahead. To ensure that future generations can grow up with the memories of woodlands carpeted with bluebells, meadows speckled with mauve scabious, clover and vetch, yellow toadflax and melilot and white marguerites, and hedgerows humming with bees, we must leave well alone and be content to admire the plants in their natural habitat. By doing so we will be playing an important part in building up the stocks, and taking many precious plants off the endangered list.

This is not to say that we can never cut wild flowers again, and bring them indoors to assemble in delightfully casual groups. We can cut them from our own gardens and windowboxes, for one of the great bonuses of the move towards wild plant conservation is that seed and plants of native species are now widely available for home growing.

CONSERVING WILD PLANTS

Conserving wild plants is the greatest excuse there has ever been for letting a patch of your garden 'go natural', and burgeon with the plants that are native to your area. For me, this means that hummocky patch beyond the stream – once neatly planted out with prim annuals – becomes a haze of speckled mist in the late spring, with a mass of sheep's parsley drawing its pretty veil over red campion; and in the summer a gently swaying sea of wild and decorative grasses splattered with vivid scarlet poppies and sky-blue cornflowers.

It is not only wild plants that are being threatened by the extension of agricultural crops, the growth of urban areas and incessant pollution. In recent years many species of butterfly, small mammal and insect have been in decline too. And so if you have a garden, however small, you can play a vital part in helping to turn back this tide. By encouraging and cultivating wild plants in the garden you issue an open invitation to butterflies, moths, bees and seed-eating birds, and thereby substantially increase your own enjoyment of the garden.

Butterflies are attracted to many wild plants. In my garden their favourite is one very small patch of stinging nettles left there solely for their pleasure. The brown argus butterfly is supported by rockrose, the green hairstreak and silver studded blue are attracted by broom, and the Duke of Burgundy's fritillary breed on cowslips. Poppies, teasel and melilot are among the many wild plants that will have your garden humming with bees.

A hedgerow harvest, which includes blackberries, wild rose-hips, elderberries, crab apples and hazel leaves, joins bush roses, mahonia, honesty and Chinese lanterns in a natural display.

GROWING NATURALLY

Wherever we live, there is a long tradition of the native plants all around us being used by local people as medicines. Until comparatively recent times, natural herb medicines were all people had to calm fevers and relieve ailments.

The golden rule in cultivating wild seed or buying plants is to match the plant as nearly as possible to its native conditions. Get to know your soil type – ask a keen neighbouring gardener if you are in any doubt – and choose seed that thrives on the diet you have to offer.

You may need to imitate the growing pattern of these plants as well. Most wild plants drop their seed in autumn. According to type, some seed germinates almost immediately, and the seedlings have to survive the winter. Other seed types do not germinate until spring when conditions are favourable.

In the latter case you have to subject the seed (hemp agrimony with its dense masses of pink flowers and clustered bellflower are examples) to its accustomed cold spell before it will germinate successfully. This means either sowing the seeds in autumn, when in the wild they would be self sown, or mixing the seeds with damp sand, and putting them in a polythene bag in the refrigerator for six to eight weeks. Once the seeds start to sprout, plant them out in pots in a cold greenhouse, or outside under a glass cloche or an upturned preserve jar. This sounds complicated, but it is not much different from growing sprouting bean shoots in a drawer. The process is called stratifying.

The seeds of all leguminous species such as vetches, clovers and trefoils need a little rough treatment if they are to germinate successfully. This is called scarification, a process which breaks down the seed coat and enables the embryo to absorb moisture. All you do is rub the seed gently between sandpaper to graze, but not completely penetrate the coating. Without this assistance the hard seed coats can take several weeks to become water-permeable.

These preliminary processes apart – which of course are required for good germination of many cultivated seed types too – wild seed is planted and nurtured like any other comparable plant type. Sow seed in seed compost in trays or boxes, water them with a fine spray, cover them with glass or polythene and keep them at a germinating temperature of about 20C (68F). A simple heated propagating tray is ideal. Or when the time comes (read the packet instructions carefully) scatter the seed thinly outside, where it is to grow – a method that seems more natural for wild seed. Keep the seed bed evenly moist and free of weeds, and be sure to put a marker to remind you of its position. Some seed types are notoriously slow to germinate, and can surprise you months later.

ARRANGING WILD FLOWERS

If you bring a few specimens indoors, how are you to arrange them? Firstly, as you cut the stems put them straight into a bowl of tepid water. Many wildings are tender creatures and wilt pathetically. Study the stems carefully. The ratio of leaves to flowers is on the high side in many wild plants – breeders having 'improved' on this characteristic in their cultivated counterparts. Strip off the leaves, and the stems may be transformed. Deadnettles, for example, hide their hoops of tiny red, yellow, mauve or white flowers under an awning of dull green leaves. Pick them off and you reveal rings of tiny flowers with all the charm of orchids in miniature. Mallow is another, whose mauve saucer-like flowers are almost swamped by foliage.

Arrange wild flowers as casually as you know how. Bunch several types loosely in your hand, pulling up one stem after another to show them to advantage, tie the stems loosely with twine and drop them into a container such as a jug, preserve jar or kitchen storage jar, or something with more panache, a silver teapot, pewter beaker or pretty glass vase.

Many of those plants with slender stems are more at home in water than in holding foam, though you can ease their passage by piercing holes in the foam with a very fine skewer or a thick darning needle.

A dainty china basket spilling over in early spring with violets, snowdrops, pulmonaria and primroses; a zingy yellow enamel pot pouring out a blaze of colourful buttercups, yellow deadnettle and melilot; a windowbox planted with cowslips and heartsease; a garden trug piled high with ornamental grasses and scarlet poppies – there are memories still to be created with wild flowers that you have grown.

Raised from seed bought from specialist suppliers, these cowslips provide a welcome reminder of open fields and country lanes.

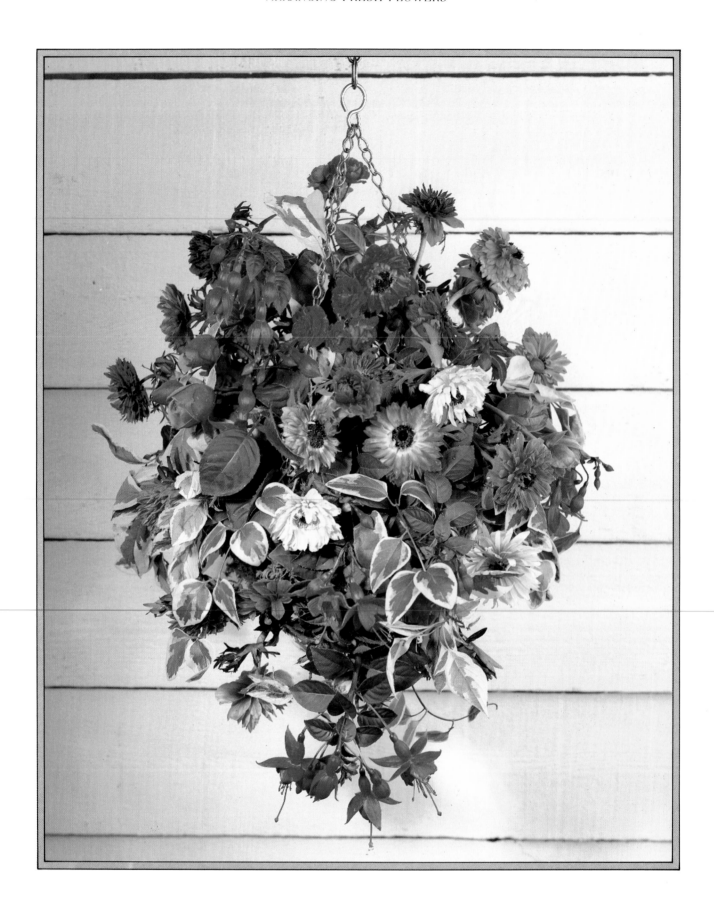

FLOWERS IN THE OPEN AIR

Whether you have supper on the balcony on a balmy summer's evening, a bubbly drinks party on the terrace, a buffet lunch in the garden in the heat of the day, or a casual barbecue, there is always an extra 'lift' to any occasion celebrated out of doors. It seems more fun, more fancy-free, more frivolous. And the ideal setting for a feast of flowers.

It isn't everyone who can boast a garden which is like a French Impressionist painting, awash with clouds of colour and the perfect background for a party. Very few, in fact. Some gardens, planned on sculptured lines, are designed to be a symphony of greens; they make good candidates for a little imported colour just for the occasion. Others might go through an awkward patch, as one burst of colour fades and another has yet to take over. Perhaps there is a dull corner that needs brightening, or just a patio or balcony to set the festive scene. Whatever the occasion or the setting, flowers can do much, much more than simply decorate the table.

Balconies look well for a little window dressing for a special party. You can weave plants in and out of the railings, loop a flower and ribbon swag over the door, or from end to end of the balcony rails, fashion flower-ball trees to stand like sentries at each end, hang shallow vases or baskets on the house wall, or arrange a simple but spectacular pedestal.

Ivy is hard to beat for trails and swags. It not only lasts well out of water – of paramount importance – but, in its various forms, can range in colour from deep buttery cream through to bright lettuce green

to the deepest of shades. Just a spray or two of the darkest greens for contrast is enough; in bright sunlight they look dreary and at dusk they merge into the shadows. Other possibilities – which will naturally depend on local and seasonal availability, and whatever you can beg or borrow – include willow, honeysuckle, lime green cupressus (avoid the dark shades), hawthorn, hazelnut, japonica, Solomon's seal and vine shoots.

To simulate climbing plants, simply weave the longest stems through upright supports, wiring the stems together where they overlap. Take matters into your own hands when it comes to deciding how 'floribunda' these plants are to be, and wire on the most accessible and long lasting flowers around. Choose from single chrysanthemums, marigolds, marguerites, zinnias and other composites or carnations and pinks. Or take the illusion a step further and use artificial flowers.

Left: *Anemones and fuchsias appear to grow in profusion from this hanging basket. There are, however, no rooted plants. The flowers and foliage are held in a block of foam concealed in spagnum moss.*
Right: *For a special occasion outdoors, consider decorating pillars, gate-posts, fences or statues with freshly cut flowers. Here a plinth bound with vine leaves and mallow supports a topknot of autumnal fruits and trailing cupressus stems.*

To make a swag, measure a piece of thick, coarse string, allowing enough length for it to hang in deep curves. Make up bunches of ivy and asparagus fern, and wire them to the string, each one overlapping the stems of the next. Fix the swag in place with ribbon bows and tuck in flowers at intervals, just before the party begins.

FLOWER-BALL TREES

Flower-ball trees, equally at home on a balcony or patio, can make a colourful impact in a small space. For each one, fix a stout 1 metre (3 feet) cane in a large flower pot, and surround it with soil or pebbles, topped with a scatter of soft-looking sphagnum moss. Shape some damp moss into a ball, cover it with crumpled wire netting and fix it firmly to the top of the cane. On a smaller scale, use spheres of soaked foam for table-top trees. Push stems of trailing leaves and flowers through the wire and into the moss, creating any effect you like. You can go for broke on colour and use brilliant pom-pom dahlias in reds, yellows and pinks, or introduce a hint of romance with pale or deep pink and cream roses and sweet

peas, clouded over with a mist of sheep's parsley or gypsophila.

For a make-believe tree with more wayward habits, fix a twiggy branch firmly in a pot and wire on large single flowers or mixed posies, or hang tiny baskets filled with fresh or dried flower nosegays.

If the table takes up all the available space, there is always the wall. Put a massive jug of flowers in the window, fix a ribbon of flowers and leaves to the windowsill or make a hanging basket. A shoulder shopping bag lined with polythene and filled with a block of soaked foam can look spectacular. Cut the most curvaceous stems you can find, trails of Russian vine and clematis perhaps, and pack the top with sweet Williams, ranunculus, or whatever is in season.

FINDING CONTAINERS

Moving on to the patio, you can carry these ideas with you and, with space to spare, fill tubs and pots with eye-catching, scene-setting flowers. Containers for the garden should be fairly substantial, to take account of wind velocity and party spirits. Earthenware jugs, strawberry pots and flower pots all have the right feel.

Hanging on bannisters, decorating a hallway, or the walls of a small courtyard, swags lend a festive air to any occasion. For a swag that is pretty, but not overfussy, co-ordinate the flowers for colour and shape and 'sprinkle' them randomly along the length.

the foam in an act of concealment. It makes a perfect decoration for a patio, to stand on a flight of steps or on top of a low stone wall.

THE COOL LOOK

When the temperature is soaring, and flowers and guests alike are feeling the heat, a watery floral scheme can be the most welcome sight. A stone sink garden, bird bath or large mixing bowl filled with water and floating with flowers, water-lily style, is pretty and practical. A collection of large glass storage jars holding cool-looking foliage and white flowers can take up a refreshing stance in a corner. Even milk bottles and old glass ginger beer bottles, each one supporting a single stem, can seem more appropriate than a crowded arrangement of any kind.

To survive the heat of the day you need to choose the toughest of flowers, as dainty wildings will not stand a chance. Spray chrysanthemums, carnations, lilies and freesia are among those that keep well. As always, but particularly in the heat, it is important to cut flowers straight into water and give them a long drink in a cool place before exposing them to the sun.

If the celebrations are likely to spill over into the evening, choose flower colours that will hold their own in the gathering dusk. White, pale lemon, pink, apricot, ice blue and pale green flowers and foliage will still be drawing admiring glances long after deep reds, dark blues and purples have faded into obscurity.

Alternatively create a pool of light with white household candles in glass jars, each one partly filled with water and bobbing with small floating flower heads. Arrange ten or more coloured nightlights on a flat white dish and scatter flowers among them. Bind tiny posies to long white candles, tie trailing ribbon bows and stick them in soil in a flower pot or straight into the ground, well out of the way of excited children.

If you decide to fill the neck of a jug with foam, for a downwardly mobile design, partly fill it with water anyway. The extra weight will help to make it more stable.

Strawberry pots that are temporarily out of commission spring to life if you fill the side apertures and wedge the top with foam. A cascade of flowers and trailing leaves at the top and simple posies of bright garden flowers all round make a stunning display.

A collection of clay flower pots makes a cheap and cheerful feature. Place a jar of water or piece of soaked foam in each and fill them with the lightest, brightest garden flowers you can find.

Garden trugs and flower baskets, wooden seed trays, a child's wheelbarrow, a watering can, even a galvanized bucket – look around for containers that are naturals in an outdoor environment. Keep alive the memory of wandering round the garden and cutting a few roses here, a few lilies there, or a spray of foliage. Do just that, but hide a block of foam in the trug first. Then push in the stems so that the flowers spray out in a fan shape, some extending way over the rim, others cut short and pushed close against

FLOWERS ON THE TABLE

Rose petals scattered on a pink voile tablecloth for a wedding shower party, a hoop of trailing vine leaves and pretty rosebuds round crisp white damask to show off a celebration cake, a garden nosegay tucked inside the table napkin at each place setting illustrate that decorating a table with flowers can extend far beyond an arrangement in its centre. Whenever there is a party in the offing – and even when you plan a special meal for just two people – consider the table as a stage on which to set the food, and a tablecloth as a blank canvas to paint with flowers.

Scattering flower heads on the table is the charming customary way to welcome guests in North African countries. One of my most vivid mealtime memories recalls a vision of a round table set under the night

sky, china, glass, silver and stars twinkling and the cloth almost hidden beneath a tapestry of fresh flower heads. Marigolds, marguerites, zinnias, geraniums, the massed effect of dozens of separate blooms strewn on the table at random added immeasurably to the enjoyment of the food and rivalled the scent of the orange groves all around. True, in Tunisia the flowers grow abundantly and are used liberally. But the idea is so delightful that it can spark off inspiration in all directions.

The random look is pretty, quick and easy to achieve, and in no danger of getting 'fussed' as the meal progresses. Match the scattered flowers to a pattern on the dinnerware. Cornflowers and chamomile tossed on to a table set with blue and white china look as if they have just fluttered down from the vegetable dish; rose or carnation petals have extra appeal, as heavenly as pot pourri in the making, and marigold and buttercup petals are an easy way of investing in a visually profitable crop of gold.

It is not, of course, the kindest thing to do to flowers, to 'arrange' them out of water. So choose the flower types carefully, according to their keeping qualities, and give them the usual good, long drink in tepid water before beheading them – that is if the decision to do so is premeditated. If it is a *crime passionele*, when you rush out in a fit of spontaneous enthusiasm and cull a few blooms to scatter willy-nilly on the table, then cross your fingers and hope they last as long as the party spirit.

Composite flowers of all kinds such as doronicum, single chrysanthemums, all the daisy types, erigeron, single and double zinnias, pyrethrums, asters (though these are rather large for this treatment) and scabious, last well. The dianthus family, all the pinks and carnations, roses in bud or partly-opened bud, separated flowers from stems of delphinium, clarkia, hydrangea and antirrhinum, flowers with wax-like petals such as lilies and camellia and the everlastings, helichrysum, ammobium and helipterum, should all continue to look fresh as a daisy out of water for several hours.

Get into the mood of using flower heads to create impact in this way, and you can advance from the imprecision of a random scattering and 'paint' geometric or abstract shapes on a table, outlining a central feature – such as a cake stand or candlestick – or dividing the surface area into place settings.

Table place settings are transformed with individual 'garnishes' of fresh flowers. Given a long drink in tepid water before being cut from their stems, alstroemerias, carnations, fuchsias and anemones will keep their appearance throughout a leisurely meal.

IDEAS FOR TABLES

When a table is for a touch-me-not display, to show off a wedding cake for example, you can simply place flower heads edge to edge, confident that they will not get jostled out of line. Ring a round cake stand with pale pink rosebuds, soft blue hydrangea florets, pastel lemon double pinks, whatever matches the colour and design of the frosting. If the cake stand is square at the base, make it the centre of criss-crossing lines of flowers, again echoing the style of the cake decoration.

Show off your prettiest silver candelabra with a hoop of flowers around the base. They will double in value as they are reflected in the metal. Place a curved or straight 'ribbon' of flowers and leaves down the centre of a dining table, well out of the way of guests reaching for the salt, or make a hoop of tiny flowers around each drinks mat at the place settings.

When the table design is going to come in for the cut and thrust of the party atmosphere, as a buffet table does, the flower ribbons need to be given more permanence, so divide a party table into sections with strips of flowers, the drinks at one end, then the first course and so on.

Measure from front to back of the table and cut to length either a piece of string (that will not show) or a piece of ribbon (that will). To work with the string, cut short sprays of leaves, and flowers with short stems. Use a roll of fine wire to bind the leaves and flowers, all pointing towards one end of the string, working as far as the centre. Turn the string round and complete the design in reverse, the flowers pointing the opposite way. Be sure to place them at equal distance, and bind each one close enough to cover the stem of its predecessor. Look critically at the strip and tuck in extra leaves to hide any gaps or tell-tale pieces of wire, and fix a special bloom to neaten the parting of the ways, at the centre.

Variegated lamium or periwinkle leaves (condition them thoroughly first) are a pretty foil to flowers used in this way. Cut the stem just above each pair of leaves

A 'shower' posy of wired carnations, freesias and feverfew, finished with satin ribbon, decorates a festive table.

to make them look like wings on a stalk, and place the smallest ones at each end of the strip, the largest ones towards the centre.

RIBBONS, SWAGS AND POSIES

Different flower types need different treatments if you are using ribbon as the base. Flat flowers with shallow calyces can be stuck on to the ribbon with modelling clay or double-sided adhesive tape. Carnations and others with long, thick calyces are best left on a short stem, made into a small posy with a spray of leaves and fixed to the ribbon with a few holding stitches.

Depending on where you live and the season, an edge-to-edge strip of flowers can be something of an extravagance. Pad it out with delicate leaves, including only a few flowers, and the word economy will never enter anyone's head.

The vertical drape of a tablecloth is such a perfect 'canvas' for flowers, you will never want to see an unadorned cloth again. As a pretty alternative to the draped swag, and exquisite for a summer wedding, transform a cloth with posies.

A large expanse of cloth, covering trestle tables for a buffet, can be covered with tiny flower posies pinned or sewn at random or in rows. Use marigold and ivy leaves, cornflowers and euphorbia, rosebuds and rosemary sprigs, lawn daisies and campanula but keep the food simple, for it will be faced with distracting competition.

For a more formal look, decorate the point of a small tablecloth with a 'shower' posy. Make a fan shape of fern-like leaves, yellow freesia, white pinks, and yellow and white feverfew. As a finishing touch, edge the rim of the display table with a geometric line of pairs of leaves and dainty flower heads such as periwinkle and chamomile.

The rim of the table makes a natural frame to set off a buffet spread. Pin long stems of ivy or strawberry leaves around the table edge and attach a few flowers at intervals. Resist the temptation to do this for a sit-down meal. Guests might resent armfuls of foliage coming between them and the food. Flatter them instead with flowers in a personal way. Tuck a single freesia or a small posy into the fold of a napkin, or make a daisy chain as a floral napkin ring.

Just one cautionary note. Use stainless-steel pins to avoid rust marks. But do not get carried away and pin flowers to your finest, most precious linen. The weight could tear the threads, so use lengths of inexpensive material or discarded bedsheets.

DESIGNING WITH LEAVES

Leaves are the unsung heroes of many a flower arrangement, unobtrusively providing a natural background against which flowers may be seen in all their glory. But foliage can be glorious too, and designs which focus attention on the wealth of variation in leaf colour, texture and shape have an especially serene quality.

A pot of herbs on the kitchen windowsill, shiny bright green lovage contrasting with woolly purple sage, with golden marjoram, with palest cream pineapple mint, with slender chive stems, will be a restful feature in a busy area. A circlet of evergreen herbs, bay, rosemary and lavender with fennel and caraway seedheads, is a theme decoration to hang on a wall or to dangle from the ceiling. In earlier days a herb wreath would have been designed as much to keep insects at bay as for its simple good looks.

Contrast in your mind's eye these charmingly nostalgic ways to group a handful of aromatic leaves with, shall we say, a 'green' pedestal of towering iris spikes, curving arcs of young beech leaves, huge fleshy misty-blue hosta leaves and ferns like complicated paper cut-outs, or a winter display of spiky rosemary, variegated ivy and dark green holly thick with scarlet berries, and the range of options begins to become apparent.

TENDING THE FOLIAGE

If it is to give long and faithful service, foliage needs special preparation and care. If you dash in from the garden with an armful of flowers and leaves and arrange them in a hurry it will be at your peril. You will find that deciduous leaves, frail and tender as they are, wilt long before almost any flowers. Only evergreens have the inner resources to withstand such shock treatment.

The immature foliage of early spring, when the sap is still rising in the plant, is most tender of all and demands the most careful preparation. Branches of yellow-green lime, so thin that shafts of light shine through them; sprays of lettuce-green oak, the scalloped leaves not yet fully grown; curving stems of beech just perfect for designs with soft, flowing lines – to enjoy the beauty of deciduous foliage, and

immature foliage most of all, you have to plan ahead and cut the leaves a day in advance to allow them time to become acclimatized. Becoming acclimatized simply means becoming full of water, a state known as turgid. With this built-in reserve, leaves can last well indoors, whether they are arranged directly in water or in soaked stem-holding foam. As leaves naturally draw moisture from two sources (taking it up through the branches and stems, and through their surface tissue), immersing them in water is the way to ensure the best results.

SOAKING TIME

Not everyone is prepared to put a 'do not disturb' notice on the bath overnight while sprays of leaves are enjoying a good long soak, but in most homes there is some container that will serve the purpose. It may be a shallow photographic developing tank, an extra large baking tin, an old drawer securely lined with a sheet of polythene, or a deep bucket. A plastic washing up bowl will house short branches and can, incidentally, usefully coax gentle curves – if that is what your design requires – into longer ones.

Prepare stems in the usual way (see page 11), keeping in mind that everything you do is designed to make it easier for the plant material to take up water. Strip off all the lowest leaves as these will eventually be superfluous and either overcrowd the design or lie below the water level.

Immerse branches of mature leaves in water for several hours or overnight, and immature foliage for a maximum of two hours; any longer than this and young leaves become sodden and limp. Transfer the branches to stand upright in a container of tepid water, again for several hours if possible, or for a minimum of two to three hours.

If, after all this, the leaves start to wilt – and immature ones are the most likely to do so – you will have to resort to drastic remedial action. Bunch the

This bounty of foliage, arranged by species in concentric circles, indicates the range of colours and textures of leaves available. With a 'flower' centre of senecio, this display includes the leaves of scented geranium, variegated ivy, carrot, vine, and acer.

branches of stems together, protect the leaves from the steam by wrapping them in newspaper, and dip the ends in boiling water for between 30 seconds and one minute. This treatment fulfils a number of functions: it breaks down air locks, sterilizes the stem ends and kills any harmful bacteria.

WATER TREATMENT

Trails of leaves on slender stems – periwinkle and Russian vine for example – also respond well to total immersion. If the leaves at the tip – the most vulnerable, and always the first to go – do flag, they may be revived by burning the stem ends in a match or candle flame. If this does not do the trick there is nothing for it but to cut off the offending tip, and the wilting leaves with it, and 'bury' the stem in the body of the design. Tipless stems are not elegant enough to feature at the top and sides.

Large fleshy leaves such as hosta, fig, and *Fatsia japonica* – so useful for providing visual weight at the base of the design and for concealing the holding material – have considerable water-retaining capacity and consequently have an exceptionally long vase life. Make their life easier, and your pleasure in them longer, by immersing the single leaves in a flat dish of water for several hours.

RESILIENT EVERGREENS

Evergreen leaves – yew, plain and spotted laurel, camellia, ivy, eleagnus and privet to name a few – all last well in or out of water. Give them an initial water bath so that they can drink their fill and they will last for a week or more fashioned into swags, drapes, ribbons, rings, hoops and other festive designs which have no recourse to water.

Decorating our homes at Christmas time with a swag of holly, ivy and other evergreens over a door or mantel is a tradition whose roots pre-date Christianity. People believed that there were magical properties in plants which could retain their leaves when other trees and shrubs had bare branches. An

Subtle but not sombre, this display includes aquilegia, purple sage, honesty, totinus, berberis, maple leaves and love-in-a-mist seedheads.

Advent ring of cupressus, juniper and yew linking the four symbolic candles, a ribbon of soft trails of ivy and honeysuckle draped in front of a buffet table, a hoop of lavender leaves and flowers to scent a clothes cupboard, are some of the countless ways of using evergreens.

Remember that leaves are quite capable of retaining water on their outer surfaces. So to prevent water dripping on to furniture and other precious surfaces, toss sprays of wet leaves gently over and over on newspaper or a piece of cloth, and pat dry large leaves – such as hosta – with crumpled kitchen paper. Any evergreens that have been covered in city grime and do not emerge from their water bath sparkling bright, will benefit from being swished gently in warm soapy water before being rinsed and dried.

LEAVES AS HIGHLIGHTS

In all its wonderful variety, foliage deserves to capture the spotlight occasionally. Try mingling shiny leaves with matt and woolly ones, plain leaves with speckled, striped or otherwise variegated ones, and colours of every tint, shade and hue from palest cream to deepest purple. You can choose to group a subtle blend of grey, green and white foliage, capture the glory of falling leaves in the bronze, red and yellow range, pick a sharp scheme in lemon and lime colours, or create a medley including all these ideas. Do not let your selection range over too wide an area, though. A display of four or possibly five species at the most will enable each to be enjoyed in detail. More would be muddling.

Take the shape and form of leaves strongly into account – tall, slender spikes for pointed outlines, soft trails for curves, large 'flat' leaves like ivy and begonia for weight at the base. And for the focus of attention, occupying that hallowed spot at the base of the stem? Round materials are easy on the eye. You can use a single succulent, or a group of three; a cluster of round leaves – some pelargoniums are like pretty multi-coloured rosettes – or end-of-stem sprays of magnolia or camellia, specially charming (if somewhat wasteful) at the bud stage.

There are many different kinds of seedheads, grasses, bracts, fruit and vegetables to use too. Long spires of delphinium seedheads, furry little lupin pods, the stately 'urns' that carry poppy seeds, clusters of lime-green or pinky-purple euphorbia and elegant stems of heavily veined Bells of Ireland bracts, rosy-green apples and pears, limes and bell peppers – when you 'go for green' there is no shortage of choice.

FASHION AND FLOWERS

Tuck a handful of flowers in your hatband just because it is a lovely sunny day or make a daisy chain for a child to wear. Pin a buttonhole to your lapel on your way to a wedding, or present a posy to a visiting speaker, and you are carrying on traditions many of whose origins are lost in the mists of time, since the use of flowers for personal adornment goes way back in history.

The choice of flowers and leaves was sometimes dictated by religious belief, often by custom. In ancient Egypt garlands were bestowed on rulers and high achievers. They were brightly coloured, and fashioned with mallow and poppies, or made of palm and papyrus leaves entwined with herbs and the sacred flower, the lotus.

The Greeks and Romans had a strong feeling, too, for wreaths, garlands and chaplets which, with a highly practical streak, they made mainly from evergreen leaves – laurel, bay, box, ivy and yew – adorned with oak leaves, acorns, fruits, and both 'sculptured' and scented flowers. Tulips, hyacinth, honeysuckle and lilies were favourites and also among those flowers which last particularly well out of water. These garlands were worn around the head, shoulders or neck, and also carried ceremonially high on staves. Flowers and petals were strewn everywhere, on furniture, floors, and over honoured guests and were maybe the origin of the custom of showering brides with rose petals and confetti.

MAY DAY CUSTOMS

It was the Romans who introduced the delightful custom of holding festivals of flowers. The most notable of these, dedicated to Flora, the Goddess of Spring, survives to this day in May Day celebrations. In some country villages in England children wearing flowers in their hair dance around a May Pole, interweaving coloured ribbons as they go. The highlight of the event is when the queen of the May – usually a small child – is crowned with flowers. In Greece on May Day you can still see elderly ladies sitting outside their houses with long necklaces of fresh flowers vividly outlined against their stark black dresses. And on every door on the first day of May

there hangs a stefani, a hoop of marguerites, marigolds, geraniums, antirrhinums, scabious, or whatever the garden or countryside grows.

In the City of London, in the 13th century, priests at St Paul's Cathedral wore floral crowns on their heads, and throughout the Middle Ages judges carried nosegays of herbs and scented flowers to sweeten the path of their procession. These delightfully named tussie-mussies were composed of herbs and aromatic flowers, with a view to their qualities as both disinfectant and air freshener. For old times' sake, they are carried still by judges in session, which proves that wearing and carrying flowers is by no means a female prerogative.

The Victorians raised the fashioning of floral posies to a fine art, leaving us a charming inheritance, a formal design of rings of wired flowers encircled with a protective layer of leaves or a lace doily. Ladies in that era wore ornate sprays of flowers in their hair and on their dresses. The buttonholes worn by the gentlemen were scarcely less showy, nosegays of mixed flowers and greenery verging on the exuberant.

Whether posies and nosegays were carried or worn, in Victorian times there was likely to be more to the choice of flowers and leaves than met the eye. For this was the age of the hidden message, and bouquets given and received would speak volumes of love, sorrow, joy, anxiety, in a language of flowers handed down from one generation to the next.

With so much tradition to draw upon, and just for the joy of it, let flowers go to your head, and your clothes. We have ideas, some conventional, some imaginative, to circle summery hats, on the spur of a magical moment, with roses, wild flowers and grasses, as a delightful notion for a carefree country picnic. We become more demure with neat posies and bouquets to carry on formal occasions and indulge in some mild flights of fancy in jewellery and buttonholes

Garlands made of flowers, such as spray chrysanthemums, are a refreshing way to enliven a dress. This thick wire hoop was covered first with willow leaves.

to match every mood. And, to make sure the flowers live up to expectations, there are detailed instructions on how to wire and fix them.

HEAD GEAR

There's a really special feeling about wearing flowers in your hair and on your hat. It is quite impossible to be your ordinary, everyday self with a red rosebud tucked behind your ear, or a bunch of primroses clipped to a hairband, celebrating the joy of early spring.

What child does not feel excitement the moment there is a daisy-chain crown or a head-dress of pink and blue cornflowers to wear? Who does not feel an extra spring in their step, an extra hint of elegance, as they pin a flower spray to a special hat to go to a garden party, or experience a spark of midsummer madness as they circle a favourite straw hat with a casual hoop of flowers? There are so many ways of expressing the mood of the moment with flowers that go to your head.

It seems the most natural thing in the world for children to link the stalks of lawn daisies, splitting each stem close to the flower and pushing the next one through it. And at that age, no-one tells you to stand the flowers in water first, to give them a refreshing drink. You can take the idea a step further, and make a simple chain in a similar way, linking marigolds, marguerites, single spray chrysanthemums and other daisy-like blooms. Make a complete circle for the child to wear as a crown, or a strip to wear as a headband. In either case, a couple of hairclips will keep it in place.

To give the decoration a little more substance – as you would for a bridesmaid's head-dress – make up small bunches of flowers and bind them with fine wire or twine to a headband that has been purchased or, for a crown, to a circle of thick cord. Arrange the posies so that each one conceals the stalks of the next, take a critical look at the nearly finished design and tuck in extra flowers or leaves to fill in any gaps that may be left.

Teenagers, and anyone who is young at heart, might prefer a floral head-dress with a wayward look. In the French countryside at festival time young girls love to wear crowns of plaited grasses, thick bunches of stalks twisted to make a circle, the long seedheads radiating out unevenly, like shafts from a Catherine wheel. These crowns are worn on the back of the head and have colourful flowers – larkspur, clarkia, cosmos, mallow, sweet peas, eschscholzia (Californian

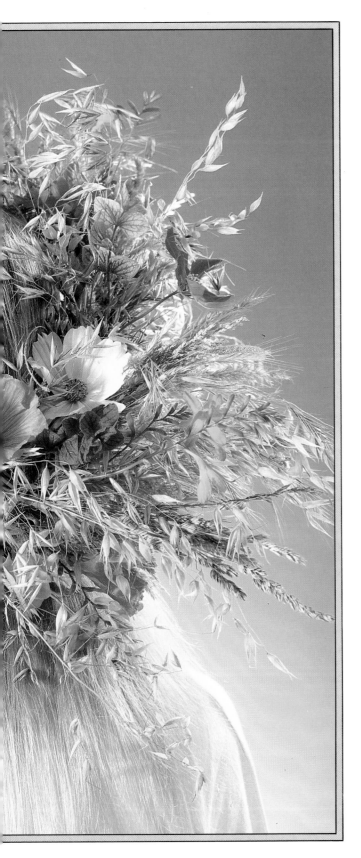

poppies) – tucked in amongst the wild, wayside stems.

Grasses in all their delicate outlines and subtle colours, from sun-bleached cream to deep purple, are a happy choice for decorating a summer hat. It's the kind of thing to wear on a leisurely day in the garden or during a picnic by the river. Choose a straw hat with a deep crown and wide brim. Measure and cut a piece of thick string to encircle the crown and join the ends. Make thick bunches of mixed grasses, 15 to 20 stems in each, cut the stems short and bind them with fine wire. Bind the bunches to the string so that the heads will flop out, higgledy-piggledy, over the brim, and slip the grassy hoop over the hat.

ALL AROUND YOUR HAT

There is an air of informality about an all-round-the-crown floral decoration. Substitute tiny posies of buttercups and daisies, candytuft and love-in-a-mist, geum and matricaria – what you have, and what you please – for the grasses, and the hat will look the part at a summer fête, a tea-party on the lawn or a country wedding.

For more formal occasions, you might prefer to emulate milliners' designs, and arrange a cluster of flowers at the back of a hat, colour-matched to a bow or ribbon band. Roses are a perfect choice. Cut them well in advance, crush or split the stems (see page 11) and leave them in a cool place in water. Make it your last task before leaving, to sew or pin the flowers to the hatband.

If you have a long journey by road, do not subject your flowery headgear to a hot and bothered ride on the back seat. It might seem somewhat excessive, but

This rural head-dress with a base of oats and wild grasses, includes godetia, clary, cosmos, mallow, montbretia, and garden pinks.

Deep salmon-coloured rosebuds and pinks in a spherical bed of primrose and pelargonium leaves, make a delightful wedding posy.

an actress who is much in demand for opening garden fêtes always travels with her latest flower creation cool as a cucumber in an insulated picnic box – a thoroughly modern version of those elegant Victorian hat-boxes.

VICTORIAN POSIES

There was nothing new, in Victorian times, in the custom of posies of leaves and flowers being offered by shy young men as love tokens to demure young ladies. For centuries that had been an accepted way of declaring undying affection. But, in keeping with the times, a new formality evolved in the design.

To achieve the tightness of the design, it is best to choose compact flowers which can easily be arranged in well-defined rows. Each flower or floret is separately wired so that the handle becomes a slender bundle of wires, each one individually bound with florists' tape and then with concealing ribbons.

Rosebuds are a natural choice, their tightly curled petals making perfect circles. (Remember, though, that the buds will gradually open even when the flowers are not in water; so allow them a little space to do so.) Small double spray carnations, love-in-a-mist, cornflowers and tight, double narcissus are among the most suitable of the 'round' flowers.

By contrast, single heads of freesia, delphinium, alstroemeria, flowering tobacco, campanula and sweet pea, with their trumpet and fan shapes, give variety, and help to lighten the design.

Leaves have an important part to play, providing natural contrast to the flowers and forming a protective ring around the outside – sometimes reinforced, in the best Victorian tradition, by a stiff lace paper doily. Your choice of materials, whether they be primrose and violet leaves, geranium and nasturtium, ivy and camellia or clematis and herb Robert, will significantly affect the appearance of the design.

Bridal and presentation posies are destined to be in the limelight for several hours so the flowers and foliage need meticulous preparation if they are to stay the course. Give all the plant material a good, long drink, overnight or for several hours, in tepid water in a cool room. Handle the flowers as gently and carefully as possible to avoid bruising, and spray the finished design with cool water. Stand the posy upright in a jar or vase and keep it in a cool place – even the refrigerator – until the big moment arrives.

WEDDING DAY FLOWERS

There is no occasion to compare with a wedding for an exuberant display of flowers to carry and wear. Weddings provide many opportunities for creative flowercraft whether you decide to make bridal bouquets, posies and head-dresses, clusters of flowers on dainty satin slippers, or a cascade of blooms trailing from a prayer book, or outlining a lucky horseshoe; extravagant corsages and flower-encircled hats for the female guests, or traditional or imaginative buttonholes for the men.

If you are entrusted with the task of designing the flower arrangement to be carried by the bride and bridesmaids, the style of the outfits, the colour and the texture and weight of the fabrics will have a bearing

The posies became completely stylized, with rings and rings of flowers and leaves arranged, like ripples in a pool, around a central flower, with never a petal out of place. Often the central bloom, slightly raised above the surrounding rows, would be a single perfect rosebud, the ultimate symbol in the language of flowers, for it signified the blossoming of new, young love.

With centuries of romantic symbolism behind them, these Victorian-style posies have been popular ever since as bouquets for young brides and bridesmaids. With their neat, compact and easy to carry shape, they are also perfect presentation gifts for visiting speakers and guests of honour.

on the flowers you choose for both bride and groom.

Sketches are a great help. Whether the dresses are being chosen from a wedding catalogue, made from a pattern or designed by a dressmaker, ask for a sketch and make tracings of the designs. Then draw outline shapes of bouquets and posies on the outlines of the dresses. You will be able to see whether the designs you had in mind are suitable for the dresses. At this drawing-board stage it is easier to modify ideas, pool suggestions and come up with finished designs.

If the dresses are being made up, take a cutting of the material to a flower shop and note down ideas for flower textures and colours that will complement the materials, but not pale into obscurity when held against them. Buy a few stems of flowers for the bride to see. Hold them against the dress materials and check that the balance is right. Heavy flowers with wax-like petals, such as tulips and lilies, may look overpowering against a fine voile or dainty net; tiny flowers such as lily-of-the-valley and snowdrops could well be lost against a self-embroidered material or intricate lace.

These sample flowers will not be wasted. Have a trial run and practise wiring them until the specific technique for each type becomes familiar and automatic to you.

If the bride's choice is for a perfect match of flowers and fabric – cream roses with cream silk, shell pink camellias with shell pink cotton – design bouquets and posies with a delicate frame of leaves or contrasting flowers that will allow the main blooms to be clearly appreciated.

These guidelines apply equally when you are

Above: *Break the conventional buttonhole habit with a purple iris, a cream orchid or a crimson rosebud.*
Right: *Imaginative flower designs for a wedding.*
Below: *Wire small bunches of flowers before attaching them to the head-dress base.*

A simple summer dress is transformed with a posy of wild roses at the waist and a ribbon of flower heads around the hem. Flowers on the hat are first wired to a strip of ribbon.

designing head-dresses, only now you have to consider not only the garments, but hair colouring as well. A delicate outline of leaves surrounding a flower headband or crown may be all you need to ensure that cream gardenias or bronze fuchsias are equally flattering to both blonde and brunette tresses.

However casual the finished effect is to be, the preparation of the flowers must be meticulous, so that they will not only look delightful but give a feeling of complete security. This is not the occasion to twist a few wild flower posies on to a stem of ivy and call it a head-dress. In almost every bridal design – or indeed for any important occasion – the flowers should be wired individually and then bound into a bouquet or a posy; on to a headband or wire ring for a crown, or grouped together into a dress spray or corsage.

Wiring flowers is surprisingly quick. Each flower head or floret is cut from its stalk and mounted on to a false stem or wire – which is much more malleable than any natural stalk. You can angle the flowers in any way you wish, twisting the wire so that the flowers face upwards, downwards or to either side. In addition, the wire stems – thinner and less clumsy to hold than a bunch of woody stalks – can themselves be shaped to give the right-angled handle grip essential for a cascade bouquet.

It may seem less important to wire flowers for a dress spray or corsage. A cluster of wild roses and a few stems of lily-of-the-valley, or a couple of stems of freesia and a rosebud, can easily be arranged, but even so the bulk of the stems may be a problem. A slender line of wires bound with narrow ribbon or florist's tape looks more elegant, and is more comfortable to wear.

SUMMERTIME FASHIONS

Memorable occasions such as a summer festival parade, a display of country dancing at an annual fair, a drinks party on the lawn or a lazy trip in a small boat are just made for the imaginative, and even slightly impractical marriage of fresh flowers and informal fashions.

Flowers have the ability to create the prettiest impact in the shortest possible time. A scattering of single blooms on a swirling skirt, sprays, posies, flower chains and flower covered ribbons all capture the mood of the moment, and are completed in a matter of moments, too.

Enhance a favourite summer dress by sewing or sticking flowers to the shoulder straps and around a frill or the hem; or scatter separate flowers across a skirt or over the bodice. Large stitches through the flower centres and fabric will hold them in place, and they can be pulled out easily when the festivities are over. Double-sided sticky tape or sticky fixing tabs can also be used.

Flowers such as marigolds, ox-eye daisies, small single spray chrysanthemums and ranunculus are suitable, since they last well out of water (after a good long drink) and being flat do not inhibit movement.

Ribbons of flowers can be worn in so many ways: Sew or stick flower heads such as scarlet busy Lizzie

(*Impatiens*) on to a white sash to encircle the waist like a waistband; or fix a few flower heads random-style, here and there along the trailing ends of a ribbon bow. Alternatively attach small mixed posies to the ends of a narrow ribbon belt. All these ideas will transform a plain dress in minutes.

In Spain and Portugal boys and girls in festival parades wear their floral sashes diagonally, over one shoulder and dipping below the waist on the other side, a style that derives from the baldric, a heavily ornamented sash worn to support a sword or bugle. Flowers are much more fun. Young children love to be decked out in this way, and the brighter the flowers, the better. Yellow and orange eschscholzia on a white ribbon, maybe, or many coloured cornflowers on pale blue enter into the fun of the fiesta. A matching circlet in a small girl's hair, or a posy pinned to a hair slide completes an outfit.

FLOWER JEWELLERY

Flower jewellery is by no means the prerogative of the very young, but perhaps just the young at heart. In country districts in Greece, for example, you can see women, when they gather together to celebrate festivals and weddings, heavily festooned with brilliant garden and wild flowers, like so many glittering and precious jewels. Small girls may wear bracelets and anklets of the brightest flowers they can find such as geranium or delphinium flowers picked from the stem and threaded on to thick cotton. Older girls may strive for more formality and elegance, and thread flowers to make a choker-style necklace or a rope of flowers, hanging almost to waist level.

Perhaps the pride of the family belongs to the oldest members. Grandmothers dress in black blouses, skirts and cardigans, and, unselfconsciously, wear the biggest, brightest flower jewellery of all, a thick rope of sunshine yellow doronicum or marigold flowers reaching almost to hip level.

When there is no time, and no need, for the more formal wiring techniques described on page 61, use the quick and easy threadneedle system. Gather together a generous pile of identical flowerheads, bright pink mallow, yellow *Kerria japonica*, golden gazania, or whatever grows in abundance. Use a thick darning needle and fine twine, and thread the flowers to make a brightly coloured, tightly packed floral rope. A long hoop of flowers that can be slipped easily over the head can be made continuous, with no fastening. Shorter necklaces can be threaded on to the twine with long ends left to tie into a bow.

Chapter 2

DRIED FLOWER CRAFT

If you have ever walked around a beautiful garden and wondered whether you could capture the magic of the shapes, colours, even the scents for ever, the good news is that you can. By a variety of simple processes you can build up a delightful collection of flowers, leaves and seedheads throughout the year, and bring them together in glorious, and almost everlasting, arrangements.

A basket filled to overflowing with dried midnight blue delphinium, silvery honesty 'moons', orange Chinese lanterns and yellow-eyed narcissus for a pedestal table; a romantic bouquet of palest pink and cream rosebuds, tiny deep red zinnias and creamy white matricaria; a miniature posy of buttercups and daisies to pin to a showy hat; a wall-hung swag that echoes the end of summer tints – with fluffy golden rod, zingy yellow tansy heads, glycerine preserved beech and oak leaves, and chestnut brown seedheads; or a glowing bowl of winter berries – all these designs and many more you can create by preserving plant materials.

Think of summer flowers as reserves in the bank. You harvest and preserve them when the gardens, hedgerows and markets are a blaze of colour and stocks are plentiful. You store them carefully and draw on them, when the gardens are empty and market supplies expensive.

THE BASIC TECHNIQUES

There are four basic preserving techniques. The first, air drying, is suitable for all types of flowers which are formed of dense clusters – such as gypsophila, tansy, sorrel – and for multi-petalled composites.

Double zinnias and double marigolds are examples. This is also the method for preserving a whole range of seedheads, from towering hollyhock to tiny rue. There are detailed instructions and descriptions for achieving this 'second harvest' on pages 80-82.

Another preserving technique, which captures and holds the shape and form of single, open flowers like buttercups and pansies, trumpet shapes like narcissus, antirrhinum and orchids, involves using a desiccant. In this method a dry powder is sprinkled gently around the flower; gradually, and without altering shape or colour, the desiccant – and several different types are available – draws out the moisture.

The art of pressing flowers and leaves is a favourite childhood hobby; it seems like magic to be able to close beautiful shapes between the pages of an album and then rediscover them, transformed but still retaining their recognizable outlines and colours. Pressed materials have many decorative possibilities – we explore these in later pages.

Preserving in a solution of water and glycerine is the fourth main technique we shall be examining in detail. This produces rich, strong colours – sprays of glowing brown beech leaves, supple lime leaves complete with their eliptical fruits, prickly stems of glistening blackberries, these and many other preserved materials will add immeasurably to your designs of fresh, dried and even artificial flowers.

Above: *Dried rosebuds make a pleasing display in a china basket.*

Opposite: *There is a wealth of plant material that can be successfully dried and will enable you to fill your home with the scents and colours of the garden.*

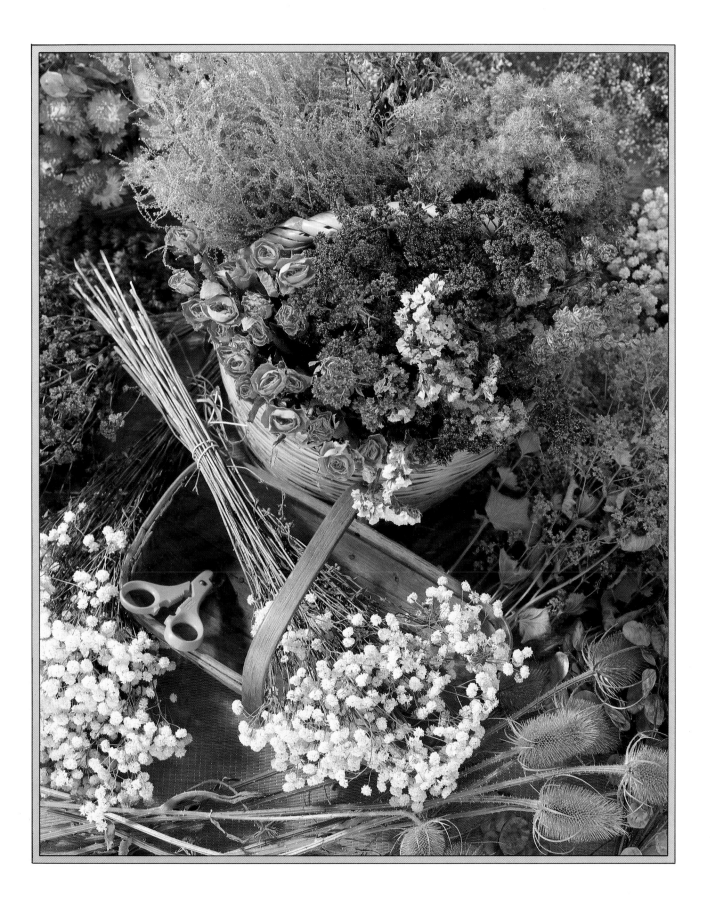

PRESERVING TECHNIQUES

The simplest of all preserving techniques is air drying. According to type, flowers, seedheads, grasses and some leaves may be dried in a warm, airy place, hanging in bunches, standing in a container or spread out on a flat surface.

AIR DRYING

In the process of drying in this nearly natural way, flower petals shrivel to become more dense. This shrinkage is almost imperceptible in flowers which are composed of a high number of petals.

The conditions under which you harvest plant materials for drying play an important part in determining the success or otherwise of the process. Choose a dry day, and as far as possible the driest time of day. This means waiting until the dew has evaporated in the morning, and gathering the materials before the dampness settles again in the evening. It is almost impossible to achieve a high standard, drawing out the natural moisture within the plants, if you have to contend with atmospheric moisture as well. Excess dampness is almost inevitably a recipe for the development of mould.

The stage of development of the plant material is another critical factor. Most flowers and seedheads for drying should be cut just before they are about to open. If you allow thistles, bulrushes and pampas grass, for example, to open fully they will explode since this is their natural process of seed distribution, and the moment for drying them will be lost. Long flower spikes should be cut when the topmost third is still in tight bud.

Next, the time scale. Plan to harvest the materials on a day when you will be able to prepare them for drying with the shortest possible delay. Put them in water, as for all fresh materials, as soon as you cut them.

The temperature and humidity of the 'drying room' also has a significant effect on successful and realistic results. Dampness and strong sunlight are the extreme conditions to avoid. Choose a well ventilated room that, if it cannot be left with closed blinds, at least has dark corners. A garage is suitable only if it is well insulated and does not get steamy in a rainstorm, a kitchen only if it never suffers from condensation.

The perfect spot will vary from one home to the next. I dry all my flowers in one end of the thirteenth century granary we use as an office – there is no excuse for lack of inspiration, sitting looking at a false ceiling of bunches of astilbe, senecio, cornflowers and helichrysum. It could be that a spare bedroom, the corner of a landing, a stairwell, a sewing room or utility room would be just the place. Although the plant materials are best left undisturbed while they are drying, there is no need to hide them away; hanging in bunches or standing in pots they make an interesting and decorative feature.

The largest candidates for air drying – long spikes of delphinium, mullein and purple loosestrife – and tightly closed rosebuds benefit from drying more rapidly at a higher temperature. The airing cupboard or the space above the boiler would be suitable.

BUNCHED OR FLAT

From the list on pages 76-78 you will see that the greatest number of plant types may be air-dried hanging in bunches. Another group, those which have tiny, delicate flowers, like alchemilla mollis, all the umbrella-shaped heads, like achillea, yarrow, fennel

An empty shelf or drawer, if well ventilated, can provide a convenient place for drying plants.

and lovage, and dainty grasses are best dried upright, their stems stuck into dry foam or standing in roomy containers. A convenient way to dry the spherical flower heads of the onion family – from the diminutive chives to the showy *Allium aflatunense* – is to push the stalks through the grid of a wire cake-cooling rack suspended between two supports.

Although it sounds like a contradiction in terms some flowers are dried most successfully by being left standing in water. Hydrangea flowers in all the heavenly shades of blue, pink and green, small paeony heads, white matricaria, heaths and heathers, and pom-pom dahlias keep their colours and characteristics best if they are left for two or three weeks with their stems standing in about 1.5-2.5 cm (½-1 inch) of water. As the water evaporates, so does the moisture in the petals. Once the flowers have dried, wash and then thoroughly dry the stems before storing them, otherwise any residual dampness will spread.

Some grasses and other seedheads supported on slender stems are best dried flat. You can use trays, box lids, sheets of newspaper, wrapping paper or open shelving, but not a closed drawer because the process depends on a free circulation of air. Turn the materials over occasionally while they are drying, so that each surface in turn lies uppermost.

Pliable stems such as broom, willow and mulberry can be twisted into a circle, tied firmly and hung on a hook to dry. When they are untied they will spring into the kind of gentle curves that give natural 'movement' to a graceful arrangement. The circular hoop of stems, just as it is dried, makes an unusual and natural alternative to a florist's wire or foam ring as a base upon which to fix herbs or dried flowers for a wallhanging.

Very few leaves preserve their characteristics when air-dried. Carrot and bay, which can both be dried hanging in bunches, are exceptions. Others, as will be seen, are best preserved by pressing or in glycerine solution.

When preparing stems for drying, strip off all the leaves, removing them carefully if you wish to treat them by another method. For hang-drying, gather the stems into bunches and tie them firmly with a slip knot that can be tightened as the stems shrink. It is better to make several small bunches rather than one overcrowded one, so that all the materials are adequately and evenly exposed to the air. Fan out the stems to dry in containers so that the heads are not touching, and arrange those to be dried flat in neat rows in a single layer.

The drying time depends on the size and density of the plant material and the temperature and humidity of its environment. When they are completely dried flowers feel and sound crisp and papery, and seedheads rattle.

Once plant materials have dried, you have several storage options. If they have been dried in overheated conditions such as an airing cupboard you must move them to normal room temperature, otherwise they will become too brittle to handle. But if you have come to appreciate the decorative properties of drying flowers around the house, you can leave them where they are – they still need a dry, warm and reasonably dark place – or store them in boxes.

USING DESICCANTS

Legend has it that centuries ago a lady discovered by happy chance the delightful art of powder-drying flowers. The story goes that she buried tiny, fresh red rosebuds in crushed sugar, hoping to create a scented sweetener for a special confection. And when she extracted the flowers she discovered that she had not only achieved her culinary aim, but had preserved the buds perfectly, their charming form and colour intact.

Drying flowers in a desiccant of some kind, crystals or powder which gradually draws out their natural moisture, greatly extends the decorative range of your dried flower collection. Many flower types, as we have seen, may be dried simply in a free circulation of warm, dry air. Many others – some large trumpet shapes, some minute specimens – can only be preserved successfully if they are completely immersed in a drying medium.

Just listing a few of the flowers which can be preserved in this way brings to mind delightful little nosegays to arrange for a dressing table, small individual groups composed in wine glasses, to decorate each place at table or tiny baskets for small bridesmaids to carry, or to take as a long lasting gift to someone who is ill or has no garden. Rosebuds, sweet peas, garden pinks, double night-scented stock, violets, buttercups, daisies, side shoots or separate florets of hydrangea and larkspur, lilac, hyacinth, broom and lily-of-the-valley – these will be enough to keep you busy throughout the season.

Preparing to dry flowers by this, as by any other method, it is important to harvest them when they are absolutely dry. If you attempt to process them in desiccant when there is residual moisture clinging to the petals or lurking deep inside a cone shape, the raindrops or dew will dampen the drying agent and render it ineffective, before it starts to draw water.

The principle is simple. You make a layer of desiccant in a plastic box or storage tin, and place the flowers well apart so that they are not touching each other. Fill deep specimens such as orchids and antirrhinum with the drying agent, and then sprinkle

desiccant gently and carefully over and around them. Another layer of the crystals or powder on top of the flowers absorbs the moisture as it rises. You then cover the box with a lid, seal it all around with sticky tape and place it where it will not be knocked.

DRYING AGENTS

There is a number of suitable drying agents and, if you are impatient to get started, you may well find you have at least one in the house. Silica gel water absorbent crystals, the kind that are used to prevent rust in cameras and clocks, are the most effective. You can buy them in chemists' shops. Large crystals are too weighty for all but the largest double flowers, so buy them already ground to very fine crystals, about the consistency of caster (fine) sugar, or process them yourself in a blender. As it is vital to the success of the operation that the desiccant is itself absolutely dry, silica gel offers a high degree of reassurance. When they are dry the crystals are bright blue. As they absorb moisture they turn pale blue and eventually they become pink – by which time they need to be reactivated.

Reactivate crystals by spreading them on a baking tray and drying them in a cool oven. Alternatively tip them into a frying pan and shake them over a low heat, until they turn bright blue again. Sieve the crystals to remove any petal particles and store them in an airtight tin for re-use.

As long as you dry it thoroughly and sieve out any stray matter you can use any drying agent over and over again, as you will certainly want to do at the height of the season.

Sand, which is considerably cheaper than silica gel, is a good choice when you want to dry very large flowers or to work with large batches. White silver sand, which you can buy from garden centres, is the easiest to use. It has small, free running particles, and is usually clean, dry and ready to use. This is not the case with other types of sand. Some sands must be washed several times in buckets of clean water until the water remains clear. These sands can be drained, spread on baking trays and dried in a cool oven. Leave them to cool thoroughly before using. Any warmth in the desiccant could scorch the petals.

Other water absorbing agents are domestic borax, salt, powdered starch, yellow corn meal, alum powder, white detergent and – returning to our innovator – fine sugar. Within this general context, these agents have varying properties. Borax and starch must be first sifted through a fine sieve, as they tend to form lumps when even slightly damp. Both are a little difficult to remove from dried petals. Sugar may prove too heavy for use on delicate flowers, and detergent, with its slight stickiness, may be difficult to remove from flowers with complex shapes.

The ideal solution often lies with a mixture of two desiccants. Tried and tested 'recipes' include: equal parts of ground silica gel crystals and sand; one part sand to two parts borax; three parts sand or alum to one part borax; two parts corn meal to one part borax; and three parts borax to one part table salt. Bear in

For an eye-catching presentation place pot pourri in an elegant bowl and scatter rosebuds on top.

mind that the smaller and more delicate the flowers are, the more the weight and stickiness of the desiccant may become a problem. But you can mix and match the drying agents to suit your own selection of flowers, and your own experiments.

While flowers dry perfectly in desiccants, most stems, apart from woody ones, lose so much moisture that they collapse. Added to this, you need deep containers indeed if you are to dry most flowers on a usable length of stem. Cut stems supporting a single flower to about 2.5 cm (1 inch) long.

Push the stems vertically into the layer of desiccant in the container so that the flowers are upright and spaced well apart. Then trickle the desiccant slowly through your fingers so that it fills every crevice in the flowers and touches every surface of every petal. Flowers with a deep 'cup' are easier to fill if you support them in one hand, sprinkle in the desiccant and then gently lower them into the box and cover them with more of the drying agent.

This is the critical stage. If you let the desiccant fall too heavily and quickly on to the flowers it will crush them. And if they are mis-shapen at this point, they will be mis-shapen when they are dried.

Flowers which are formed in clusters along a stem, such as lily-of-the-valley, hyacinth and larkspur, are treated in a slightly different way. Whatever shape of container you use, hold the stem so that the flower bells are inverted and fill the flowers with desiccant. If you are using an upright container – such as a coffee jar – push the stem into the layer of desiccant covering the base and sprinkle in more drying agent

to build it up around the stem. If you are using a shallow box, gently tilt the container and the stem, and lay the stem flat on the desiccant layer without tipping out the contents of the flowers. Cover the flowers completely, then cover and seal the container in the usual way.

STORING AND SUPPORTING

The drying process takes from about two days (for buttercups, daisies and pansies) to five days (for pom-pom dahlias and double African marigolds). Test the

Fine, white sand which has been washed and dried can be used as an efficient desiccant to draw the moisture from multi-petalled flowers.

flowers as soon as you think they should be ready. Gently brush aside the top layer of desiccant and if the petals sound papery, remove the flowers from the box. Once they are dry they should not be left any longer as they will become too brittle.

Use a small, fine camel hair paint brush to flick away any crystals or powder clinging to the petals. Push a stub wire (you can buy them in packets from florists) up through the short stem and out through the flower head. Make a short, thin hook in the top and draw it carefully back through the flower to secure it. Long flower spikes such as hyacinths simply need a wire pushed through the stem. Store the dried flowers with their false stems stuck into dry florist's foam, taking care that they do not crush or damage each other.

You now have the makings of a varied collection of realistic looking dried flowers on the most unrealistic looking stems. This imbalance is easily rectified. Bind the wire stems neatly and tightly with a thin strip of green or brown crepe paper, or with florist's tape, gutta percha.

The stems probably will not show. Dried flowers look prettiest when they are arranged close together, but not overcrowded, the stems supported in dry brown florist's foam or crumpled wire mesh.

A silver bon-bon dish packed with tiny cream rosebuds, sprays of golden broom and delphinium flowers; a glass cake stand piled high with a pyramid of camellias and Mexican orange blossom, a Victorian cup and saucer overflowing with godetia in every shade of pink – that imaginative and experimental cook really started something with her scented sugar.

USING YOUR COLLECTION

As your collection of dried flowers grows – with, for instance, lavender hanging from coat hooks and coathangers, pots of water dried hydrangeas and foam blocks that have been pierced with myriad wire stems of powder dried blooms – the time will come to create lovely long lasting designs for your home and for gifts.

The wonderful thing about dried flowers is that you can arrange them in or on any kind of container from a priceless vase to a wooden spoon, since water retention is not a consideration.

Dried flowers of all types seem to have a will of their own because they are so light. Place a few stems in a narrow vase, turn your back, and they will have popped out or shot upwards. And so you need to take a firm hand and employ a few tricks of the trade.

Designs created with bunches of dried flowers rather than single blooms look fabulous; dried cornflowers or matricaria are, for example, more stunning if massed rather than arranged so that each stem is placed separately. Not only that, the bunches are a great deal easier to handle.

You probably will not need any holding material if you arrange bunches in wide-necked containers such as earthenware pots, deep shopping baskets or copper preserving pans. Wide shallow containers can be a problem. If the bunches will not stay anchored, fill the container with a piece of crumpled wire mesh, twist a wire round each flower bunch and hook it over the netting.

Crumpled netting in the neck of narrow containers tames dried stems just as it does fresh ones. Dried stems or false stems of wire are much more slender than fresh ones however, and so will need a base of netting which has smaller spaces.

There is a special stem-holding foam for use with dried flowers. It is usually brown, has a tight, compact texture and takes a much firmer grip on stems than does the standard green type. Use the brown foam and you can create designs with dried materials akin to all those described for fresh flowers, with the added advantage that, with no maintenance at all, they will give lasting pleasure.

Whether you decide to fashion an equal triangle design in a classic urn container or an armful-of-flowers effect with foam wedged into the neck of a pottery jug, maximize the impact of the dried flowers and avoid a 'spotty' look by grouping several of each small type together. A cluster of pink or white rhodanthe, a handful of chamomile, a clump of lavender or sea lavender make a stronger impact.

Take a critical look at dried flower arrangements of all kinds and carefully fill in any gaps that reveal spindly stems. Generous profusion is the effect you are after.

Foliage does not feature prominently in dried flower design, for of course very few leaves can be dried successfully. Small sprays of foliage preserved in glycerine provide a hint of sheen in a group of flowers where the charm is in their matt paperiness. Take care not to overdo it, though: the deep strong shades of preserved leaves can all too readily become dominant.

Other dried materials can perform the 'neutral background' function normally required of foliage. Clusters of lime green alchemilla mollis, pale green bracts of Bells of Ireland, silvery honesty 'moons', parchment coloured seedheads and delicate grasses all complement the modesty of dried flowers.

FOAM TECHNIQUES

When a design will give joy for months to come it is worth spending a little time in its creation. By using foam shapes you can fashion dried flower cones, trees, circlets and swags. Place a pyramid of foam on a cake stand, cut short the stems of dried flowers such as helichrysum, rosebuds and poppy seedheads, and arrange them in a pattern. Fix a sphere of foam to the top of a cane, 'plant' it in a flower pot and make concentric rings of dried flowers around it. Buy a plastic posy ring ready-filled with foam and fill it to capacity with your prettiest blooms. Short snippings of golden rod, clarkia or larkspur tucked in tidily break up the 'all round' effect. Fix a hook to a slice of foam, hang it from a ribbon and create a flower sculpture to hang over a bed, in an alcove, or over a mantel. Brush a picture frame or the edge of a piece of mirror-glass with adhesive and press on flowers to make a floral border. This is a thrifty way of using small cuttings and snapped off flower heads.

For the most delightful gift of all, take some ideas from the fresh flower section and shape a perfect posy with dried flowers. All the rosebuds, camellias, and lily-of-the-valley, dried in crystals or powder, are posies in waiting, their stems already wired.

A medley of dried flowers and seedheads, bunched in a deep basket, makes a pleasing, long-term feature indoors.

FLOWERS FOR AIR DRYING

Flower	Method	Notes
Acanthus	Hang in bunches	Tall arcs of pink, white and mauve flowers
Achillea or Yarrow	Upright, or in bunches	Small young flowerheads are most successful
Agapanthus	Upright	Allow plenty of space between seedheads. Hollow succulent stems take weeks. Can be varnished
Alchemilla mollis	Upright or hanging in small bunches	Flowers gradually fade from lime green to mustard yellow
Allium species	Stand upright, supporting heads on racks, or flat in boxes	Wide range of sizes and colours including white, yellow and purple
Anaphalis	Hang upside-down	Harvest before full-blown. Do not strip off foliage. Dries well
Astilbe	Hang in bunches	Long, feathery stems give a misty look to arrangements
Ballota	Dry flat	Cut when young and green. Keep leaves on
Bay leaves	Hang in bunches; can also be glycerined	The leaves turn brown after both drying and preserving in glycerine
Bells of Ireland (*Molucella laevis*)	Hang singly. Can also be preserved in glycerine	Strip off leaves. Fade to rich parchment colour

Bluebell (*Scilla*)	Seedheads – hang or stand upright in container to dry	Pick seedheads when becoming dry and papery.
Broom	Hang dry stems	Can be twisted into a circle, tied firmly and hung on a hook to dry. When untied the stems will spring into gentle curves
Bulrush	Hang dry	Pick spikes when they are half developed, and spray with hair lacquer to prevent seeds bursting
Burdock	Hang dry	The burs dry well and keep their colour
Carrot	Hang-dry leaves	Useful to give a feathery softness to small designs
Chamomile	Hang in bunches	Pick flowers before they reach full bloom
Chinese lantern (*Cape gooseberry*)	Hang-dry seedheads in bunches	Cut when not all the calyces have ripened. Strip off leaves. When dried, hang some stems in sunlight to fade the bright orange 'lanterns'
Chive	Dry flowers upright, with the stems through wire mesh to support the heads	Quick-drying in an airing cupboard helps to preserve colour
Clarkia	Dry hanging or flat	Flowers dry extremely well and keep their colour. Seedheads can also be dried
Clematis	Hang dry	The fluffy seedheads dry well. Spray them with hair lacquer to prevent them from disintegrating
Columbine (*Aquilegia*)	Hang dry	Wait to harvest seedheads until they open and start to curve outwards
Cornflower	Hang in bunches in airing cupboard	Pink, blue and white flowers all keep colour well
Cow parsnip (*Heracleum*)	Dry upright in containers	Harvest just as seedheads are formed
Dahlias (*Pom-pom*)	Stand in 1.5-2.5 cm (¾-1 inch) water	Petals dry as water evaporates. Once flowers have dried wash and thoroughly dry stems, otherwise dampness will spread
Delphinium and larkspur	Small young flower shoots can be dried in desiccant. Flowers (in an airing cupboard) and seedheads can be dried hanging or flat	Dry both flowers and seedheads. Pick flowers for drying when some buds are still unopened and dry in a heated room
Dock	Hang dry. Can also be glycerined	Seedheads change from lime green to deep red when dried

Fennel	Dry seedheads upright	Stick stems into dry foam or stand in roomy containers
Feverfew (*Matricaria*)	Hang in bunches	Pick just before fully open. The small white flowers are most effective arranged in clusters
Figwort (*Scrophularia*)	Hang upside down	Candelabra-like clusters of seedheads are good for outlining
Foxglove (*Digitalis*)	Hang-dry seedheads	Can snip off seedheads for use singly in small designs
Fritillary	Dry seedheads flat. Can then be varnished	Harvest early in the season
Globe artichoke (*Cynara scolymus*)	Dry individual stems by hanging, or standing upright in containers	The huge purple flower heads, like great thistles, dry well and turn glistening cream
Globe thistle (*Echinops ritro*)	Hang dry	Cut the steel blue globular flower heads as they are just beginning to open. Later in their formation they disintegrate as they dry
Godetia	Dry seedheads flat	Harvest late summer, strip off leaves and dry clustered seedheads
Golden rod (*Solidago*)	Hang dry or upright in a container	Cut stems in various sizes. Sprays of the laterals can be snipped off for small-scale designs
Grape hyacinth (*Muscari*)	Dry seedheads flat or upright	Once dried, the seedheads look like papery bluebells
Grasses	Dry by hanging in bunches, upright in containers, or flat	'Top heavy' grasses on slender stems are best dried flat
Gypsophila	Hang dry loosely in bunches	The minute flowers give a misty look to designs
Heathers	Stand in 1.5-2.5 cm (¾-1 inch) water, or hang dry	Pick stems when flowers have just opened
Helipterum	Hang in bunches	Harvest the everlasting flowers just before fully open
Hollyhock (*Althaea*)	Seedheads – hang dry or can be dried flat	You can clip off and use individual seedheads in miniature arrangements
Honesty (*Lunaria*)	Seedheads – hang dry or dry upright.	Cut stems when the centre of the seedhead, like silver tissue paper, is still protected by two brown outer skins. Rub these layers between thumb and first finger when arranging the sprays
Hop (*Humulus*)	Hang upside down or can be glycerined	The pale olive flowers fade only slightly. These papery blossoms are useful in dried arrangements, providing neutral green colouring
Hyacinth – giant summer (*Galtonia*)	Hang in bunches	Harvest as last petals are falling – except in hot Indian summer, when they can dry on plant
Hydrangea	Stand flower heads in about 2.5 cm (1 inch) water. Separate florets can be powder-dried	The petals dry as water evaporates. Once flowers have dried wash and thoroughly dry stems, otherwise dampness will spread
Jerusalem sage (*Phlomis*)	Dry flat	Seedheads dry quickly. Do not strip off the white woolly leaves.
Knapweed (*Centaurea*)	Seedheads dry upright or hang in bunches	Gather as soon as seedheads open (midsummer – early autumn). Cut some buds and varnish them
Larkspur (*see Delphinium*)		
Lavender (*Lavandula*)	Can be dried by hanging, or upright in containers, both dry or in a little water	Cut the stems before the flowers are fully open
Lovage	Dry seedheads upright	Stick stems into dry foam or stand in roomy containers
Love-in-a-mist (*Nigella*)	Hang dry	Harvest late summer. Remove most of the frondy leaves. The globular seed capsules look like purple-striped lanterns
Maize (*or Sweetcorn*)	Dry cobs in an airing cupboard, flat on racks. Spray with lacquer or paint with varnish once dried. Hang-dry seedheads and leaves	The leaves dry to a pale avocado green colour and look like crepe paper. The seedheads turn to pale parchment
Mallow	Hang dry	The long spikes of silver-grey seedheads are like closed-up stars
Marigold	Double flowers can be dried by hanging in an airing cupboard. Both double and single marigolds dry successfully in desiccants	Harvest flowers for drying just before they open fully
Montbretia (*Crocosmia*)	Dry long spikes of seedheads flat	The stems, with the small, pale cream seedheads, are good 'points' in an arrangement
Mullein	Hang-dry the long spikes of seedheads, or lay them flat. Large subjects like this are best dried in an airing cupboard	Such long spires are useful for large displays in public places

Narcissus	Cut the stems short and dry flat in an airing cupboard. Can also be powder dried	All snub-nosed flat-flowered kinds retain their colour well. Mount the dried flower heads on false wire stems	**Senecio**	Hang the flowers in bunches, and dry sprays of leaves upright in containers in about 2.5 cm (1 inch) of water	The silver-grey leaves retain the delicate tones well
Paeony heads (small)	Stand in about 2.5 cm (1 inch) water, or can be powder dried	Petals dry as water evaporates. Once flowers have dried, wash and thoroughly dry stems otherwise any dampness will spread	**Smoke tree** (*Rhus*)	Hang dry	When dried, the seedheads look like a puff of smoke and soften the outline of an arrangement
Pampas grass (*Cortaderia*)	Hang dry	Should be cut before they start to shed. Can be kept in shape by spraying with ordinary hair lacquer	**Sorrel**	Hang flower spikes in bunches. Can also be preserved in glycerine	Pick in full bloom preferably. If picked after formation of seed it will easily disintegrate unless sprayed with hair lacquer. Colours vary from pale green to dark brown
Pinks	Dry upright. Can also be powder dried	Cut before the flowers are fully open. To retain the natural colour it is important to keep them in a dark place	**Spiraea**	Dry upright	The white flowers of the variety Meadowsweet dry a pale parchment colour
Poppy (*Papaver*)	Hang dry the seedheads	All kinds of poppy provide excellent seedheads which are invaluable in any collection of dried material. Colours range from pale cream, through pale green to deep purple	**Stonecrop** (*Sedum*)	Hang dry	The flowers dry to a subtle pinky-beige in soft sprays
Rodanthe	Hang dry	These pinky-white everlasting flowers retain their colour well	**Straw flowers** (*Helichrysum bracteatum*)	Hang in bunches	These daisy-shaped everlasting flowers are among the most useful of dried plant material. If the brittle stems snap off, or where height is needed, attach false wire stems to the flower heads
Rosebuds (tightly closed)	Hang dry in airing cupboard. Can also be powder dried	Only small, very compact buds can be successfully air dried	**Sweet William** (*Dianthus*)	Dry upright, in dry containers or with a little water	Pick the flower heads just before they are fully open; they will dry into balls of muted coloured flowers
Rue	Hang seedheads in bunches	Seedheads look like little wooden nuts	**Tansy**	Hang dry the flower heads	The brilliant golden heads are especially useful for large arrangements
Sage	Hang seedheads in bunches or dry upright. Sprays of leaves and flowers can be dried in an airing cupboard	Leaves retain their aroma even after drying	**Teasel** (*Dipsacus*)	Hang dry	The long stems with seedheads like hair brushes, dry well. They are good subjects for drying
Salvia	Dry flowers and seedheads upright or flat – flowers in an airing cupboard	Delicate spikes of seed capsules are attractive 'neutrals' with more colourful subjects	**Thistle** (Scotch or cotton)	Hang dry	Cut before fully open or they will explode
Santolina	Dry upright in containers in an airing cupboard	If dried quickly the tiny flower heads will retain their bright yellow colouring	**Sycamore**	Hang dry	The 'keys' should be cut before they are ripe
Sea holly (*Eryngium*)	Hang dry	Dry the pale blue round flower heads on the stems, with the leaves	**Willow**	Hang dry stems after leaves have fallen	Can be twisted into a circle, tied firmly and hung on a hook to dry. When untied they will spring into gentle curves
Sea lavender or statice (*Limonium*)	Hang dry in small bunches	Harvest when flowers are just open. The everlasting flowers dry very well and the neutral shades give a misty, cloudy effect. Bright colours fade in strong sunlight – which can be an advantage	**Xeranthemum**	Hang dry	Everlasting flowers with strong wiry stems which retain their colour well after drying. Varnish some buds
			Yarrow	Dry flowers or seedheads upright	Stick stems into dry foam or stand in roomy containers

DRYING FLOWERS IN DESICCANTS

Flower	Notes
Antirrhinum	Pick off and dry each separate flower
Broom	Cut when not quite in full bloom. Lay short sprays flat. Retains both colour and shape well
Buttercup	Retains colour well. Use lightweight powders such as borax to avoid crushing

Camellia	The double blooms dry best and retain their colour and elegance. Leaves can be glycerined
Carnation	Cut before fully in bloom
Choisya (Mexican orange blossom)	Powder dry short sprays, flat in desiccant
Dahlias	Small pom-pom dahlias give best results. To dry very large ones, use sand as the desiccant
Daisy (lawn)	As the dried flowers are so small and brittle it is best to mount them on a short length of stub wire before drying
Delphinium	Choose small young shoots. Large blooms and seedheads can be hang dried
Forsythia	Dry short sprays horizontally
Hollyhock (Althaea)	Powder dry open flowers or tightly-closed buds. Double flowers dry more successfully
Hyacinth	Push a wire through stems before drying
Hydrangea florets	These separate florets can be very useful in miniature designs
Laburnum	Cut when not quite in full bloom. Lay short sprays flat. Retains shape and colour well
Larkspur (see delphinium)	Dry small young shoots
Lilac	Dries very well. Cut before heads are fully open
Lily-of-the-valley	'Fades' to deep cream
London pride	Very useful shape for points in, for example, triangular arrangements
Marigold (Calendula and Tagetes)	Dry face down in the desiccant
Narcissus (Yellow-eyed)	Flowers can also be air dried flat
Orchid	The flowers retain their form, shape and colour but lose the waxy sheen of the petals
Pansy	Mount flowers on short lengths of wire for stems before drying
Paeony	Dry large, double flowers in sand. Can also be dried upright in a little water
Pinks	Single pinks should be powder dried. Double ones may be air dried, upright
Polyanthus (Primula)	Push a short length of wire into the calyx before drying
Rosebuds	Small, tight buds can also be hang dried in an airing cupboard
Stock (double night-scented)	Double flowers give best results
Sweet pea	Red colours strengthen considerably
Violet	Keeps colour well
Wallflower	Sprays may be laid flat in desiccant
Zinnia	Dry face down. Small varieties dry most successfully

A HARVEST OF SEEDS

There is no cause to sigh wistfully as flowers in gardens and fields around you fade; no need for a hint of self reproach if you missed the magic moment to preserve them. For as the petals fall they give way to seedpods which in many cases are almost as attractive as the flowers themselves and a versatile second harvest.

Add to these a collection of delicate and ornamental grasses, a dramatic selection of vegetable and herb seedheads such as onion and lovage for example – not forgetting the cereal harvest to be gleaned along the waysides – and you have a wealth of varied plant material which is rich in shape and subtle in colour.

If you find the deep buttery golds, the sun bleached creams, the misty blues and purples and the pure unabashed silver (of honesty pods) a shade too understated, you can take the colour law into your own hands and dip-dye or spray paint seedheads to your own preference. I would not go so far as to say that these colouring techniques actually improve on nature, but they do give you a helping hand.

It takes a trained eye to see the decorative potential in a flower border or vegetable patch that has gone to seed. But once that eye is in training, even the rubbish heap in a friend's garden can be the most fruitful place on earth. Many is the time I have scrabbled among the prunings and thinnings of late summer and emerged triumphant with a handful of mallow stems, the seedpods like puffed up stars; lupins, like pairs of silver-grey rabbits' ears; rue like clusters of tiny chestnut coloured wood carvings, and acanthus, like a sturdy ladder with rungs on each side of the central stem. It is amazing what some people will throw away.

PICKING YOUR TIME

As with any plant materials for drying, the harvest time is critical. It goes without saying that you should cut seedheads when they are outwardly dry, before, not after, a rainstorm. But that is not all. Seedheads are so fascinating because many of them significantly change shape, form and colour as they develop, and it is up to you to keep an eye on them and choose which stage you wish to capture.

For instance, soon after the unremarkable mauve flowers of honesty fall, this plant develops clusters of flat, fleshy blue-green discs, each pair of which is supported on a short spiky stem. At this stage the pods are very useful in foliage and 'green' groups, bringing their unique shape and texture. As the seeds inside the discs ripen, the pods turn first purplish – when they blend beautifully with blackberry and red maple leaves – and then gradually bleach to beige. At this stage you can rub off the outer covers between your fingers – or leave them on the plant and nature will do it for you – to reveal the translucent silvery 'moons'.

If you grow honesty plants and can watch this evolution from your kitchen window, it is a good idea to cut some stems at each milestone. When the pods are still moist – at the green and purple stages – you can preserve them in glycerine solution. They emerge glistening bright and a deeper shade of the original colour. Or, at any stage, simply hang them in bunches to dry.

SEED ART

Plants which form numerous flowers along a long stem are a treasure trove for the floral artist. Stately spires of delphinium, mullein, foxglove and delicate stems of parchment coloured grape hyacinth seedheads seem to give best results if they are dried flat; hollyhock, sage, dock, lupin, giant summer hyacinth and clarkia hanging upside down; and agapanthus, sometimes called lily of the Nile, standing upright in containers. If you harvest agapanthus before the pods burst to release their seeds, be prepared for a shock. They explode with a crack that is almost indistinguishable from rifle shot. Once dried the pods can be painted with varnish.

The fact that some of these stems rise to towering heights does not mean they are suitable only for grand displays in church and other public places. There is no need to use them in all their stately glory. Each stem can be snipped and clipped into a number of small elements. The short and slender side shoots are useful for 'uprights', and individual seedpods, on their own stems or pushed on to false wire ones, can be delightful in small and miniature designs.

You can raid the vegetable patch as well as the flower garden for umbrella shaped seedheads, and keep a look out for other species – giant hogweed, cow parsnip, fennel and yarrow – that grow freely in the wild. Angelica, caraway, carrot, chervil, lovage with its deeply ridged stems, all these umbellifer seeds aquilegia with brown tulip-shaped pods; flag iris with long blue-grey tubes; campion, not unlike a smaller and less substantial version of poppy heads, and by far the most spectacular, Chinese lanterns, which are bright orange on the plant and fade to a much more sociable shade of pale apricot. They all add interest and variety to dried arrangements, or can be mixed with fresh flowers.

In an end-of-season frenzy of garden clearance many people are apt to throw away a whole group of seedheads that have highly attractive chunky shapes. But once their petals have fallen, sunflowers, gaillardia, scabious and knapweed, vastly different in scale, leave a legacy of humpy centres that dry well hanging in bunches. Other favourites of mine are Jerusalem sage, with hoops of pale cream or green seed capsules around the stem, candytuft with whorls of seeds in clusters, and Greek spiny spurge, the seedheads for all the world like crisp brown lawn daisies. Many is the time I have braved unfriendly terrain in Greece to bring home a bunch of my annual souvenir.

The most graceful and slender seed carriers of all are wild and ornamental grasses, and cereals – wheat, oats, barley and rye – which perhaps you can gather from roadsides. Birds are helpful seed broadcasters and tend to scatter a crop far and wide enough to enable it to be harvested by flower craft enthusiasts without the need to trespass. All these materials are easy going candidates for drying, and the option of either hanging them in bunches, standing them in containers or spreading them out on racks, is dependent upon what is most convenient. Only those with the slenderest stems show any preference and these give the best results if dried flat.

A jug of dried grasses, wheat and wild oats, with a colour burst of paper poppies, can evoke the golden days of harvest. A sun-bleached arrangement of seedheads emphasizing the fascinating variety of shapes can be a symphony of neutral creams and browns, the long lasting equivalent of a foliage display. This second harvest of seed capsules has plenty to offer just the way it is.

dry successfully when left standing upright. I keep a collection of used bottles and place one stem in each. They make an interesting group standing in an empty grate and have even been mistaken for a deliberate arrangement. Again, there are no constraints on any floral artist to use these huge protective heads as they appear on the plant. Snip off several of the tiny stems, cluster them together and push them into stem-holding foam as you build up a mini arrangement. In close-up they look quite impressive.

PODS AND GRASSES

There is a whole range of plants which rewards the eagle eyed arranger with a collection of various urn shaped seed capsules that dry perfectly hanging in bunches. Grey-green poppy seedheads, probably the most 'classic' shape of all, and prickly spiky teasels are among the best known. But there are many others, such as love-in-a-mist, the purple and green striped 'lanterns' criss-crossed with a net of green whiskers;

DYEING AND SPRAYING

To the adventurous and imaginative floral artist a collection of dried plant materials also presents a wealth of opportunity for experiments with colour, as exciting a challenge as a piece of unbleached calico to a tie-dye enthusiast. Colouring plant materials, by dip-dyeing or spray painting, can never be an exact art with precise recipes and methods timed to the minute. The colour tones achieved will depend on the absorption properties of the various plants and whether they have retained any residual moisture.

For dip-dyeing I like to use natural dyes since they give more sympathetic results. Not having any woad or dyers' poke-weed in the garden, I have turned instead to readily available fruit juices and flower petals. The juice strained from stewed blackberries, mulberries, raspberries, redcurrants and gooseberries (which makes a pale amber dye) work splendidly. The more you dilute the juice with water the softer the colour will be. Onion skins simmered in water make a brown dye, and marigold petals (one cup of petals in one cup of water, simmered for one hour) give a pale yellow colour.

I find that the heathery shades obtained with the black fruits and the soft pinks and corals made possible with the red fruits give the prettiest effects. You simply leave the juices to cool, pour them into jars and dip in the dried plants.

DYEING SEEDHEADS

A collection of seedheads in all shapes and sizes dyed in a single colour makes a charming group. It does not take much practice to realize that the furry surfaces of lupin pods and ballota, for instance, absorb dye most readily and emerge with the deepest shades. Teasels, Jerusalem sage, knapweed, grape hyacinth and many others have what I term medium absorption, and the shiniest and toughest examples – honesty moons and poppy pods – grudgingly accept the colour. Honesty gives the most delightful effect, looking as if it has been spattered with coloured rain.

Dip-dye the seedheads for a few seconds only, or else they will go soggy. Shake them gently over several layers of absorbent paper and hang them to dry in a warm place, with protective newspapers underneath. When they are dry, store them in the usual way.

Spray painting offers different possibilities – bright and shiny colours and a cloak of gold or silver for Christmas arrangements, for instance – and is yet another way of preserving flowers.

A GLEAM IN WINTER

There could scarcely be two more contrasting methods of preserving plant materials than drying and treating them in glycerine solution. Whereas drying – whether it is achieved in a free circulation of air, in powder or crystals, or by pressing between absorbent paper – draws out the natural moisture from the plant, the other method replaces that moisture with a heavy liquid which will not evaporate.

Not surprisingly, the results are quite different, too. As we have seen, dried flowers retain their colour and shape but become crisp, papery and almost invariably have a matt texture. Materials preserved in glycerine, on the other hand, are soft, pliable, and positively glow. Leaves take on a sheen they may never have had in their fresh state, berries radiate colour and gloss, and grasses and bracts have a velvety softness.

Where alternative preserving methods are recommended, it is interesting to treat some materials, such as Bells of Ireland and hydrangea, undeveloped honesty seedheads, dock and sorrel, grasses and cereals, bay leaves and others in each way, and note the different effects. Since there will be differences in both colour and texture, it is useful to have examples of both methods in your collection. It is this contrast, matt with shiny, light colour tints with deep shades, which gives the many forms of flower craft such lively visual interest.

By repute the art of preserving leaves was first practised by Queen Alexandra, whose fondness for gardens, and for flowers in the house, is well known. Like many who are new to the technique, the Queen began by preserving sprays of beech. As her skill and enthusiasm grew so, it is said, did her ever more varied collection of leaves, which she liked to use as a background to winter flowers brought in from the hothouses.

Preserved leaves are naturally at their most useful in winter, when the gardens can offer nothing but evergreens and florists have very little foliage indeed. But there will be other times throughout the year when a spray of deep cream preserved eucalyptus, chestnut brown maple or yellowed birch can provide just the contrast needed to complement a design.

The process of preserving in glycerine gives deciduous leaves many of the characteristics and colours they naturally acquire at the end of summer, in what a New England gardener friend calls the golden days. But you must not wait until the leaves are about to fall before you cut them. It will be too late when the sap is receding in the plant and, on the other hand, too early in spring, when the immature leaves lack the veins and fibres needed to support them.

Gather the branches of deciduous leaves in high summer (in practice, in Britain and the United States this means late June, July and most of August). Evergreens can be preserved over a longer period,

By contrast with plants that are dried with desiccants, leaves, berries and seedheads will shine when preserved with glycerine.

but avoid the time when the tree or bush is forming new shoots of tender young leaves. At this stage they will be totally resistant to a sustaining drink of glycerine.

As you can use the glycerine solution over and over again – you simply need to strain it now and then, and eventually store it in a stoppered bottle – this method of preserving can be easily repeated.

If you have a garden it seems almost wasteful not to keep your pots of glycerine constantly topped up with leaves becoming more glorious day by day. And there is no need to call a halt when you have enough for your own use. To a flower arranger without access to laurel and bay, broom and bergenia, a bunch of preserved foliage is a welcome gift or an irresistible bazaar stall purchase.

THE GLYCERINE TECHNIQUE

To make the preserving solution, mix one part of glycerine with two parts of very hot water and stir or whisk it vigorously until it is thoroughly mixed. You might use a cup as the volume measure to start with, and then increase your stock as your enthusiasm gains momentum.

To preserve sprays of leaves, pour the solution into containers to a depth of 5 cm (2 inches). As the stems take it up, you need to keep the mixture topped up to this original level, so transparent containers such as preserving jars and bottles are an advantage. Large fleshy leaves like bergenia, *Fatsia japonica* and fig are very slow to preserve on the stem, taking up to six weeks, and will sit in your glycerine solution for an undue length of time. To avoid this you can preserve separate leaves, two or three at a time, immersed in a flat dish of the solution. This cuts the time to 10-14 days. Only perfect specimens are worth picking, since flaws that may be scarcely noticeable in the fresh state will be magnified after preserving.

Cut sprays of leaves such as beech, silver birch or whitebeam, that have graceful curves. Snip off damaged leaves and criss-crossing stems which confuse the main outline. Treat woody stems in the usual way, cutting them at a slant, making deep slits or lightly crushing the stem ends and scraping 5 cm (2 inches) off the bark. If you intend to preserve very thick fleshy leaves on the branch it helps to rub them first with cotton wool soaked in the glycerine solution. This prevents leaves at the extremities from drying out before the solution reaches them.

Stand the prepared stems in the solution, taking care that they actually reach the base of the container.

Place individual leaves in a dish of the mixture and press them down to ensure complete immersion.

Patience is a useful virtue while the next stage takes its course, though the process never lacks interest. You can see the progress of the glycerine as it travels up the stems and reaches first the lower leaves and finally the topmost ones. When the leaves at the top, or the tips of large immersed leaves have turned brown and glossy, the time has come to remove them. Wipe the leaves and stems with a clean cloth to dry them and remove any oiliness. Tie stems into bunches and hang them upside down for a few days to 'firm up' the tips. You can continue to store them this way or flat in boxes, whichever is more convenient.

Preserved plant material does not need to be arranged in water. Dry foam, a pinholder or crumpled wire mesh in a dry container is all that is needed to hold the stems. If you wish to use sprays of preserved leaves to complement fresh flowers in water or soaked foam, paint the stems with two coats of nail varnish to protect them from mould.

MATERIALS TO PRESERVE

The materials you preserve will depend of course on what is available. If you have only one tree, shrub or flower patch in the garden it is worth giving it a try. A few notes on preserving times and results will serve as a general guide. Sprays of beech leaves are preserved in four to seven days; ferns, oak, pittosporum, rose and whitebeam in 14 days. They all turn attractive and varying shades of brown. Variegated holly (about 21 days) turns chestnut brown; laurel and broom (14 days) almost black, and box (21-28 days) becomes beige.

Teasels harvested and preserved when they are green, pussy-willow catkins, lime flowers (stripped of the leaves), sprays of blackberry and strawberry tree both in fruit, or spruce with cones take from 14-21 days, and add interest and variety to your collection.

You can capture the magic of berries and other fruits by preserving them on the stems in glycerine solution. Holly, rose hips, snowberries, skimmia, japonica, hypericum, spindle tree, pyracanthus, all give rewarding results. In general the colour deepens and the gloss is retained. Give the shine an extra boost by spraying preserved berries with hair lacquer or painting them with varnish.

For short-term keeping, for Christmas and other winter decorations maybe, simply paint fresh berries with varnish. This will extend their vase life by several weeks.

PRESERVING IN GLYCERINE

Material	Preserving days	Notes
Aspidistra	14-21 immersed, about 70 upright	Immersion gives better results
Bay (*Laurus nobilis*)	14	Leaves may turn dark olive green or chestnut brown
Beech (*Fagus*)	3-7	Cut in midsummer when fully mature
Bells of Ireland (*Molucella*)	21	Preserve then hang upside-down to dry.
Berberis	21	Treat long stems. Leaves turn deep brown
Bergenia	14	Preserve the large leaves
Berries	14-21 depending on type	Treat sprays of berries and leaves together
Blackberry	21	Treat leaves and fruit
Box sprays	14-21	Small, compact sprays are useful fillers
Camellia (leaves)	14-21, immersed 21-28, upright	The flowers can also be powder dried
Choisya (leaves) (Mexican orange)	21-28	Treat only mature leaves
Clematis	14-21	Treat sprays of leaves and seedheads.
Cypress	21-28	Treat flat fan-shaped sprays complete with 'cones'
Dock	14	Cut small spikes of flowers.
Escallonia	14	Sprays of minute leaves are ideal for shape outline
Fatsia (*Fatsia japonica*)	14-21, immersed about 70, upright	The evergreen foliage turns mid brown
Fig	7-14, immersed about 45, upright	Treat leaves singly
Gum tree (*Eucalyptus*)	14-21	Leaves turn grey-mauve
Hellebore (*Helleborus corsicus*)	21	Leaves turn light brown
Holly (*Ilex*)	21	Spray berries after preserving with hair lacquer
Hop (*Humulus*)	14-21	Sprays can be hang dried
Ivy (*Hedera*)	10-14, immersed about 21, upright, depending on length	Long sprays are best immersed. Berries can be treated also
Laurel (*Laurus nobilis*)	21-28	Store individual preserved leaves between blotting paper
Lime	18-21	Treat sprays of leaves and keys
Mahonia	21-35	Leaves darken progressively
Maidenhair fern (*Adiantum*)	14	Cut at any time except when new growth is forming
Maple (*Acer*)	14	Treat single leaves and clusters of keys
Mistletoe	14	Berries wither in time
Oak (*Quercus*)	14-21	Oak apples and acorns preserve well on the stems
Old man's beard	14	Gather before flowers open
Paeony (*Paeonia*)	14	Leaves turn pale olive green with dark, contrasting veins
Pyracantha	21	Spray berries with hair lacquer
Raspberry	14	Cut young perfect leaves
Rhododendron	21	Preserve sprays of leaves with young, tight buds
Rose briars	14	Young shoots of wild roses preserve well
Rose hips	14-21	Spray hips with hair lacquer after preserving
Rosemary (*Rosmarinus officinalis*)	14	Stems after preserving vary from dark green to silver grey. Leaves retain aroma
Mountain ash		Spray berries with lacquer
Shoo-fly plant (*Nicandia*)	14	Hang upside down to dry after preserving
Silver birch (*Betula*)	28	Cut with catkins on twigs. Use solution at boiling point
Snakeweed (*Polygonum*)	14-21	Fine sprays of dark red flowers keep colour well
Snowberry (*Symphoricarpos*)	14-21	White snowberries deepen in colour
Sweet chestnut (*Castanea sativa*)	10-14	Preserve in three stages with tiny chestnuts, and with and without catkins
Sycamore (*Platanus*)	7-10	Treat leaves and keys
Tree paeony	10-14, immersed	Totally immerse short sprays or separate leaves
Viburnum	21	Leaves turn deep brown with olive brown undersides
White cedar (*Chamaecyparis*)	21	Leaves turn orangey-brown. Do not remove from solution when they are just brown
Yew (*Taxus*)	21-28	Berries do not always preserve well

PRESSING FLOWERS

What memories are stirred by opening the pages of a forgotten book and coming across some pressed pansies or bell-shaped foxgloves, nasturtiums or poppies, and other charming reminders of seasons long since past. It is just as delightful to browse through a second-hand book and turn to a single precious flower enclosed between its pages.

Drying plant materials by pressing presents an artistic challenge of two completely different kinds. First, the thrill of the hunt, for flowers and leaves that will retain their characteristic shape and, if not their original colour, a hue that is pleasing. Then after the pressing process comes the creative joy of arranging petals, flowers, stalks and leaves into representational or abstract designs, for anything from a gift tag to a full scale picture. One of the most evocative pressed-flower pictures I have seen depicted a thatched cottage surrounded by massed herbaceous borders, and a herb-filled, crazy-paving path leading up to the entwined roses round the door. It must have been a joy to create.

PRESSING EQUIPMENT

The equipment you need for pressing is minimal, though you may choose to enlarge your kit as you progress. Highly absorbent paper is the main essential item. Blotting paper is hard to beat, though somewhat expensive now. Kitchen roll and toilet tissues are suitable for small, thin subjects – be sure to choose a smooth paper without a waffle or ridged surface – and newspaper is serviceable for large leaves, which may be pressed under a mattress, sofa cushion or carpet.

Large books were traditionally used for pressing. Flowers may be enclosed directly between the pages, but check that the printing ink is not likely to transfer to the petals – not a pretty sight – and remember that the reverse can happen. It is a pity to spoil a valued book with chlorophyll stains. To be on the safe side, it is better to interleave the folios with absorbent paper.

As an advance on the book technique you can buy or make a flower press. This is a series of alternating sheets of flat card and blotting paper enclosed top and bottom between boards and held together at each corner by thumb-screws. The trick is to exert similar pressure on each screw so that the materials are efficiently and evenly dried.

It is useful to have plastic tweezers to pick up subjects before and after pressing, and a small camel-hair paint brush to move them about on the page. Handling delicate petals and flowers can all too easily cause bruising and result in an ugly brown stain.

The greatest asset to a beautiful collection of pressed materials must surely be a garden. There cannot be many craft activities which offer more sheer delight than wandering from plant to plant, cutting a spray of leaves here, a handful of flowers there, some buds, a few supple stalks. But a garden is not the be-all and end-all of the art. Take a calculating look at your house plants; there is plenty of potential there. A mixed bunch of flowers bought from a stall, or flowers in prime condition from a gift bouquet might also be used.

It goes without saying that plant materials must be dry and in perfect condition when you press them. If you gather flowers from a friend's garden or pick weeds in the countryside, give them a reviving drink when you get home. But keep the time between cutting and pressing as short as possible. Better still, take your books or presses with you on day trips and press on site. A word of caution; a gust of wind plays havoc with carefully arranged pages, so position yourself with this in mind.

CHOICE OF MATERIALS

The world is your oyster when it comes to deciding exactly what to press, and it is fun to experiment with new subjects now and again. Flowers and leaves with thin tissue are likely to give consistently good results. Moist, fleshy leaves and flowers with thick centres (which prevent the absorbent paper coming into contact with the petals) are a disappointment. Buttercup and clematis stalks are the best choice for natural curves in pressed flower designs and it is worth trying to obtain these in preference to any other.

Kits for pressing flowers need only include a heavy book and absorbent paper, but an attractive flower press adds to the interest.

Snip off flat flowers such as borage, daisy and hydrangea florets, just below the calyces. Pull off petals from thick flowers such as carnations and press them separately. One flower yields a multitude of petals that can be reassembled more sparingly to create the illusion of a natural flower. Snip off leaves or leaflets for pressing separately.

Arrange flowers, petals and leaves of a single kind, or at least of equal thickness, on each sheet of paper. Take care that they are well apart, not touching and certainly not overlapping. A page spread with plant materials both before and after pressing is a beautiful feature of the craft.

Lower the covering sheet of absorbent paper or close the pages of a book carefully. The slightest whoosh of air disturbs the placement. Close the press, or weight books with a pile of additional volumes and leave the 'pressing workshop' in a warm, dry room for at least six months, longer if possible. The longer that you leave them the less likely they are to fade when they are eventually exposed to light.

KEEPING THE COLOUR

Colour retention – in flowers more particularly than in leaves – can be a problem. I have found that changing the blotting paper layers two or three times during the first few days and transferring the subjects to dry paper, helps considerably. And, of course, you can dry the papers for re-use.

Dampness is always an enemy. Once your materials are pressed and dry, layer them between fresh tissues and keep them in boxes in a warm, dry place. They are only too ready to reabsorb moisture, and that

Flowers such as daffodils may be sliced in half for pressing, but the petals of bulky flowers, like carnations and roses, need to be separated from the heads. The calyces of daisies may need slitting to allow the heads to lie flat.

means discoloration and mould. A spoonful of silica gel crystals in a twist of muslin helps.

Blue has the reputation for being the most difficult colour to 'hold', but there are many subjects that will retain this hue. Tiny sprays of speedwell pressed on the stem, single delphinium flowers, borage with their star shaped calyces, alkanet (anchusa), lobelia, pansies and *Geranium ibericum* are a galaxy of sky-blue colour.

Bright sunshine yellow flowers are a great success. Use buttercups pressed singly and as buds on the stem, marigold petals for later reassembly, celandine, Iceland poppies – complete flowers or separate petals – primroses, cowslips, chrysanthemum petals and daffodils. The technique with trumpet shaped flowers in the narcissus family is to slit them through with a sharp knife and press each half, making two perfect shapes from one bloom.

Pink and red flowers tend to fade or deepen slightly. Bright red poppies soften to an attractive shade of old rose pink, and carmine old rose petals often deepen to strong purple. Fuchsia flowers make charming bell shapes, and wallflowers look like miniature flag iris. London pride emerges like toy flowering shrubs.

White flowers usually take on varying tones of

cream, with lawn daisies and sheep's parsley the exceptions. Used whole or snipped into florets, the latter – also known as Queen Anne's lace – looks just like delicate snowflakes. Green flowers and bracts such as the large trumpet shaped tobacco plant and fluffy alchemilla mollis, retain colour well.

Many leaves deepen in colour or turn varying shades of brown. Grey leaves such as senecio, anthemis, lavender, sage and cineraria are useful in design, and keep their neutral colour well. But colour is not everything in pressed flower work. Select leaves as much for the variety and interest of their shape. Clover, sheep's parsley, herb Robert, buttercup, achillea and aquilegia with their decorative cut shapes, slender wallflower and willow, feathery fennel and cosmos, young rose leaves and variegated ivy, fallen leaves of chestnut, beech, lime, in glorious shades of red and gold, all add natural variety.

DESIGNING ON THE FLAT

Think of a collection of dried and pressed flowers, leaves and stalks as a kaleidoscope of colour and shape. Spread out several examples on a page, move them around with the tip of a small paint brush and a design will begin to emerge.

You might decide to criss-cross several stalks to simulate a basket and 'fill' it with buttercups and daisies, some buds dipping over the rim as they would in a 'real' arrangement. Or represent a circular table-top with poppy petals, adding a classic urn vase with three foxglove flowers and an exuberant bouquet of mixed blooms in the best Regency tradition.

For a more abstract approach, select a graceful stem and, with no attempt at realism, arrange flowers and leaves on each side of it, a study in pleasing balance and shape.

You might like to create a scene – perhaps a waterside impression with striped grasses for rushes, slender willow leaves for sailing boats and sheep's parsley florets for the glistening foam on the water.

Whatever design you choose, rearrange the materials on a card or coloured paper background until you are satisfied with the effect. Work on one section at a time and dab each leaf, stalk or flower at intervals with Copydex on the point of a wooden cocktail stick. Position the material, cover it with a small piece of clean paper and press it gently in place. When you are overlapping petals and flowers – a daisy makes a pretty centre for a composed flower – let one layer dry before imposing the next. Cover your completed work with a sheet of paper, then glass or

a board and some books to weigh it down overnight.

Pressed flower designs always need protection from dust and scuffing. Cover greetings cards and tags with film wrap, pictures with glass or transparent iron-on mount. And to fight the battle against fading, display them away from direct sunlight.

SKELETONIZING LEAVES

Until you see a leaf which is skeletonized you cannot appreciate the intricacy of the vein structure. You can sometimes find these 'outline leaves', stripped of the green plant tissue, under holly, magnolia or laurel trees and bushes, but perfect examples are rare.

They make a delicate contrast for blending with evergreens, a happy choice with dried flowers and a dainty 'frill' surrounding a posy.

To strip evergreen leaves – the only ones with a sturdy enough structure – boil them for 30 minutes in 500 ml (1 pt) water to which you have added 100g (4 oz) blue biological household detergent. Strain the leaves, rinse them under the cold tap and place them on newspapers. Use an old toothbrush to brush off the leaf tissue, working from the central vein and out to the sides. Rinse them again, dry them and press them between sheets of blotting paper for about 14 days. Store the leaves as for pressed flowers.

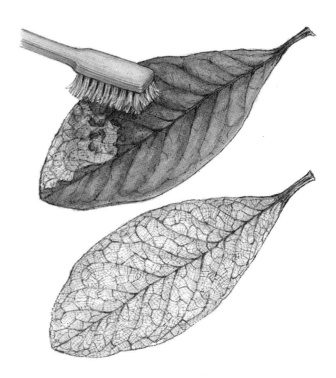

PRESERVING THE FRAGRANCE

Ponder for a moment on the tranquillity of days gone by, when the big country houses had a still-room. Flowers and leaves hung in bunches to dry, others lay on wooden racks, shelves were filled with spices and fixatives and there was a still, to extract the essential oils from plant materials. In large households there would be a mistress of the pot pourri, whose job it was to make the aromatic blends to scent the rooms, some in priceless covered bowls and some sewn into fine linen bags and pillows.

Conditions have changed and there is no longer the need to strew our floors with dried mint, lemon balm, sweet cicely and other herbs to mask unwelcome odours, nor the necessity to place large bowls of pot pourri at strategic points around a room, for the same purpose. But the delight of pot pourri lingers still and the gentle therapy involved in capturing the scents of a garden is more valuable to us than it ever was.

MAKING POT POURRI

Pot pourri is a medley of dried flowers, petals and herbs – some chosen for their scent and others for their shape and colour. To those decorative ingredients are added grated dried fruit rinds, powdered spices, fixatives, essential oils and salt. With such a wide choice of components, you can vary basic recipes to suit your personality and preference, and create a blend which is uniquely your own.

There are two basic types of pot pourri, the 'moist' and the dry kinds. In the past, rose petals formed the foundation of both. Old-fashioned roses which grew in abundance in Elizabethan gardens were highly fragrant and rose petals have the advantage that they hold their fragrance for several months. American gardeners especially prized the Provence or cabbage rose, which they aptly named the hundred-leaved rose.

MOIST POT POURRI

For the moist method the petals are partly dried until they are leathery, not crisp and brittle, and have been reduced to about half their original bulk. They are then packed into a jar with a lid, or a crock (never

use a metal container) between layers of coarse salt, usually in the proportion of three cups of petals to one of salt. The mixture is left in a dry, dark, well ventilated place for about 10 days. During this time the salt will draw out the residual moisture in the petals and the mixture will ferment, sometimes froth, and eventually form a block.

The fragrant block is broken up and other ingredients added, to be sealed into a container and

left to 'work' for about six weeks. Opening the lid on the mixture to stir it daily, and noticing the gradual blending and mellowing of the fragrances, is one of the pure joys of the craft.

After this, other dried materials may be added, together with a few drops of essential oil. Another two weeks of harmonizing and stirring and the 'moist' pot pourri – now completely dry – made to a centuries old method, is ready to use.

Above: *As soon as they are partly dried, rose petals can be 'matured' in a container of salt.*
Right: *Spices and essential oils will enhance and fix the fragrance of scented roses for pot pourri.*

*A traditional dry pot pourri of pink carnations combines
rose petals with cloves and cinnamon.*

DRY POT POURRI

The dry pot pourri method is simpler. The rose petals
and other plant materials are thoroughly dried until
they are cornflake crisp, blended with the other
aromatic ingredients, the spices, fixative and oils,
placed in an airtight container and left to mellow for
at least four weeks.

SOME FLORAL INGREDIENTS

A pot pourri is essentially a personal pleasure. Choose
the floral ingredients according to your own

preference for scent and colour. You may like to attempt a blend to resemble the perfume you wear, or colour match a bedroom or sitting room scheme. And what more romantic a way could there be to preserve petals from a bridal bouquet or a Mother's Day posy?

To scent the pot pourri mixture select from the petals of roses, carnations, flowering tobacco, honeysuckle, sweet pea, night-scented stock, orange blossom and clove carnation (the gillyflowers of old). To dry lily-of-the-valley, jasmine, sweet violet, verbena, hyacinth and lavender, first pick off the flowers and florets. And for the most charming touch of all, include some powder dried rosebuds.

Many of these flowers are graced with both perfume and beauty, but there are countless other possibilities. Choose from forget-me-not, delphinium, larkspur, golden rod and cornflower, and pansy, marigold, clematis and zinnia petals. They add more colour, texture and shape interest.

FRAGRANT LEAVES

Dried herbs are a traditional and delightful part of any pot pourri, their soft green tones blending attractively with both vibrant and modest petal colours, their aroma linking and complementing the floral scents. There is much to choose from in the herb garden – rosemary, sweet marjoram, oregano, lemon verbena, scented geranium, lemon balm, mints of all types, lemon thyme, sweet basil, tarragon and sweet cicely.

In an ideal world the floral and herbal ingredients for pot pourri would be dried on muslin racks on still, dry, warm days under the all enveloping shade of a tree. To be more realistic, spread each flower and petal type separately on racks or trays in a warm, dry room, or in a cool oven. The more quickly the flowers dry, the more perfume they will retain. According to type and moisture content, flowers and petals will dry within two to 10 days in a warm room or airing cupboard. On trays in the oven at the lowest setting and with the door ajar they take only three to four hours. Stir them often and remove them as soon as they feel crisp.

You can dry sprays of herbs hanging in bunches – in the airing cupboard again – or strip the leaves from the stems and dry them flat.

A thoroughly modern way is to dry herbs in a microwave oven. Spread herb sprays or leaves on three layers of absorbent paper, cover them with more paper and dry them in 15g (½ oz) batches in the oven at 100 per cent (high) for three to four minutes. Allow them to cool completely before blending them with other materials.

When fresh herbs are unobtainable, you can use commercially dried ones, but make sure that they are 'fresh' enough to have retained their colour and aroma. Long-term keeping in a warm and steamy kitchen robs them of their volatile oils and effectiveness.

THE ADDITIVES

Raid the spice rack for powdered mace and ginger, and grind or crush whole allspice, cardamom, coriander, fennel and cumin seeds and cinnamon sticks. For all but the daintiest of sachets (when the sharp edges would be an annoyance) use whole cloves and star anise.

Dried citrus rind adds a sharp aroma that contrasts well with sweet floral scents. Thinly pare the rind of oranges, lemons and limes and dry the strips in a cool oven. Use thin strips or grind them to a powder in a blender or food processor.

The fixatives are a vital element in the making of pot pourri. These are the ingredients that absorb and hold the scent of plants. There are some evocative names among traditional fixatives – frankincense, myrrh, sandalwood and patchouli. Those most popularly used now are powdered orris root and gum benzoin, which you can buy at herbalists and chemists.

Essential oils are extracted from strongly perfumed flowers and herbs and may be considered as pot pourri seasonings. You can use them 'like with like' to strengthen the existing fragrance – a few drops of oil of roses to enhance rose petals – or to add fragrance to blends chosen more for texture and colour than for fragrance. And when eventually the magic aroma of a pot pourri fades and becomes musty, a few drops of pure flower oil, stirred in, will revive the mixture.

Good herbalists sell a delightful range of essential oils. Among the ones I would choose to line a still-room shelf are oil of rose, rose geranium, rosemary, citronella, lemongrass, pine, tangerine, vetiver, musk, violet, lavender and lemon verbena.

The pot pourri recipes that follow are selected as a springboard to many others you will want to make from the ingredients available to you. As a general guide, to four cups of fresh flower petals and herb leaves, allow just over one cup of salt (if you are making pot pourri by the moist method) at least 30 ml (2 tbls) spices, one-third cup of fixative, and two to three drops of essential oil.

HOLDING THE SCENTS

Gathering an aromatic harvest of flowers and leaves to dry is the first stage in a craft which branches off in many directions. If you have a workbox full of bits and pieces of material, ribbons and lace, you have all it takes to make sachets, bags and pillows filled with fragrance. If even simple sewing is not one of your interests, you can keep alive a delightful tradition and tie lavender stems into crisp bundles. And if the idea of fragrant fruit appeals to you – and clove apples and clove oranges are surely irresistible – wrap these spicy pomanders in pot pourri. It's a notion that captures the essence of flower craft.

POMANDERS

In the 15th and 16th centuries pomanders – known as clove oranges – were carried to cloud unpleasant odours, ward off fevers and generally sweeten the air. It would have been the height of luxury to consider that they were also delightfully ornamental. Now that their original *raison d'être* has evaporated in a wave of health and hygiene awareness, we can enjoy them for the pure pleasure of their aroma – reminiscent of a waft of orange blossom on the warm summer air – and for their decorative properties. Studded with nut-brown cloves, sometimes with dried flowers and grasses too, and prettily ribboned, pomanders look well piled in a bowl, hanging in a bedroom and, at Christmas time, on the festival tree.

For the spherical base you can use any long lasting fruit. Thin-skinned oranges are traditional, but cooking apples such as Bramley seedlings have their champions and were our choice. Small grapefruit and limes are other possibilities.

An unblemished cooking apple that is not too ripe makes a good base for a lightly scented pomander.

THE 'CLOVE APPLE'

Bramley seedling apples or any cooking apple may be used for the pomander base. The cloves can be packed closely on the fruit, even though apples do shrink more than oranges.

1 large cooking apple
30 cm (12 inches) of 1 cm (½ inch) wide tape
a few needlework pins
1 wooden cocktail stick
25 g (1 oz) whole cloves
5 ml (1 tsp) dried orris root powder
5 ml (1 tsp) powdered cinnamon
1 small metal curtain hook or loop
60 cm (24 inches) of 1 cm (½ inch) wide satin ribbon

1. Mark the apple into four equal sections, or quarters. Cut the tape in half. Place one piece around the apple from the stalk end, underneath and back to the top and pin it in place to divide the apple – visually, that is – in half. Pin the second piece of tape crossing the first, so that you have four quarters.

2. Use the cocktail stick if necessary to pierce holes in the skin. Working in one section at a time, press the cloves into the apple in a line closely following the line of the tape on the left of the section and then on the right. Keep the rows even and gradually fill in the section towards the centre, until it is completed. Fill in the other sections in the same way.

3. Put the orris root and cinnamon into a paper bag and shake the studded apple in the mixture. Close the bag tightly, pressing it around the apple, and put it in a box to mature for two weeks.

4. Unwrap the pomander, remove the tape – which will look very grubby – and press the hook or loop into the top. Pin ribbon in place of the tape and tie a bow as a final flourish on the top.

Spicy variety

Variety being the spice of life, it is fun to take the original concept, of packing a piece of fruit with spices and leaving it to dry, and to develop it in different ways over a period of time. Instead of dividing the fruit into sections with ribbons, section it with rows of dried flowers or grasses. When you take off the masking tape, fill in the lines with dried glixia or santolina flowers, helichrysum buds or hare's tail grass. Or use these and other dried materials from your collection to make other patterns. Concentric circles or wavy lines, for instance, will make your pomander distinctive, and perhaps a conversation piece.

It is not quite so easy to hold the fruit in your hand and stud it with brittle flowers so pierce the fruit with a knitting pin, stick it into a piece of modelling clay on a saucer and you can rotate the design and have both hands free.

Closer to the original concept, play down the design element and maximize on the aromatic spices. Stud oranges or apples all over with cloves (you will need rather more for each, of course) and roll them in spices. Add grated nutmeg, ground allspice and powdered cloves to the mixture for extra piquancy. Wrap the fruits, leave them to mellow, and then pile them pyramid fashion in a bowl. Alternatively place two or three – more sparingly – on a large bowl of lavender flowers or pot pourri to make an attractive feature that will last.

Pomanders and pot pourri were made for each other. Here is another spicing trick. Roll the pomander first in spices, then in pot pourri before setting it aside. The petals will cling delicately to the cloves, and look attractive when the pomander is placed in a bowl.

LAVENDER BOTTLES

For centuries people have delighted in making bundles, bags and sachets of sweet smelling flowers to scent their linen cupboards. There is a strongly sensual pleasure in taking out clothes and household items with a waft of the heady scents of summer. And a practical application too. Moths do not find the powerful perfume at all attractive, and so will not be tempted to lay eggs among clothes.

Lavender bundles – or lavender bottles, to use the traditional and descriptive term – are simple to make and compact enough to tuck into a drawer, suspend from a clothes hanger or hide in a trousseau suitcase. They also make delightful gifts and profitable bazaar stall items.

Cut fresh lavender flowers on a dry day, cutting the stalks as long as possible. Gather the stalks into bunches of about 20-24, depending on thickness, with the flower heads level. Tie the stalks together just under the heads with fine thread and bind the two ends round and round the flowers to enclose them in a tight web. Secure and tie the thread ends and cut them off.

Bend the stalks just below the flower heads, upwards and over the binding and the flowers so that the lavender is enclosed completely. Neatly bind the stalks together, well above the tips of the flower heads – the design will now strongly resemble a baby's rattle. Cut off the stalk ends to make a neat finish.

Cover the binding with a generous bow of narrow pale mauve, white or mint green satin ribbon. Or – as in our photograph – weave ribbon under and over each group of four stalks covering the flowers. The ribbon binding not only adds a look of luxury. It ensures that once they are dried and have consequently shrunk and fallen from the heads the flowers cannot fall out between the stalks.

SCENTED PILLOWS

Heart shaped sachets, muslin dolly bags, drawstring bags trimmed with flowers, patchwork pockets, lacy pillows, tartan triangles, come in all shapes and sizes, and they can all possess a soothing aroma.

30 ml (2 tbls) dried lavender flowers
30 ml (2 tbls) dried rosemary leaves stripped from the stalks
10 cloves, lightly crushed
2.5 ml (½ tsp) powdered dry orange peel

Mix the ingredients together and spoon them into a bag or sachet. A small pillow case made of muslin placed inside a linen case will retain the fragrance.

Scent variations
Any medley of fragrant flowers, petals and leaves, whether it is a full scale pot pourri or an aromatic duet, can be enclosed in the fabric – in small sachets to slip into a drawer, bags to hang with a suit or dress, or pillows to send you to sleep on a waft of perfume.

Throughout the ages some herbs have been especially associated with inducing sleep – so when making a mixture for headrest pillows try to include dried leaves of angelica, sage, dill, bergamot, lemon balm, tarragon, scented geranium or rosemary, and chamomile, lavender or elder flowers.

ROSE POT POURRI

This fragrant mixture is made by the moist method.

8 cups fragrant rose petals
175 g (6 oz) block salt
175 g (6 oz) table salt
30 ml (2 tbls) ground mace
30 ml (2 tbls) ground cloves
30 ml (2 tbls) ground allspice
30 ml (2 tbls) ground nutmeg
1 stick cinnamon, crushed
175 g (6 oz) dried, powdered, orris root
1 cup dried red rosebuds
4 or 5 drops oil of roses

Dry the rose petals until they are leathery. Mix the coarse salt and table salt. In a glass or earthenware container, make layers of petals and salt, beginning and finishing with petals. Cover and leave for 10 days in a dry, airy room, stirring the mixture each day. The petals will ferment and by the end of this stage of the process will form a crumbly block.

Break up the petals and stir in the spices, cover and set aside for six weeks, stirring frequently. Stir in the oil of roses. Transfer the now dry pot pourri to bowls, scattering a few dried rosebuds on top.

LEMON-SCENTED GOLDEN POT POURRI

The sharp citrus aroma and the brilliant yellow colouring of this pot pourri makes it especially refreshing.

1 cup dried lemon verbena leaves
1 cup dried lemon balm leaves
1 cup dried forsythia flowers
1 cup dried marigold petals
thinly pared rind of 1 lemon, cut into fine strips
65 g (2½ oz) dried, powdered, orris root
1 cup dried chamomile flowers
6 drops oil of lemon verbena

Mix together all the ingredients except the oil of lemon verbena. Put them into a container with a lid, and set aside in a warm, dry, airy place for six weeks. Stir or shake the pot pourri daily. Stir in the oil.

KEEPING THE FRAGRANCE

Traditionally open bowls are used for the display of pot pourri. Not only can you readily appreciate the colours and texture of the dried plants, you can also

Made by the dry method, lemon-scented pot pourri gives lasting fragrance with a difference.

stir them with your fingers as you pass, and release scents as strong as those of a herb garden in the evening. Porcelain bowls, pedestal cake stands, bon-bon baskets are charming containers, but somewhat wasteful. The fragrance will more readily evaporate on constant exposure to the air. Check it frequently – be sure to remember just how lingering it once was – and stir in a few drops of oil from time to time.

Pretty glass jars, heart-shaped bowls with lids, and ginger jars are thrifty alternatives. Take the lid off the container just before friends are coming, to offer them a fragrant welcome.

Pot pourri has a natural affinity with aromatic pomanders (there are ideas for pomanders on the following pages) and with dried flowers. Fill a glass container – a cylindrical vase or a deep rectangular bowl – with pot pourri and use this as stem holding material. Arrange dried flower stems in the mixture and you have a perfect visual partnership. If the container has a wide neck, bury a piece of foam near the top to give the stems a better grip.

Pot pourri can be used for wall, table and hanging decorations. Buy dry foam rings, heart shapes, strips and spheres and brush them liberally with glue, then press on the dried leaves and petals. Tie the pot pourri ball with ribbons to hang like a pomander.

You could fill a deep, round basket with pot pourri, or cheat and cram the basket with crumpled tissue paper, with a thin layer of flower petals on top. Make a dried flower ring to rim the basket and you have a delightful small arrangement for a bedroom or hearth.

In a beautiful house beside the Thames I saw bedroom hearths used to display pot pourri. Each small blackened iron grate was heaped with petals gathered from the rose garden beneath the windows. It looked and smelled like the enchanting luxury it was.

THE LANGUAGE OF FLOWERS

For hundreds of years a single flower or a simple posy could speak volumes between two people. The language of flowers has its roots deep in the past. In Victorian times many people conveyed their messages with flowers. When a single flower was given and inclined to the right, the pronoun 'I' was indicated,

but 'thou' when it was tilted to the left. If the flower 'asked' a question and the recipient touched it to her lips, the answer was yes. If she pulled off a petal and let it flutter to the ground, the answer was no.

Our illustration shows the depth of feeling that could be conveyed in a nosegay. You can use our own extracts from the dictionary to compose bouquets to offer for an anniversary, as a thank you gift, an expression of sympathy, or indeed love and affection. Just one word of warning: it is a good idea to copy out the specific flower meanings and enclose them on a card. There may be several and conflicting meanings attached to some flowers.

An eloquent posy uses ranunculus to say 'I am dazzled by your charms', ox-eye daisies for 'here is a token of love', and bluebells for 'to show constancy'. The message ends with 'do not refuse me', shown by the presence of eschscholzia.

LOVE, UNDYING LOVE

Amaranth, globe	*Undying love*
Ambrosia	*Love returned*
American linden	*Matrimony*
Catchfly red	*Youthful love*
Canterbury bell, blue	*Constancy*
Carnation, pink	*Woman's love*
Chinese primrose	*Lasting love*
Chrysanthemum, red	*I love*
Eschscholzia	*Do not refuse me*
Forget-me-not	*True love*
Gorse	*Love for all seasons*
Lemon blossom	*Fidelity in love*
Lime	*Conjugal love*
Myrtle	*Love*
Pink, red double	*Pure and ardent love*
single	*Pure love*
Rose	*Love*
bridal	*Happy love*
Rosebud, red	*Young love*
Tulip, red	*Declaration of love*
Violet, blue	*Faithfulness*

AFFECTION, FRIENDSHIP

Acacia	*Platonic love*
Bluebell	*Constancy*
Daisy wreath	*Childhood's affection*
Geranium, oak-leaved	*True friendship*

Heliotrope	*Faithfulness*
Hyacinth, blue	*Constancy*
Immortelles	*Never-ceasing remembrance*
Ivy	*Friendship*
Pear blossom	*Affection*
Periwinkle, blue	*Early friendship*
Valerian, pink	*Unity*
Veronica	*Fidelity*
Wallflower	*Fidelity in misfortune*

SORROW, GRIEF

Aloe	*Affliction, grief*
Anemone, garden	*Forsaken*
Balm	*Sympathy*
Columbine	*Anxious and trembling*
Harebell	*Grief*
Hyacinth, purple	*Sorrow*
Marigold	*Grief*
Poppy, red	*Consolation*
Tulip, yellow	*Hopeless love*
Yarrow	*Solace*
Yew	*Sadness*

GRATITUDE

Agrimony	*Thankfulness*
Bellflower, white	*Gratitude*
Campanula	*Gratitude*

UNDERSTANDING AND HOPE

Almond	*Hope*
Elderflower	*Compassion*
Geranium, scarlet	*Comforting*
Rose, stripped of thorns	*There is nothing to fear*
Snowdrop	*Consolation and hope*

REJECTION, HATRED

Basil	*Hatred*
Birdsfoot trefoil	*Revenge*
Bur	*You weary me*
Burdock	*Touch me not*

Carnation, striped	*Refusal*
white	*Disdain*
Chrysanthemum, yellow	*Slighted love*
Garden anemone	*Forsaken*
Larkspur, pink	*Fickleness*
Lobelia	*Malevolence*
Love-lies-bleeding	*Hopelessness*
Pink, variegated	*Refusal*
Indian double	*Aversion*
Rue	*Disdain*
Snapdragon	*'No'*
Tansy	*I am your enemy*

ADMIRATION

Alyssum, sweet	*Worth beyond beauty*
Fennel	*Worthy of praise*
Garden ranunculus	*You are rich in attractions*
Garden sage	*Esteem*
Geranium, apple	*Present preference*
Orange blossom	*Your purity equals your loveliness*
Pansy	*You occupy my thoughts*
Peach	*Your qualities, like your charms, are unequalled*
Pineapple	*You are perfect*
Ranunculus	*I am dazzled by your charms*
Rose, Austrian	*You are all that is lovely*
full red	*I admire your beauty*
centifolia	*Your charms are manifold*
Salvia, blue	*You are wise*
Sweet William	*Gallantry, a smile*

OLD-FASHIONED VIRTUES

Acacia, pink	*Elegance*
American cowslip	*Divine beauty*
Ash, mountain	*Prudence*
Azalea	*Temperance*
Bachelor's button	*Celibacy*
Bel orchis	*Industry*

Centaury	*Delicacy*
Broom	*Neatness, humility*
Clove gillyflower	*Dignity*
Cowslip	*Divine beauty*
Dock	*Patience*
Fuchsia, scarlet	*Taste and gracefulness*
Hibiscus	*Delicate beauty*
Lilac, white	*Purity, modesty*
Marshmallow	*Mildness*
Mint	*Virtue*
Mugwort	*Tranquillity*
Mullein	*Good nature*
Pasque flower	*Devoid of pretension*
Rose, campion	*Gentility*
Roses, crown made of	*Reward of virtues*
Rose, single	*Unaffected simplicity*
moss	*Superior merit*
Sage	*Domestic virtues*
Salvia, red	*Energy*
Speedwell	*Female fidelity*
Star of Bethlehem	*Purity*
Violet, white	*Innocence, modesty*
Water lily	*Purity of heart*

OLD-FASHIONED VICES

Abatine	*Fickleness*
Bramble	*Envy*
Bugloss	*Falsehood*
Cherry blossom	*Insincerity*
Deadly nightshade	*Falsehood*
Fool's parsley	*Silliness*
Foxglove	*Insincerity*
French marigold	*Jealous*
Mesembryan-themum	*Idleness*
Narcissus	*Self-interest*
Primrose, evening	*Inconstancy*
Rose, yellow	*Infidelity*
Sunflower	*Haughtiness*

Chapter 3
ARTIFICIAL FLOWERS

It is the most natural thing in the world for any artist to want to capture the beauty of garden and countryside flowers, and convey something of the emotions and moods they arouse. Flowers of every kind, the primary coloured flowers of spring, delicate, dew-splashed rosebuds, bright golden sunflowers, or bold, brilliant red poppies splattering colour through a crop of corn have inspired artists and craft workers throughout the ages. Oils, watercolours and acrylic paints; clay, wood and stone; wax, wire, plastics and paper; silk, nylon and cotton materials; fondant icing, almond paste, yeast dough and 'play-dough' – there is scarcely a material that has not been used to portray love and appreciation for the flowers around us.

In this section we have gathered together a harvest of designs for flowers you can make quite simply at home from paper, fabrics and even bread dough. And we hope the accompanying photographs will sow the seeds of a wealth of ideas for the many ways you can display and use your crop of handcrafted blooms.

Paper is the most versatile of materials for making flowers; high quality crepe paper – the kind which can stretch well – being the most useful of all. Our designers prove just how many shapes and effects can be achieved with it, from the smooth, sculptured look of tulips, and the exaggerated, generous size and floppy habit of huge field poppies to the trumpet-profile of crisp golden yellow and snow-white narcissus and the deep bell shapes of fuchsia. We include some fine, spider chrysanthemums and delicate roses, showing how such flowers can be made to look realistic and attractive.

In these practice sessions it is fun to experiment with colouring techniques too. You can smudge pale coloured paper petals with crayon, dabbed and smeared on with cotton wool. The tulips shown on page 101 demonstrate just how effective this colour application can be, adding not only a hint of shaded colour but an illusion of shape and extra fullness. By contrast, with the utmost care and wearing protective gloves, use a weak solution of household bleach to subtract colour from petal papers in deep, dark shades. Pale bleached streaks give a dramatic two-tone or bi-colour petal effect – the cream and blue anemones on page 113 demonstrate this well. Try also dipping petal and stamen tips in bleach for colour-lightened edges or spattering flowers with cotton wool buds soaked in bleach for specks and flecks.

FABRICS OF ALL KINDS

You have the chance to introduce a variety of texture with a range of materials – the delicate, pale-coloured art-deco-inspired herbaceous flowers (page 124) were made of nylon, and the shamelessly shiny sunflowers were made of plastic (page 121). What many fabrics have in texture and sheen, however, they lack in malleability, very few can be twisted and stretched like crepe paper. This means that you need to apply hidden supports in the form of wires around the edge or through the centre; only then can you coax the petals into the shape of, for example, camellias, iris or poinsettias.

Paper and fabric flowers have one common bond – they are all usually mounted on wire stems, or thin slivers of wood if you do not wish them to be bendable. Mounting the flower head firmly on to the false stem wire, wrapping the petals around the stem and then binding it along its length with florist's self-adhesive binding tape are all stages in flower making which take time and attention to perfect. Time spent in practising these stages is well spent in terms of finished appearance.

Anyone who is more at home with a rolling pin than with a pair of scissors will be delighted to find among our flower harvest a festival loaf crafted from ordinary bread dough. The design may look daunting at first sight, but it is not difficult to achieve. For a start you may like to try rolling and shaping off-cuts of dough (a favourite pastime with children) to make the irresistible golden brown roses, bluebells, campanulas and daisies – bread rolls which are lovely to look at, and tasty to eat.

Paper tulips will bring springtime freshness to your home (see overleaf).

TULIP TIME

Tulips will add a perennial touch of spring to your home. Our design was inspired by the tulip variety Angelique, the white paper petals softly tinted green and pink with crayon. Deeper shades, simulating the stripes, splashes and flecks that give these stately spring flowers such appealing variety, may be added with poster paint.

Materials you will need
(for 12 flowers)
1 pack heavy craft flower paper, white (or chosen petal colour)
1 pack heavy craft flower paper, leaf green
1 pack crepe paper, leaf green
1 pack crepe paper, black
roll of fine wire, for binding
stub wires, for stems
coloured crayons, green and pink
cotton wool balls
paste

Cutting and using the templates
Trace the patterns of the leaf and petal on to card and cut out the templates. Place the petal template straight on the grain of the white paper, draw round it and cut six petals for each flower you wish to make. You will find that to save time you can cut through four layers of the craft paper, and six layers of the crepe paper. From the green craft paper cut two leaves for each flower.

Making the flower centres and stamens
Make the flower centres from green crepe paper. For each one, cut a strip of paper 8.5 cm (3½ inches) long and 6.5 cm (2½ inches) wide. Fold it in half across the grain. Fold over the top 2.5 cm (1 inch) of a stem wire to make a tight loop. With the folded edge of the strip facing upwards, roll it tightly around the wire loop so that it is completely hidden. Secure the end with a dab of paste. Shade the top with a light green crayon. To achieve a natural effect rub the crayon on to a ball of cotton wool and then dab this on to the paper.

To make the 'stamens', cut a strip of black crepe paper through all thicknesses of the pack 5 cm (2 inches) wide. Make straight cuts along one edge 4 cm (1½ inches) deep and 4 mm (³⁄₁₆ inches) apart. Round off the top corners. Cut the strip into lengths

petal
⟵⟶

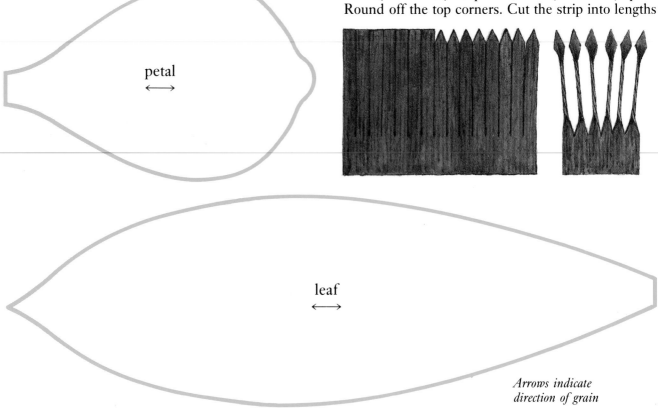

leaf
⟵⟶

Arrows indicate direction of grain

of six 'stamens' for each centre. Twist each 'stamen' separately, starting 5 mm (¼ inch) from top. Wrap a stamen strip around a green flower centre. Space out the stamens evenly with the black tips 10 mm (½ inch) above the green roll and paste them in place.

Treating the petals
If you wish to colour the petals, do this before shaping and fitting them. Dab the base of each one very lightly with the cotton wool coloured with the green crayon. Apply the colour gradually, building it up until you achieve the depth of colour you wish. Streak the top of the petals lightly with cotton wool rubbed on the pink crayon.

To shape each petal, hold it about 4 cm (1½ inches) above the base between the forefingers and thumbs of both hands. Gradually stretch it carefully and evenly all around the width to make a full cupped shape.

Assembling the flower
To assemble each flower, arrange three petals, evenly spaced, around the green and black centre. Bind them on tightly with binding wire, allowing the parts which

bulge to lie just above the fastening. Place the remaining three petals to form a second row. Make sure that the centres of this layer cover the overlapping edges of the first layer of petals, and that they are all level at the top. Bind the petals tightly around the base. If you wish to strengthen the stem or make it thicker, insert another stem wire. Push it into the base of the flower and twist the two wires round each other in two or three places.

Covering the stem
From the green crepe paper cut a strip 15 mm (¾ inch) wide through all thicknesses of the pack. Secure the end of the strip with a dab of glue just above the binding wire securing the base of the petals. Bind the paper strip tightly over the base of the petals and down the stem, overlapping it neatly and keeping it taut.

Inserting the leaves
Towards the base of the stem, insert the two leaves, on opposite sides, binding them in place with roll wire. Continue binding the stem wire with the green paper strip. At the end of the wire, cut the paper strip and secure it with a dab of glue. Bind a second strip to cover the first in the same way.

Final touches
Insert your fingers and thumb into the flower and stretch the petals a little more to give the flowers the characteristic cup shape. To store the flowers before arranging them, pack them in a box between layers of tissue paper, or push the stems into a block of dry foam.

A piece of foam in the base of a deep vase will hold the stems in place when you arrange them. Wire tulip stems have a great advantage over natural ones – you can ease them into gentle curves or have them completely vertical – just as you wish.

MEXICAN POPPIES

Flowers as big, bold and beautiful as these paper poppies are a passport to festivity. Make them as an eye-catching feature when you are planning a special party; stand them in a stone pot outdoors on a balcony or terrace, to be the most exotic blooms in any garden; or cluster them in a room corner to brighten dull winter days. Wherever they are, these larger-than-life flowers will steal the limelight.

Materials you will need
(for 6 flowers)
cardboard, for petal template
1 pack crepe paper, bright orange
1 pack crepe paper, black
6 x 2.5 cm (1 inch) diameter buttons
6 stub wires for stems
2.75 metres (11 feet) thick wire, for stems
roll of fine wire, for binding
1 knitting needle
florist's green binding tape, to bind stems
cotton wool balls

Cutting and using the templates
Trace the pattern of the petal on to card and cut out the template. For each flower, cut eight 14 x 11 cm (5½ x 4½ inch) pieces of orange crepe paper and, using the template, cut out the petal shapes.

Making the flower centres and stamens
Push a stub wire through the holes in a button and twist the ends underneath. Cover the top of the button with a small piece of cotton wool. Cut a small square of black paper, cover the top of the button, shaping the cotton wool to make a mound, and bind the paper beneath the button with fine silver wire.

Cut a strip of black paper 32 x 10 cm (13 x 4 inches) and fold it in half along the length. Cut narrow slits 4 cm (1½ inches) long from the fold through both thicknesses all along the length of the strip. Gather the strip around the button and wire it beneath the button to the stem.

Hold the knitting needle against the outside of the cut strip and wrap the slits in the paper around it, several at a time, to give a frilled effect.

Assembling the flower
Bind on the first four petals one at a time, spacing them equally around the stem. Bind on the next four petals at equal intervals between them, then bind them all securely on to the stem. Using the forefingers and thumbs, stretch the lower part of each petal to give the flower a natural cupped shape.

Frill the top edge of each petal: hold the edge between the forefingers and thumbs of each hand. Push the paper away from you with one hand and pull it towards you with the other, stretching it carefully. Work all around the top edge of each petal.

Making the stem and calyx
Cut 45 cm (20 inches) of the thick wire and push it up through the wired-on 'stamens' to the base of the button. Twist the two free ends of the stub wire tightly around the stem wire. Wrap a little cotton wool around the stem beneath the button to simulate a calyx. Cover it with binding tape and then bind the length of the stem.

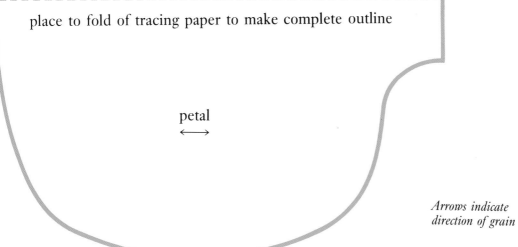

place to fold of tracing paper to make complete outline

petal
⟷

*Arrows indicate
direction of grain*

GOLDEN DAFFODILS

Our sunshine bright narcissi are made from one of the simplest of paper flower patterns, and you do not need particularly nimble fingers to assemble them. They could be displayed in a cylindrical white vase, a piece of bleached driftwood or a shallow basket.

Materials you will need
(for 12 flowers)
cardboard, for flower and leaf templates
1 pack heavy craft flower paper, yellow or white, for petals
1 pack heavy craft flower paper, lemon, for trumpets
small amount crepe paper, beige, for sheath
small amount crepe paper, yellow
1 pack crepe paper, leaf green
roll of fine wire, for binding
stub wires, for stems
coloured crayon, green
cotton wool balls
paste

Cutting and using the templates
Trace the patterns on to card and cut out the templates.

For each flower cut six petals, one trumpet, one sheath and one or two leaves.

Making the flower centres and stamens
To make the centre, bend over the top of a stub wire for 2.5 cm (1 inch) to form a narrow loop. Cut a 5 mm (¼ inch) strip of yellow crepe paper. Secure one end to the top of the loop and bind it round to about 2.5 cm (1 inch) below the loop to conceal it.

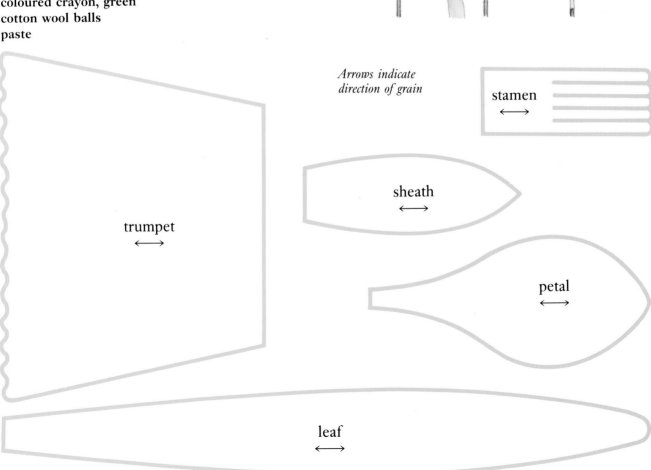

Arrows indicate direction of grain

stamen

trumpet

sheath

petal

leaf

To make the stamens, cut a strip of yellow crepe paper 4.5 cm (1¾ inch) wide. Along one side make cuts 3 mm (⅛ inch) apart and 2.5 cm (1 inch) deep. Snip the tops of the narrow strips to round off the corners. Cut the strips into sections, each with five 'stamen' divisions. Using binding wire, bind one stamen section to the wrapped wire, just below the base of the loop.

Treating the petals

To achieve a natural effect, slightly curl the top edges of each petal. Rest the back of a knife blade on the underside of the petal tip and, with your thumb on top, draw the blade up and outwards so that the paper springs into a curl. Lightly colour the base of the petals pale green. Rub green crayon on to cotton wool and brush it gently over the petals, building up the colour gradually.

The trumpet

To make the trumpet, flute the uneven edge of the shaped material. Hold the edge of the paper between forefingers and thumbs of both hands close together. Stretch the paper by pulling forward with the left hand and pushing away with the right hand, taking care not to tear the paper. About 2.5 cm (1 inch) from

the base of the trumpet strip, and with the inside facing you, stretch the paper between your fingers and thumbs so that it bulges and will form a cup shape. Wrap the trumpet to form a tube, overlapping the straight edge slightly. Paste the edge.

To give the beige sheath the look of dried plant material, gently crush the paper shape, then smooth it out.

Assembling the flower

To assemble each flower, place the trumpet over the stamen centre and gather it tightly, just below the bulge. Secure it with binding wire so that the stamens are 10 mm (½ inch) below the fluted edge.

Bind the petals on about 15 mm (¾ inch) from the base, just above the point where the base narrows. Space the first three petals evenly around the trumpet and bind them securely. Then bind the remaining three in a second row, spacing them between the petals of the first layer. Make sure that all petals are at the same height. Snip off any surplus paper just below the fastening to neaten the base.

Covering the stem

Cut a 15 mm (¾ inch) strip of green crepe paper to wrap the stem. Bind the stem with the paper strip as described for the tulip (page 103). Wrap the stem with a second paper strip, adding the sheath 4 cm (1½ inches) below the flower. Using the binding wire, bind the leaves on opposite sides of the stem towards the base, then continue wrapping the stem with the paper strip.

LASTING SUMMER ROSES

A few of these flowers and buds in a pottery basket or in a glistening crystal rose bowl, twined, rambler style, around bare twigs in a flower pot or pinned to a looped 'ribbon' of greenery to decorate a table will give you lasting pleasure.

Materials you will need
(for 12 flowers or buds with leafsprays)
cardboard, for petal and leaf templates
1 pack heavy craft flower material, apricot (or chosen petal colour)
1 pack heavy craft flower material, leaf green
1 pack crepe paper, leaf green
roll of fine wire, for binding
12 No. 18 wires
steel knitting needle
paste

Cutting the templates
Trace the patterns of the petal, calyx and leaf on to card and cut out the templates.

Making the petals
Place the petal template straight on the grain of the apricot craft paper, draw round it and cut 12 petals

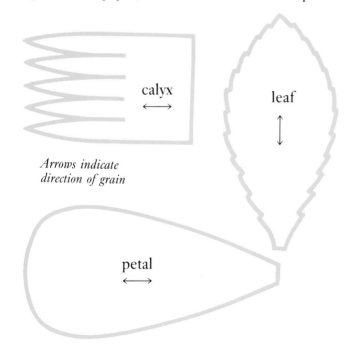

Arrows indicate direction of grain

for each flower. Divide the petals into three groups.
Group 1: Stretch two petals deeply near the top, by holding each side of the petal with both thumbs and forefingers – this is called 'cupping'. Gradually stretch the entire width of the petal, carefully and evenly into shape.
Group 2: Curl the top edges of six petals over a knitting needle. Cup them slightly in the centre, curled top facing away from you.

Group 3: Curl the remaining four petals deeply at the upper sides and cup them two-thirds of the way down.

Cut one calyx for each flower from the green craft material. Roll each tip into a point between thumb and forefinger.

Assembling the flower
To assemble the flower, take one of the wires and bend the top over about 2.5 cm (1 inch) to form a loop. Take one petal from Group 1 and roll it closely round the loop with the base of the petal 15 mm (¾ inch) below the loop. Secure the petal tightly with a twist of binding wire just below the loop. Arrange the other petal around it, overlapping about halfway, so that the wire is hidden.

Arrange the six petals of Group 2 evenly around the first pair and bind them on in a similar way, with the tops of the petals a little higher so that the centre will be slightly recessed.

Arrange the four petals of Group 3 at intervals around the others. Bind them in place and cut off the binding wire. Ease these petals outwards to make a slightly open flower. Trim off the surplus paper beneath the flower. The bulk below the petals will form the calyx.

Brush paste around the base of the flower and adjust the calyx.

Making the leaves and stem

Cut the leaves from the green crepe paper. Make one or two leaf sprays for each flower. Each leaf spray consists of one large leaf, cut using the template, and two slightly smaller leaves.

To make the leaf sprays, cut a piece of binding wire 11 cm (4½ inches) long for each large leaf and 7.5 cm (3 inches) long for each smaller leaf. Bind the wire with a 5 mm (¼ inch) wide strip of green crepe paper. Paste the wires to the centre backs of the leaves, so that they reach about halfway along the leaves. Wrap the wire 'stem' of the long leaf with another strip of the green crepe paper, binding in the smaller leaves on opposite sides of the stem about 2.5 cm (1 inch) below the large leaf. Mark veins on the leaves with a steel knitting needle, held like a pencil.

Bind the main flower stem with a 15 mm (¾ inch) strip of green crepe paper as described for the tulip (see page 103). Wrap the stem with a second paper strip, binding in the leaf spray or sprays, one on each side of the stem about 5-7.5 cm (2-3 inches) below the flower.

Making the buds

To make a rosebud, cut two petals, one calyx, and one leaf spray if you wish. Also cut one 20 cm (4 inch) square of crepe paper in the petal colour.

Loop a stem wire as for the rose. Double the paper square diagonally and roll it around the loop into a cone shape, overlapping and pinching it together 15 mm (¾ inch) from the bottom. Tightly bind this cone on to the stem. Trim off surplus paper.

Cup one petal deeply near the top. Curl the upper sides of the other over a knitting needle and cup deeply near the middle. Roll the first petal around the cone, then place the curled petal around it, overlapping it about halfway. Secure the petals with binding wire. Make a calyx as for the flower. Brush the base of the bud with paste and secure the calyx. Wrap the stem with a 15 mm (¾ inch) strip of green crepe paper, adding a leaf spray or sprays if desired.

A MASS OF COLOUR

Making paper flowers allows you to acquire blooms which span the seasons, and are all shapes and sizes. The colours of your 'instant' plants could complement each other and be chosen for one glorious arrangement. Here we give details for making anemones, bluebells, fuchsias and spider chrysanthemums.

Materials for all species
cardboard, for templates (for four species)
1 pack crepe paper, mid green
roll of thick green wire, for stems
roll of fine wire, for binding
wire cutters
paste

ANEMONE

Materials you will need
1 pack crepe paper, in chosen petal colour(s)
1 pack crepe paper, black
household bleach (optional)

Cutting and using the templates
Trace the patterns of the petal and the sepals, transfer them on to card and cut out templates.

Cut a strip 5 cm (2½ inches) wide through a pack of crepe paper in your chosen petal colour. Moving the petal template along, cut out the petal shapes right across this strip, through all the layers of the folded paper. If you wish, dip the base of the strip in a weak solution of bleach and leave to dry. Open out the strip and cut off eight petals for each flower.

Making the flower centres and stamens
For each flower, cut a 22.5 cm (9 inch) length of green wire. Cut a 2.5 cm (1 inch) strip through all layers of the black paper. Open out the strip, cut off 15 cm (6 inches) and screw it into a flattened ball shape to cover the top of the wire. Cover this with a small length of the black strip, stretched across the centre and gathered in to the top of the stem. Glue in place.

Cut a 4 cm (1½ inch) strip through the black paper and make narrow, regular cuts along it. Open out the strip and cut off 10 cm (4 inches). Tightly twist each cut section along the strip to make stamens. Glue around the flower centre, and trim the stamens.

Assembling the flower
Gather the petals around the flower centre and glue in place. From the mid-green paper, cut a strip 4 cm (1½ inches) wide. Moving the sepals template along (or cut out freehand if you prefer), cut out the sepal shapes right across this strip, through all layers. Open out, and cut off two 10 cm (4 inch) sections for each flower. Gather two sepal strips around the flower base and glue in place.

Covering the stem
Cut a 2.5 cm (1 inch) strip through the green pack. Use a length of this to bind the base of the flower and 2.5 cm (1 inch) down the stem. Twist another 10 cm (4 inch) sepal section round the stem 2.5 cm (1 inch) down. Bind the full length of the stem twice with the green strip and secure with glue.

BLUEBELL

Materials you will need
1 pack crepe paper, blue, or chosen petal colour(s)
1 fine knitting needle

Cutting and using the templates
Trace the pattern of the bluebell heads, transfer on to card and cut out a template.

From the blue pack, cut a strip 4 cm (1½ inches) wide and, moving the template along the strip, cut the bluebell pattern through all layers. Open out the strip and cut off six petals for each bell.

Making the stem and buds
For each stem, cut a 30 cm (12 inch) length of green wire. Cut a 2.5 cm (1 inch) wide strip through all layers of the mid green crepe paper, and of the blue or petal colour.

Open out the blue strip, cut off a 10 cm (4 inch) length, fold it in half lengthways and shape it to make a small bud. Glue it to the top of the stem. Make another slightly smaller bud and glue this beside the first.

Open out the green strip, cut off about 43 cm (18 inches), glue the end to the top of the stem and tightly bind the buds and stem along the length as you build up the design.

Making and attaching the flowers
Cut a 5 cm (2 inch) length of fine wire. Stretch the petal strip to cup it along its length, roll it around a finger, slip the bell shape over the wire and bind it tightly with fine wire.

Cut a 1 cm (½ inch) strip through the mid green pack and cut off enough to bind the bell and stalklet as tightly as possible. Curl each petal by rolling the top over a fine knitting needle.

Make five more bells in the same way. Add the bell flowers one by one to the main stem at regular intervals, binding them in place with the green paper strip. Bind to the bottom of the stem, then bind it again with a second paper strip and secure the end with a dab of glue. Gently bend the top of the main flower stem into a curve.

Making and attaching the leaves
To make the leaves, cut a 22.5 cm (9 inch) length of green wire. Glue it between two layers of green paper and cut out a narrow spear shape. Gather the paper at the base and glue in place on the stem.

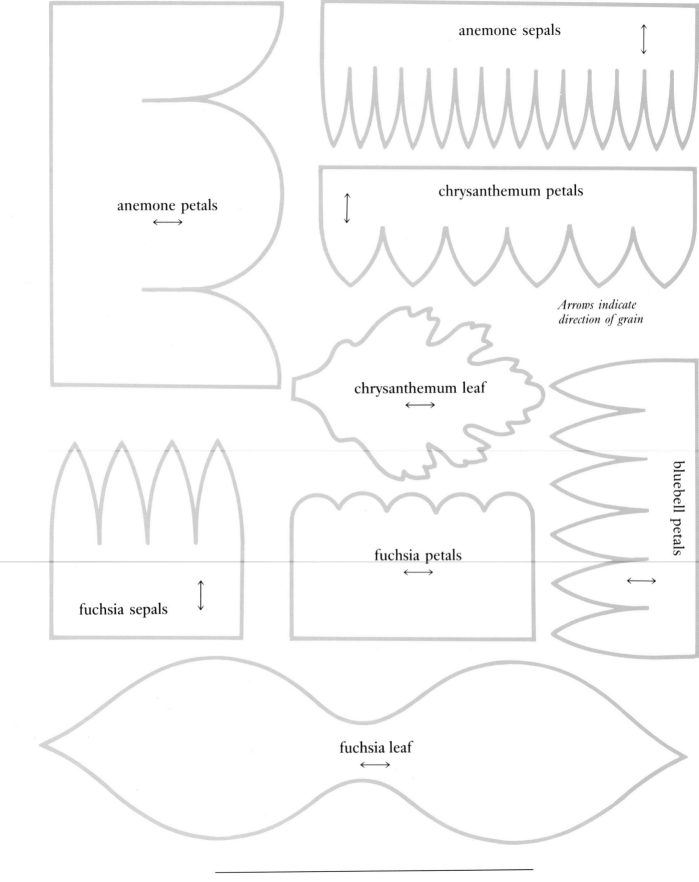

anemone sepals

chrysanthemum petals

anemone petals

Arrows indicate direction of grain

chrysanthemum leaf

bluebell petals

fuchsia petals

fuchsia sepals

fuchsia leaf

FUCHSIA

Materials you will need
1 pack crepe paper, white, for petals
1 pack crepe paper, scarlet, for sepals
1 pack crepe paper, light brown
1 fine knitting needle

Cutting the templates
Trace the pattern of the leaf, petals and sepals, transfer on to card and cut out templates.

Making the flowers
Cut strips 4 cm (1½ inches) wide, 10 mm (½ inch) wide and 5 cm (2 inches) wide through white pack. Moving the petal template along the 4 cm (1½ inch) strip cut out the shape through all layers. Open out the strip and cut off four petal sections for each flower. Twist one length and cup it to form a bell shape. Bind the base with fine wire, leaving a short end to attach the flower to the branch.

From the contrasting colour, say scarlet, cut strips 5 cm (2 inches) wide and 10 mm (½ inch) wide. Moving the sepals template along the 5 cm (2 inch) strip, cut out the shape. Open out the strip and, for each flower, cut off one 4-sepal section. Gather the strip around the base of the flower and glue in place.

Open out the narrow contrast strip and use a short length to bind over and over the ends of the sepals. Open out the narrow white strip and use a short length to cover the join and bind the flower stalk.

From the 5 cm (2 inch) wide strip of the main colour (white) make regular narrow cuts through all layers. Open out the strip and cut it into sections of six stamens for each flower. Twist the stamens tightly, roll up the strip, dab glue round the base and push it well down into the flower centre. Cut five stamens short and bend the end of the sixth.

Making the buds
To make a bud, cut a 12.5 cm (5 inch) length from the 5 cm (2 inch) wide strip of the main colour (white). Shape it to form a bud and bind the base with fine wire, leaving a short end to attach the bud to the branch. Add sepals in the contrast colour, and bind and finish as for the flower. Bring the four points of the sepals together and glue at tip.

Making the leaves
To make the leaves, cut out the pattern three times through double thicknesses of mid green paper. Cut three 10 cm (4 inch) lengths of green wire and glue one down the centre of each leaf. Press the two thicknesses together while the glue is wet to make double leaves.

Making the stem
For each stem, cut a 35 cm (14 inch) length of green wire. Cut a 2.5 cm (1 inch) wide strip through all thicknesses of the light brown crepe paper. Glue one end of this strip to the top of the wire and bind the stem, stretching the strip tightly. Cut off and secure the end with glue.

Assembling the flower branch
Twist a double leaf shape to the top of the main stem. Bend over the brown stem at the top to hold it firmly. Add three flower stalks to this point at the top of the branch, using another length of the light brown paper strip, and glue them in place. Working down the branch, add another pair of leaves. Bind and glue in place. Continue down the branch, adding another pair of leaves. Secure the binding at the base of the branch with a dab of glue. Curl back all the sepals.

SPIDER CHRYSANTHEMUMS

Materials you will need
1 pack crepe paper, in chosen petal colour
1 pack crepe paper, dark green
pinking sheers
household bleach

Cutting the templates
Trace the patterns of the sepals and the leaf, transfer them on to card and cut out templates.

Making the flowers
Cut a 7.5 cm (3 inch) wide strip through a pack of paper in the petal colour. Cut into the strip at regular intervals through all layers of the paper.

Open out the strip to double the packet width, about 20 cm (8 inches), and trim down about 1 cm (½ inch) with pinking shears. Do *not* cut this off. Continue to open out the strip to four packet widths – about 40 cm (16 inches) – and then cut off from the remainder. Twist each individual petal between finger and thumb to make spikes.

Take the pinked edge of the strip and begin to roll it up, pinching and gathering as tightly as possible. Roll up the rest of the spiky petals.

Cut a 30 cm (12 inch) length of green wire and twist the top round the base of the flower head, pulling the stem downwards. Trim off excess paper at the base of the flower head. Dip the ends of flower spikes in weak bleach to lighten the tips.

Making the sepals
From the dark green pack of paper, cut strips 30 mm (1¼ inches) wide and 10 mm (½ inch) wide through all layers. Moving the sepals template along the 30 mm (1¼ inch) strip, cut out the pattern. Open out the strip and cut off an eight-sepal section for each flower. Gather the sepal strip around the base of the flower head and glue it in place. Fan out the sepals and glue four of them to the underside of the flower head, making it fairly flat.

Covering the stem
Glue the top of the 10 mm (½ inch) green strip to the top of the stem and bind it down about 4 cm (1½ inches). At this point make a loop of paper (to form a leaflet later) and continue to bind the stem for another 2.5 cm (1 inch). Cut off the end and glue the binding down.

Making the leaves
To make a leaf, use the template to cut the pattern through two layers of the dark green paper. Glue and bind to the stem with another length of the dark green strip. Continue to the bottom, cut off and secure with glue. Shape out the loop to make a small spear-shaped leaflet. Shape and refine the main leaf. Mark veins with the point of a knitting needle.

A GIFT OF GRAPES

There are so many ways to display these bunches of silky grapes that you will be tempted to make a bumper harvest. Turn a bottle of wine into a vintage gift by decorating it with appropriately pale green or red grapes and a clinging tendril of vine leaves.

Materials you will need
(for one bunch of 24 grapes)
cardboard for leaf template
piece of fine, grape coloured material, silk or cotton lawn, about 75 cm (30 inches) square
small piece of coarse dark green fabric, such as flock material, about 25 cm (10 inches) square
roll of medium-gauge wire, to outline leaves
roll of fine wire, for binding
1 stub wire
florist's binding tape
cotton wool balls
glue

Making the grapes
Cut 24 x 3 cm (1¼ inch) squares of the fine material for the grapes. Tear off 24 small pieces of cotton wool, roll each one in a square of the material and bind with a length of fine wire, leaving about 5 cm (2 inches) trailing.

Cover one end of the stub wire with binding tape, wrapping it tightly to conceal the stem. Add one of the grapes to extend beyond the wire end, and bind the trailing wire around the stem. Add two more grapes close against the stem, twisting the fine wire ends around the stem and covering them with florist's tape as you work down the length. Add three more grapes in the same way, and continue until they are all in place. Make sure that the bunch fills out neatly from the tip to make a full cone shape.

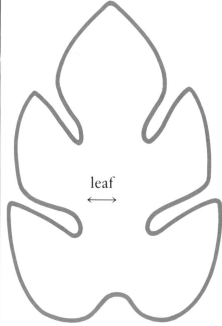

leaf
←→

Making and attaching the leaves

Trace the pattern of the leaf on to card and cut out the template. To make one leaf, fold the green material in half and cut out the template shape through both thicknesses. Stick the medium gauge wire along the length of one leaf shape, leaving 5 cm (2 inches) trailing for the stem. Glue the second leaf shape on top of the first leaf shape.

Twist the leaf wires around the stem near the top and bind to the end of the stem with the tape. Finish off the end neatly.

Ease the grapes into a neat shape and twist the leaves so that they look realistic.

RIBBON ROSES

A few strips of ribbon and a few moments to spare are all you need to make these dainty ribbon roses. They are a good stepping-stone for readers who are new to the craft of making artificial flowers – there are no patterns to cut and very few materials are needed.

Make the ribbon roses to trim a pretty parcel, and they become a lasting keepsake. Make a spray of the flowers in pink, red, cream, yellow or white, and wear them on a lapel or a summery hat, and they are a flattering fashion accessory, or mount the flowers on long stems and use them to decorate a bedroom.

LARGE ROSES

Materials you will need
(for one flower)
87.5 cm (35 inches) double sided satin ribbon
width of the ribbon may vary from 4-7.5 cm
(1½-3 inches) according to size of flower required
stub wire, for stem
roll of fine wire, for binding
florist's binding tape, for stem

Making the flower
Bend the stub wire into a narrow loop at one end, making a hairpin shape about 10 cm (4 inches) in length.

Starting from one end of the strip of ribbon, fold it over at a right angle. Continue folding from each side in turn, folding towards you and forming the ribbon into a square with a small hole in the centre. Hold the ribbon square firmly as you work, or it will spring up and out of shape. Continue until only 5 cm (2 inches) of ribbon is left unfolded.

Hold the ribbon square firmly in one hand and push the looped wire up through the centre opening. Thread the remaining 5 cm (2 inch) strip of ribbon through the loop and twist it clockwise so that the ribbon coils round and round the loop and forms a realistically rose-like centre. Pull the wire gently until it is concealed in this centre coil.

Take the first fold underneath the flower and bind it securely to the stem with fine wire.

Bind the base of the rose, and the length of the stem with florist's binding tape.

If you wish to mount the flower on a long stem, push a length of thicker wire up into the centre of the flower, bind it to the stub wire with fine wire, then cover it all neatly with the florist's tape.

SMALL ROSES

Materials you will need
(for six flowers)
1.8 metres (72 inches) satin ribbon
2.5 cm (1 inch) wide
45 cm (18 inches) medium string, for stems
needle and thread
12 small rose leaves, from craft shop
florist's binding tape, green

Making the flower
To make each flower, cut 30 cm (12 inches) of ribbon and 7.5 cm (3 inches) of string. Make a knot close to one end of the string.

Twist one end of the ribbon around the knot, fold over the corners and stitch the ribbon to enclose the knot. Tack 10 cm (4 inches) along one edge of the ribbon with running stitch and pull up the stitches to gather the ribbon.

Wrap the gathered ribbon around the flower centre (the covered knot) and stitch in place.

Tack along the next 10 cm (4 inches) of ribbon, pull up the thread, wrap it round the flower centre and stitch in place. Repeat with the last 10 cm (4 inches) of the ribbon, sewing it in place.

Wrap florist's tape 10 times around the base of the flower to form the calyx, making sure to cover the base of the ribbon. Wrap the tape for another 15 mm

(½ inch), insert the leaf wire and continue taping to the base of the string stem.

SUNFLOWERS

Made from ordinary furnishing quality pvc and bright and brazen as can be, these blooms make a bold splash of colour with all the impact of a field of sunflowers on a golden summer's day.

Materials you will need
(for six flowers)
cardboard, for petal template
100 cm (40 inches) stiff pvc material, 62.5 cm (25 inches) wide
6 x 2.5 cm (1 inch) diameter buttons
small piece of brown material, to cover centres
roll of fine wire
6 stub wires
roll of medium-gauge wire, for stamens
roll of thick wire, for stems
florist's binding tape, green
brown poster paint
cotton wool balls
glue

Cutting the templates
Trace the petal pattern on to card and cut out the template.

Use the template to cut 24 petal shapes for each flower – that is for 12 double-thickness petals.

Making the flowers
Cut 12 x 15 cm (6 inch) lengths of fine wire. Glue a piece of wire down the centres of half the petals so that the wire extends 5 cm (2 inches) below the petal. Glue the other 12 shapes on top so that the wire is enclosed in double-thickness petals.

Push one end of a stub wire up through one hole in the button and down through another. Twist the ends underneath the button.

For each flower, cut a 7.5 cm (3 inch) square of brown material. Cover the button with a small piece of cotton wool and then with the brown material. Bind the fabric tightly under the button with fine wire.

For each flower, cut 20 x 6 cm (2½ inch) lengths of fine wire, to make the stamens. Twist a very small piece of cotton wool tightly around one end of each length and cover it with green binding tape, wrapped round very tightly and finished off neatly. Dab the stamen ends with brown poster paint and leave to dry before assembling the flower centre.

petal
⟵⟶

Arrange the stamens around the button representing the flower centre, spacing them evenly. Bind the stamens beneath the button with fine wire.

Arrange the petals evenly around the stamens and flower centre and bind each one in place.

For each flower, cut 50 cm (20 inches) of the thick wire. Push the wire up through the ring of wired-on petals until it reaches the underside of the button. Twist the exposed length of stub wire around the thicker wire.

Starting at the base of the flower bind the stem tightly and neatly with the green binding tape. Press the plastic forming the base of the petals tightly to form a neat calyx shape as you work. Continue binding to the end of the thick stem. Cut off the tape and bind the stem over again. Make the other five flowers in the same way.

CHRISTMAS TIME

A stocking trimmed with a brilliant poinsettia, evergreens and baubles will be a delightful surprise for Christmas, but do not give this decoration to a very young child as the wires and stamens could be dangerous.

Materials you will need
(for one poinsettia)
cardboard, for petal template
75 cm (30 inches) red flock ribbon 8 cm (2¾ inches) wide
25 cm (10 inch) square green felt
6 red artificial stamens
5 yellow artificial stamens
stub wire
roll of fine wire
florist's green binding tape, to bind stems
1 cotton wool ball
glue

Cutting the templates
Trace the pattern of the two petal sizes on to card and cut out the templates. Fold the ribbon in half lengthways. Use the templates to cut three large and nine small pairs of petals from the double thickness of the ribbon. Make the holly leaf template and cut five pairs of leaves from green felt.

Making the flowers
Glue a length of fine wire down the centre of one side of each petal, dab glue around the edge and stick down the other petal halves, so that you have double thickness petals with wire in the centre. Set aside to dry.

Bind the four lengths of stub wires together with fine wire to form the stem. Arrange the stamens around the top and bind them on with wire.

Bind the nine small petals at equal intervals around the stem one at a time, evenly spaced around the inner ring. Lastly bind on each of the three large petals, spacing them equally around the others.

Wrap a small piece of cotton wool around the base of the flower, to represent the calyx. Bind from the base of the flower, over the calyx and down the length of the stem with florist's wire.

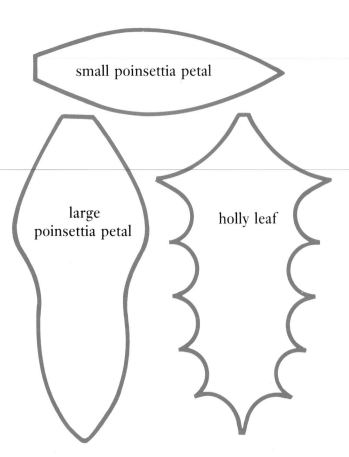

small poinsettia petal

large poinsettia petal

holly leaf

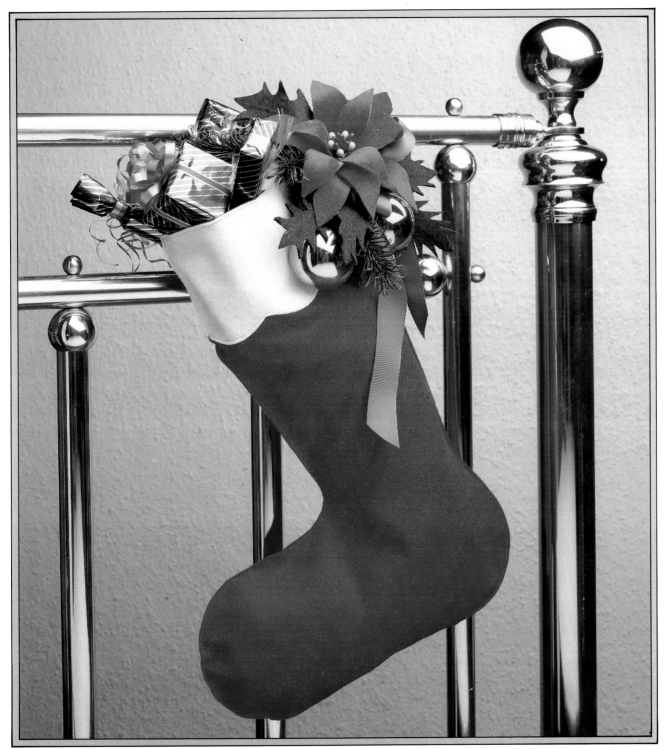

Making the leaves
Glue a length of stub wire down the centre of one leaf from each pair, then dab glue around the edge of each wired leaf. Place a matching leaf over each glued leaf and bind the stem with florist's tape. Twist the leaf stems around the poinsettia stem.

To assemble the decoration, make a fan shape of the holly leaves, adding fresh springs of evergreen if you choose, around the poinsettia. Sew the poinsettia decoration and baubles to the top of the stocking.

SIMPLY ELEGANT

There is more than a hint of the 'twenties and 'thirties in these elegant nylon flowers. Pale, romantic shades of pink, lilac and cream combine in a way that sets the imagination racing.

Display a bunch of these beautiful blooms in a classic urn-shaped vase to stand on a pedestal, arrange them in a long, low container to grace the centre of a dining table, cluster a few blossoms in a pretty china basket under a lamp or on a dressing table, or fix them to a picture or mirror frame.

Materials you will need

(for six flowers)
very fine stretch material, such as nylon stockings or tights, georgette or chiffon, in petal colours, and in green, for leaves
bunch of artificial stamens with coloured, silver or golden tips
roll of fine wire, for binding
copper, galvanized or millinery wire to outline petals (the wire must be easy to manipulate)
stub wires, for stems
florist's binding tape, green

Making the flowers and leaves
Arrange five or six stamens around one end of a stub wire and bind them tightly in place with fine wire. From the wire used for the petal and leaf shapes, cut lengths of about 12.5 cm (5 inches) for each petal and slightly shorter lengths for the leaves. Bend each piece of wire into a loop and twist the ends to secure them, leaving some length to attach to the stem.

Push the wire loop into the fabric and stretch it tightly. Draw the fabric into the base of the loop, bind it tightly with fine wire and cut off the surplus.

Tightly bind each petal on to the stub wire and stamens group, taking care that it is firmly attached and will not slip.

Start binding the flower high up on the stem, where the calyx would be, making sure that all the binding wires are completely concealed. Bind tape down the full length of the stub wire stem, cut off the tape, then bind the calyx and stem again.

Make leaves in the same way as petals, using fine green stretch material. Bind the leaves on to the stem with fine wire and cover the joins neatly with tape.

You will find it surprisingly easy to shape the petals, twisting and bending the wire outlines. This final shaping of the flowers is the most important stage, giving each flower a distinctive form.

Sprays of small, tight buds are a useful feature in a group of these dainty flowers, especially if you are arranging them in a shape – such as a long, low horizontal or a triangle – that benefits from having clearly defined points.

Make the buds in the way described for the grapes (page 116), spacing them at intervals on each side of the stem, in pairs, not quite opposite each other.

READY-MADE FLOWERS

Ready-made flowers can be all things to all people. You can buy some which are so convincing, visitors just cannot resist touching them to see if they are real. There are also improbable blooms, that are obviously fakes and in frankly fantastic or dazzlingly outrageous colours. Our purchases from department stores include both.

Those artificial flowers which resemble garden varieties look especially pretty arranged with preserved leaves or long lasting evergreens. Often the leaves on sprays of artificial plant material do not reach the same high standard of texture, shape and colour that is achieved with the flowers, and are disappointing in an otherwise aesthetically pleasing group. Strip them off, add natural foliage, and the arrangement becomes softer, prettier and more believable.

Containers for realistic artificial blooms can be chosen without regard to the flowers' pedigree – or lack of it. Choose any holder that would complement fresh or dried flowers. Silky sweet peas might tumble from a pretty china teapot; you could pile roses into a glistening crystal bowl; allow freesias and bluebells to form gentle, natural-looking curves in a pedestal vase or fill a shallow willow basket with poppies or paeonies.

BUILT-IN ADVANTAGES

Ready-made flowers with wire stems will stand upright, but use a strong pair of wire cutters or pincers from the tool box if you want to cut such flowers as you arrange them; or have a pair of pliers to hand if you decide to bend back the stems to shorten them. This way you can unravel the stems to their original full length when rearranging the flowers later. Shortened wire stems can be extended another time by twisting them on a florist's stub wire.

Anchor wire stems in a pinholder – useful for an arrangement in a shallow dish or on a wooden board – in dry, brown stem-holding foam or a handful of glass marbles.

The stems of the peaches and cream coloured flowers arranged in a basket (see title page) are held in a block of foam which is tied securely, parcel fashion, with fine twine taken through the basket base.

Arrange the leaves first to give the triangular, curving or casual outline you have chosen. Glycerine preserved leaves such as beech, lime and oak blend particularly well with artificial flowers, the curving branches giving a graceful look to the design, their suppleness and sheen perfectly complementing the silky petals. For the 'long points', the natural shape contrast to full, round flowers, choose preserved stems of rosemary (which retains its aroma), berberis and yew. And for the visual weight at the base of a design, arrange a cluster of single leaves in preference to one or two very large ones – such as preserved maple, magnolia, camellia or geranium. Bleached preserved leaves, in all the deep, buttery-cream tones, are preferable to those in very dark shades. Large, dark coloured foliage can dominate delicate colours and 'fragile' flowers, and artificial ones are no exception.

FANTASY HARVEST

For a complete contrast to the pastel shades of the flower-basket design, we shopped around and produced an improbable harvest of poppies, paeonies and lilies all in black and grey – with just one colourful highlight, a glowing red poppy.

Contrast in texture and good lighting are the secrets to displaying them with style. Glittering, shiny containers are just the thing. Polished silver, brass and copper, chromium plated and tin items catch every glint of light and add sparkle to the group. Chunky glass containers are good too, providing just the right textural contrast. Conceal a piece of dry stem-holding foam in a heavy glass vase, fill it with shiny marbles and give the darkest of artificial flowers a good send-off.

Consider the background carefully. These flowers look best against the shiniest of surfaces such as gloss paint, metal window blinds, plastic-coated fabrics and mirror glass. These are the surfaces that attract and hold the light, reflecting it back on to the flowers – and those flowers in deep, midnight shades need all the limelight they can get. Place them in the full glare of the sun, so that every shaft of light from the window reaches deep into the centres and brings out the detail in the petals; arrange them in directional light from a wall or ceiling spotlight or table lamp, under a strip of fluorescent lighting or on a glass surface which is lit from below.

Shop-bought poppies, paeonies and lilies will make an effective feature held with heavy marbles in a large glass container.

FLOWER LOAF

Celebrate a festival of flowers with a glorious thanksgiving loaf. Our spectacular flower-spray loaf is the horticultural equivalent of the traditional harvest festival sheaf-of-wheat loaf. Designed and made by a master baker, each stalk, leaf and flower is formed separately and arranged on a base of yeast-leavened dough. The whole bouquet is left to rise in a warm place, the flowers expanding and spreading as if they were blossoming under the heat of the summer sun.

A loaf like this would make a spectacular centrepiece for a buffet party, or indeed a display item for a church or chapel. Beginners might like to start by shaping the individual flowers as bread rolls.

THE DOUGH
40 g (1½ oz) fresh yeast or 25 ml (1½ tbls) dried yeast and 5 ml (1 tsp) caster sugar
1 litre (1¾ pints) warm water
2 kg (4½ lb) strong white bread flour
15 ml (1 tbls) salt
THE GLAZE
3 eggs, beaten with 90 ml (6 tbls) milk and 5 ml (1 tsp) salt
poppy seeds
sesame seeds

1. If you use fresh yeast, put it into a small bowl and gradually stir in the warm milk. For dried yeast, put the water into a bowl, stir in the sugar, sprinkle on the yeast and stir well. Set aside in a warm place for 15 minutes until the mixture is frothy.
2. Sift the flour and salt into a large bowl. Make a well in the centre and pour in the yeast mixture. Mix to a firm dough that will leave the sides of the bowl.
3. Turn the dough out on to a clean working surface and knead it for 10 minutes; or knead it in an electric mixer, using the dough hook, until the mixture is smooth and pliable.
4. Return the dough to the mixing bowl, cover with a piece of greased polythene and leave for about one and a half hours at room temperature, until the dough has doubled in size.
5. Remove the dough from the bowl and press it firmly with the knuckles to remove any large pockets of air.
6. Divide the dough into two pieces, one slightly larger than the other. Roll out the larger piece to form a rectangle 55 x 30 cm (22 x 12 inches) and cut out the bouquet shape. Place the dough on a large, greased baking tray.
7. Roll out the second piece of dough. From this piece and the trimmings, cut about 24-30 flower stalks with strips of dough rolled into long, thin sausage shapes.
8. Brush the dough base with water and arrange the stalks on top, twisting some, and crossing some stalks over others in a realistic way. Roll three long, thin strips of the dough, press them together at one end and plait them loosely to make a braid. Dampen the stalks and press the braid over them, twisting and knotting it in the centre. Shape a leaf and press it over the stalks.
9. Shape the remaining dough into flowers and leaves – you can see the detail more clearly in the individual bread rolls. Make some round shapes, some full-blown ones like roses, some trumpets and bells.
10. Brush the base shape with water and press the flowers into place, arranging them to make a generous display. Press a knife point into the dough to mark petals and flower centres. Trim the base shape around the outline of the flowers.
11. Cover the dough with greased polythene and leave it in a warm place to rise for about one and a half hours. It is ready to bake when it springs back when pressed lightly with a finger.
12. Brush the bread with water and sprinkle the seeds on some centres. Bake it in a preheated oven at 220C (425F) gas 7, for about 50 minutes, until it is golden brown. The loaf should sound hollow when tapped underneath. Leave the loaf to cool completely before removing it from the baking tray. Brush the loaf with the glaze, however, as soon as you take it out of the oven and when it is still warm.

If you wish to dry out the loaf completely (which will make it last longer but render it inedible) leave it in the oven at 130C (250F) gas 1/2, for a further two hours. Cover the top with foil if it is showing signs of becoming too brown.

Flower-shaped bread rolls

Use one fifth of the dough recipe, that is 400 g (14 oz) flour, make the dough as described and leave it to double in size. Roll it out and cut it into small pieces, using scissors. Shape it into flower outlines, mark in petals and centres with a knife point. Leave to prove for the second time for 20 or 30 minutes. Brush the dough with water and scatter poppy seeds and sesame seeds in some flower centres. Bake in the preheated oven for 10-15 minutes, then brush it with glaze.

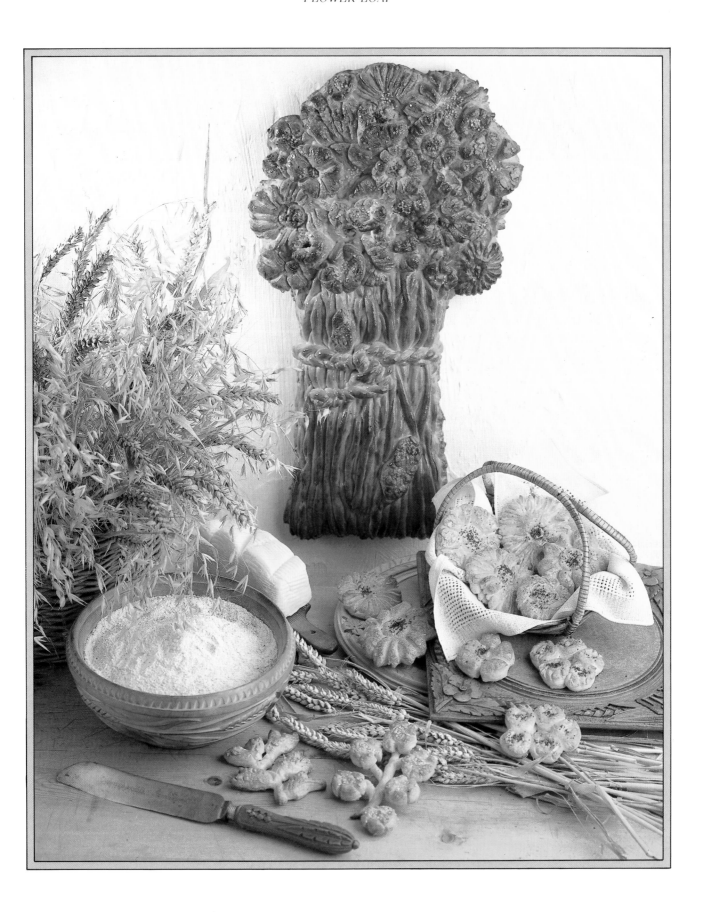

Chapter 4
HEALTH AND BEAUTY

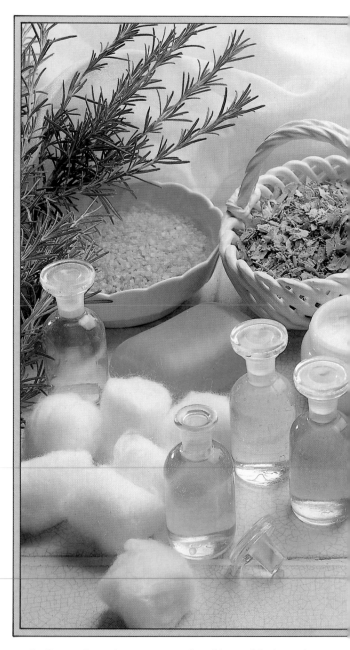

For thousands of years flowers have formed a hallowed part of our cultural heritage. They have been grown for the beauty care of queens – kings, too – and regarded as symbols of purity. Their fragrance has been used for personal enhancement and, in the form of aromatic oils, has had deep significance in religious ceremonies. The wonderful colours that can be extracted from plants have for centuries been used to dye yarns of wool, cotton and silk, for weaving into clothes, rugs and other furnishings.

The earliest use of flowers and other plant materials in all these ways was, of course, making a virtue out of necessity. People were entirely dependent on the natural products to be found locally or, in the case of spices, what could be easily obtained from imports. Today, when every fragrance and hue can be accurately reproduced in a laboratory, we can preserve our complexions, and waft about on a wave of tantalizing aromas, draping ourselves and our homes in brilliant colours, entirely without recourse to a single natural product.

But 'beauty from a bottle' may not match the personal satisfaction of capturing the aroma and colour of the natural products from the world around us. If you love nature and have reservations about the methods used for some laboratory and research experiments, and have even a little leisure time to spare, why not make your own beauty – and beautiful – products and share this delight with your friends.

EARLY COSMETICS

As befits any woman's beauty preparations the exact composition of the first cosmetic products is veiled in the mists of time. What is clear is that these recipes were known in one form or another to most ancient peoples. In some cases the use of aromatic ointments and oils was largely to protect the skin and hair against the ravages of hot and dry climates; some preparations were used as status symbols; some had a religious significance; and others had magical associations, as in the case of warriors who smeared their bodies with pungent oils before going into battle, relying on the oil's mystical powers to bring about rapid victory.

The base of all the earliest cosmetics must have been natural vegetable oils and animal fats which were available. The first known cleansing cream, a mixture of olive oil, wax and rosewater, was blended by a Greek physician, Galen. All along the Mediterranean

Home-made soaps, herbal oils and shampoos are a cheap and delightful alternative to commercial products.

cleansing steam bath, and so keep wrinkles at bay.

Fashion played its part, and in every society there was a natural pacesetter. Cleopatra built up her confidence – and presumably weakened the political resolve of her adversaries – by appearing awe-inspiringly decorative at all times. History tells us that she used floral scented face masks to soften and clarify her skin, and cosmetic creams coloured with saffron. She rubbed fragrant oils into her body, painted her lips and cheeks with red ochre and accentuated her eyes with generous applications of kohl. Other beauty tricks of the trade at the time included the use of butter and barley flour paste scented with flower oils to eradicate skin blemishes (the Romans used heavily perfumed white lead and chalk for the same purpose) and henna, a deep, reddish-brown dye, to colour the hair, nails and palms of the hands and soles of the feet. To this day, henna is regularly used in this way in North African countries. This author had a narrow escape from a friendly group of Bedouin tribeswomen in Tunisia who made every attempt to transform her appearance from top to toe with a pot of the omnipotent dye and a menacingly wide brush!

PETAL AND SPICE BATHS

The Egyptians considered frequent and fragrant baths a prerequisite to purity and good health, and in Syria and Rome it was the custom for kings and emperors to join forces with their loyal subjects in bathing pools. In Syria, on these occasions, the water was lavishly strewn with rose petals, a water-borne red carpet spread before the monarch. Roman emperors vied with each other to distribute publicly the most fragrant of oils. The emperor Heliogabalus, renowned for his personal extravagance, bathed in saffron scented, golden coloured water, emerging with a glowing though temporary tan imparted by the powdered stigmas of blue-violet autumn crocus flowers.

One of the oldest known body lotions, Queen-of-Hungary water, is said to have won the approval of that particular royal lady not only as an after-bath refresher but because, she believed, it had cured her paralysis. A precise list of ingredients has not survived the passage of time, but flowering rosemary, grated spices, dried lemon peel and pure alcohol were among them.

Perfumed baths attained wide popularity in England in the seventeenth century, when women would gather flowers into bath posies to scent the water, and splash themselves with flower scented wine or vinegar. Recipes for these posies were as individual as the

ladies came to value sesame oil as a skin food that penetrated and softened the skin and, since it absorbed most of the ultra-violet rays, protected the skin from the sun.

Athenian ladies liked to burn a little powdered myrrh on a stone, allowing the astringent resin fumes to penetrate the skin in the form of a fragrant, gardens where they grew. They would include some fragrant flowers such as rose, honeysuckle and lily, and herb leaves such as scented geranium and lemon balm. In those days the posies were tied with ribbons and trailed in the water. Today they might be hung beneath the bath taps. Marie-Antoinette's chosen bath fragrance, which was made up into 'muslin bonnets', consisted of equal measures of wild thyme flowers, rosemary leaves and sea salt.

Fresh petal and spice mixtures, the equivalent of dried pot pourri blends, were widely popular as bath fragrances. Some would be sweetly scented, including rose petals, thyme and lavender flowers, crumbled bay leaves or mint tied into muslin bags; others would be more pungent – and carried by fashionable males – and include, besides rose petals, marigold and lemon balm leaves, crushed juniper berries and fenugreek seeds. (Middle Eastern harem ladies, it is worth noting, preferred to eat their fenugreek seeds, in the

Cosmetics blended at home with natural herbs and oils can be made to suit your own preferences.

belief that they were the secret of rounded plumpness of the body.) Perhaps the best bath aromatic of all – one you can achieve when, on a sudden whim, you feel like pampering yourself – is simply that brought about by scattering rose petals and a few drops of oil of roses into your bath water.

ASH AND LAVENDER

Soap is reputed to have been first discovered by accident in Rome about 1000 BC, when the fat from sacrificial animals combined with ashes from the fire and set into blocks. Gradually spices and floral scents were added to colour and scent this soap, making its use as much a pleasure as a practicality. Examples of the soapmaker's craft have been found in excavations in Pompeii, Italy.

Lavender, (the plant name derives from the Latin, *lavare*, to wash) has had a long association with bathing and also with relaxing the mind and body. An old herbal book invites its readers to boil two handfuls of lavender flowers in water with a little salt, strain the infusion and put it into a bath 'not too hot, in which to bathe the body in the morning and at the same time to cleare the minde'.

Town dwellers who were denied the therapeutic luxury of stepping into the herb garden and cutting lavender flowers for the bathroom and boudoir could step outside their front doors and buy them. 'Sweet-smelling lavender, six fine bunches for one penny' was one of the frequently heard flower cries of London and other cities. Roses, marigolds, myrtle, stocks, mignonette, rosemary and thyme were other flowers sold and 'cried' on the streets.

FRAGRANT OILS

Natural oils impregnated with the aroma of flowers, leaves and seeds are the key to many cosmetic and beauty preparations, soaps, bath fragrances, hair lighteners and conditioners, skin care creams, scented candles and, as we shall see in a later chapter, traditional country recipes. As each season brings its harvest of aromatic plants, several batches of fragrant oils can be made. You will soon build up a delightful collection to ring the personality changes on a range of beauty crafts.

Extracting the essential oils from plants is a job for specialists. The mistresses of the pot pourri, on the great estates, spent a lifetime in the still-room perfecting their craft. But by infusing pure vegetable oils with fragrant plants you can make pleasing substitutes; or, for a more concentrated aroma, you can buy mini bottles of 'the real thing' in herbalists' shops.

FLORAL OIL

To make floral oils first select your fragrance according to preference and availability. Rose, carnation, hyacinth, jasmine, lilac, stock, lily and honeysuckle are but a few of the options.

300 ml (½ pint) oil (such as sunflower, safflower, almond, corn or olive)
10 large cupfuls petals
5 ml (1 tsp) liquid storax
5 ml (1 tsp) tincture benzoin

1. Pull off the petals of large flowers, and strip small petals from the stalks. You will need enough petals to pack into 10 large cups. Measure two cupfuls and store remaining petals in a polythene bag in the refrigerator.
2. Pour 300 ml (½ pint) of your chosen oil into the top of a double boiler or a bowl, over a pan of simmering water. Heat the oil, then add two cups of flowers or petals. Stir, cover tightly and leave on very low heat for two hours. Strain and keep the flowers. Add another two cups of flowers to the oil and repeat the process. Then repeat this three times more.
3. Pour the oil and all the flowers into a pan, bring it slowly to the boil and simmer over low heat for about one hour, or until the flowers are dry. Strain the oil through muslin, pressing the dried flowers with a spoon against the sieve.
4. Stir the liquid storax and the tincture of benzoin to fix the aroma. Bottle and cover the oil, label it and store in a dry, dark place.

HERBAL OIL

Making herbal oil is a simpler but longer process. Applemint, eau de Cologne mint and peppermint, lemon balm, sweet cicely, rosemary and fennel seed oils can be kept to hand in the kitchen for culinary as well as beauty craft purposes, provided they are kept in a dry cupboard.

300 ml (½ pint) oil
45 ml (3 tbls) herbs
30 ml (2 tbls) wine or cider vinegar

1. Gather fresh herbs, strip the leaves from the stalks and crush or grind them until they are like coarse grains. For each 300 ml (½ pint) oil you will need 45 ml (3 tbls) herbs. Half fill a jar with the herbs and oil, and add 30 ml (2 tbls) wine or cider vinegar.
2. Cover and shake the jar and leave it on a sunny windowsill or over a radiator for three weeks. Shake the jar every day.
3. Strain the herbs, add 45 ml (3 tbls) fresh herbs and leave for a further three weeks. Do this once more, then finally strain the oil through muslin. Pour it into a clean bottle, cover and label it, and store in a dry, dark place.

SCENTED SOAPS

Decide to delve into the fascinating craft of soapmaking and, in the kitchen, you will become not a cook but a practising chemist, chopping herbs, selecting bottles of fragrant oils and mixing everyday ingredients such as honey, oatmeal and vegetable oils.

Making 'real' soap is a task that needs meticulous care because it involves using caustic soda (lye), a powerful alkali which can cause serious skin burns. It is important that you can work without distraction and be sure that there will be no flying leaps on to the table from curious cats, or children anxious to help. You will need to protect your hands with rubber gloves, and the working surface with newspapers, and be sure that you can measure and handle the ingredients carefully. If you do spill even the smallest amount of caustic soda on your skin, wash the affected area immediately with cold water and dab liberally with lemon juice or vinegar.

In soapmaking the caustic soda is blended with fatty acids which neutralize the alkali. Originally tallow, a saturated animal fat, was used. This could be melted in advance, strained and kept ready in the refrigerator. It is more convenient and more flexible however to substitute vegetable oils. Our recipe uses coconut, sunflower and olive oils, but you could use others.

If you do not wish to make soap in this way, there are simpler alternatives. Our ideas include adding your own distinctive fragrances to pure, unperfumed castile soap, and making a 'loofah' soap with fine oatmeal.

BASIC SOAP

Make variations of this recipe, as suggested below, and at the end of an absorbing experiment you will have a collection of soaps in a combination of shapes, colours and fragrances.

300 m (½ pint) water
60 ml (4 tbls) caustic soda
45 ml (3 tbls) coconut oil
45 ml (3 tbls) sunflower oil
45 ml (3 tbls) olive oil
a few drops of food colouring (optional)
a few drops of fragrant oil or essential oil

Put the water into a glass bowl (do not use a metal container) and very carefully stir in the caustic soda with a wooden spoon. Stir until it dissolves, then set the solution aside to cool – the caustic soda will have heated spontaneously.

Warm the vegetable oils in a small saucepan. When the soda solution and the oils are at the same lukewarm temperature (test by putting your hand underneath the containers) pour the oil slowly and steadily into the soda, stirring constantly. Stir in the colouring if you use it, the flower oils and any other ingredients. Beat the mixture with a whisk, watching carefully for the sudden transition from a shiny liquid to a thick, opaque substance.

Pour the mixture quickly into prepared moulds (see below), stand them on a cake-cooling tray and leave in a warm, dry place for about 24 hours, until the soap has set. Remove the mixture from the moulds, wrap it in greaseproof paper and leave in a cool place for two to three weeks to harden.

Variations on the recipe

To vary the basic recipe, add three to four drops of an essential oil, bought from a herbalist, or 7.5 ml (1½ tsp) of your own make of fragrant flower or herbal oil. You can also add about 60-75 ml (4-5 tbls) of chopped herb leaves or flower petals.

With so many possible additions, the fragrance permutations are endless. Here are just a few ideas to inspire you. Oil of roses and two to three drops of red food colouring; oil of lemongrass and a pinch of powdered saffron (for yellow soap); homemade elderflower oil and honey for a cream coloured soap; finely chopped marjoram or other herb with a complementary oil and two to three drops (if you wish) of green colouring.

Vary not only the fragrance but the shape of your soap. Use small jelly and trifle moulds, yoghurt pots, candle moulds or small foil baking dishes lined with polythene. You can decorate plain shapes after the soap has set by carving initials, flowers or leaves on the surface. Collect the soap shavings and use them in a metal soap saver.

Coloured soaps can be easily made by incorporating food dyes or herbs chopped and mixed with oil.

OATMEAL SOAP

An old country favourite, this variant of the basic soap is not usually given a heavy fragrance.

Basic soap mixture
60 ml (4 tbls) fine oatmeal
30 ml (2 tbls) clear honey
a few drops of fragrant oil or a pinch of sandalwood powder, if desired

Make up the basic soap mixture, as described, adding the oatmeal and honey.

ADDING PERFUMES

If you buy unperfumed castile soap you can transform it by adding any fragrance you please.

120 ml (8 tbls) grated soap flakes
15 ml (1 tbls) vegetable oil
15 ml (1 tbls) clear honey
a few drops of fragrant oil or essential oil

1. Put the grated flakes into the top of a double boiler or a bowl fitted over a pan of simmering water. Stir with a wooden spoon until the soap has melted.
2. Add vegetable oil and honey and stir over heat for five minutes.
3. Add the fragrant or essential oil and pour the soap into moulds. Leave it to harden, as for basic soap.

LOOFAH SOAP

The notion of lathering yourself with a dry, powdered soap on a loofah is as old as the hills.

45 ml (3 tbls) fine oatmeal
45 ml (3 tbls) kaolin powder
5 ml (1 tsp) household borax
a few drops of fragrant oil or essential oil

Stir together the oatmeal and the kaolin powder (bought from chemists). Sift in 5 ml (1 tsp) household borax and add any fragrant or essential oil of your choice. Pack the mixture into small, lidded pots. A collection of these soaps makes an unusual gift.

Spicy variations
This type of natural looking, refreshing soap is best scented with a spicy oil such as patchouli, semmel, vetiver or sandalwood.

BEAUTY IN THE BATH

Great beauties of the past have lavished fortunes on ingredients for luxurious baths. Cleopatra made no secret of her fondness for a deep, soothing bath of asses' milk scented with expensive aromatic oils – a kind of all-enveloping floral milk shake. Catherine the Great sent herb gatherers far and wide throughout Europe and the Far East to discover ever more exotic fragrances for her daily dip. Madame Tallien, an 18th century courtesan renowned for her delicate skin, took to bathing in crushed strawberries and raspberries, before rubbing down in rose scented milk. Madame Pompadour, reputedly one of the greatest beauties of all time and mistress of Louis XV, languished so frequently in baths scented with herbs and strewn with flowers that it worried the king. He feared that this over indulgence would spoil her beauty.

There is some truth in this theory, which generations of schoolboys have been at pains to point out. Some people do find that taking frequent baths has a drying effect on the skin, destroying the acid mantle which forms a protective layer against disease. A simple way to redress this balance is to add a little cider vinegar, sunflower or sesame oil to the water.

Certain herbs and flowers are accredited with specific properties, so we can select not just for fragrance, but for the 'mood' of the bath we take. Are you in need of complete relaxation? Choose chamomile or lavender flowers. Feeling slightly jaded? Try elderflowers. Just cannot get to sleep? Opt for valerian. Lovage and mint have been found to be helpful for skin disorders, and both are refreshing. Marigold leaves have been relied on in times past to soothe varicose veins and fade thread veins. Rosemary and angelica are considered stimulating, hyssop and houseleek nourish the skin, and both dandelion and nettle leaves can aid that other function of bathing – they help to cleanse the skin.

TYPES OF OILS

In order to enjoy the fragrance and derive the benefits from aromatic leaves and flowers you need to extract the oils. There are a number of ways of doing this, apart from the method which involves using a still to produce what is known as essential oil.

Firstly you can make disposable muslin sachets of fresh or dried herbs and flowers – bathtub bouquet garnis – and, for appearance sake, put each one in a pretty outer covering when you use it.

It is not advisable to scatter tiny blue rosemary flowers, spiky rosemary leaves, minute cream elderflowers, lavender and small petals directly into the bath water, as scraping them from your skin is a very time-consuming, messy business.

Dispersing and floating oils made with petals or herbs and used as 'steamers' will add a touch of luxury to bathtime.

A more effective way to extract plant oil is described on page 133, where details are given for a versatile range of fragrant oils. You can use these, or essential oil from herbalists, to make your own scented bath oils that have a touch of luxury.

Choose from two types of oil for the basis of the bath oil. If you like one that dissolves in water (and incidentally leaves no telltale ring around the bath) use a dispersing oil such as Turkey red which is treated castor oil and the most readily available type. If you prefer to emerge from the bath with a healthy glow, with a glistening preparation still clinging to your skin, choose a floating oil. Almond oil and avocado – rich in skin-nourishing Vitamin E – are examples.

Mix one part of homemade fragrant oil with three parts of the dispersing or floating oil; or sprinkle a few drops of the more concentrated essential oil into the basic type. Mix well, pour the bath oil into attractive bottles and jars, such as those that originally contained herbs and spices, and label them with the names of the fragrances. Carnation and almond, jasmine and avocado, or Turkey red rose oil will make a delightful collection for your own bathroom, and would be thoughtful gifts for friends. On each label make a note of the quantity to be used; normally this is 5 ml (1 tsp) for each bath.

USING VINEGAR

Oil and vinegar may not seem natural ingredients for bathtime beauty, but each has its part to play. The addition of vinegar helps to tone the skin by restoring the natural acid balance and counteracting the alkali effect of soap. To make an infusion, use equal volumes of plant material and white distilled vinegar. Pack the leaves or flowers into a heatproof preserving jar, and pour on an equal quantity of boiling vinegar. Close the jar, leave it on a sunny windowsill or in a warm place and simply shake it once or twice a day.

Strain the vinegar, pressing the plant material against the sieve to extract the maximum fragrance, and pour it into a stoppered bottle. Label the bottle with the fragrance type. Use about 150 ml (¼ pint) for each bath. As a skin toner, dilute the fragrant vinegar with eight parts water and use it as an after-bath splash.

Herbal and flower infusions in water, known as tisanes, are as beneficial in the bath as they are in the teacup. Make them in the way described on page 162. For maximum relaxation pour one cupful of, say, chamomile tea, into your bath and drink a second cupful.

HAIR CARE

Look along the shelves of hair-care products in any shop or supermarket and it is easy to see that those products obviously employing herbs and flowers, and fruits and vegetables, are very popular. Natural ingredients have made a big and welcome return in recent years. It is worth reading the labels carefully, however, for not all the fragrances have their origins in a herb garden. Generally it is only the more expensive products that are as 'natural' as those you can make for yourself. So, beyond the therapy and satisfaction, this is another reason for adding hair shampoos, conditioners and rinses to your repertoire.

Herbal and floral shampoos are rewardingly quick and easy to make, and the range of fragrances and benefits is enormous.

BASIC SHAMPOO

This simple soap can be varied by the addition of different flowers: chamomile flowers hold the secret to many a head of beautiful fair hair, as they have a lightening effect; rosemary and sage leaves and lavender flowers – used separately – are time honoured shampoos for dark hair, and marigold petals have just the coppery glow that is needed for red hair.

90 ml (6 tbls) castile soap
1.5 litres (2½ pints) water
1 cupful herbs or petals
2 eggs (optional)

1. Grate castile soap. Pour boiling water over herb leaves or flower petals, stir well, cover and set aside to infuse for two hours.
2. Strain the liquid into a saucepan, pressing the plant material against the sieve so that you do not waste a scrap of fragrance.
3. Add the grated soap, whisk over low heat until it has dissolved, cool, then pour into decorative bottles, and label. Shake the bottle well before using. Rinse the hair thoroughly after shampooing. The slightest trace of soap imparts a dull look.

Adding protein
The addition of two eggs, whisked into the shampoo one it has cooled, adds valuable protein. Add only the egg whites for use on greasy hair.

SOAPLESS SHAMPOO

If your hair reacts badly against soap, there is a herb you can use instead, called soapwort. You can buy the dried, powdered root in herbalists.

90 ml (6 tbls) powdered soapwort
one cup of herb leaves or flowers, such as elderflowers, wild thyme or lime flowers
1.5 litres (2½ pints) boiling water
one egg (optional)

1. Mix the dry ingredients in a bowl and pour on the boiling water. Stir well, cover and leave to infuse for two hours.
2. Cool and strain. Whisk in an egg for extra protein, if you wish, before bottling and labelling the mixture.

RINSING AND CONDITIONING

After the shampoo comes the conditioner and rinse – and fragrant oils (made according to the instructions on page 133) and fragrant vinegars (page 138) find yet another use. A treatment of warm oil rubbed into the scalp is an excellent conditioner, and any vegetable oil is suitable. If it is fragrant, so much the better. Treated castor oil is good for strengthening the hair, and both avocado and almond oil are rich in protein. And so homemade bath oils (pages 136-8) are just the ticket. For maximum benefit, rub the oil in thoroughly, cover your head with a piece of aluminium foil and then with a towel. Leave for at least 15 minutes, longer if your schedule allows.

For another after-shampoo conditioner, and one that is easy to make, mix 75 ml (5 tbls) plain yoghurt with one egg and 5 ml (1 tsp) fragrant oil or one drop of essential oil. Apply to the hair as described above.

Most people remember being told in childhood that vinegar in the rinsing water leaves hair 'squeaking clean'. Multiply that benefit by using an infused vinegar (see page 138). As with shampoos, rosemary, sage and lavender vinegars are good for dark hair, chamomile for blond tresses and marigold for brunettes. Comfrey leaves infused in vinegar have disinfectant properties; peppermint leaves, nettle leaves, elderflowers, yarrow flowers (which also help to combat greasiness) and fennel seeds are all recommended to fight or prevent dandruff. Use about 45 ml (3 tbls) in the final rinsing water. If you are using dried herbs or flowers, perhaps bought from a herbalist, halve the stated quantities.

COLOUR CHANGE

Herbal and floral preparations can be beneficial not only in restoring and maintaining the hair in a healthy condition, they can also be used to alter the colour. A paste, made by mixing a plant and water infusion with kaolin or other powder, is likely to be more effective than a rinse when applied to the hair.

To give fair hair that sun-kissed look, try chamomile and rhubarb for the best chance of success. Infuse one cup of chamomile flowers in 600 ml (1 pint) of boiling water (use rainwater if possible since it leaves the hair soft). Stir well, cool, strain and pour the liquid on to 120 ml (8 tbls) kaolin powder, stirring constantly. Beat in one egg yolk. Using half the quantity at a time, rub the paste thoroughly into the hair, leaving it on for 20 minutes. Then rinse in clear water, adding a little vinegar to the final wash.

The use of walnut skins for deepening brown hair goes back to Roman times when infusions of walnut leaves were also used. For the paste method, mix 120 ml (8 tbls) chopped walnut skins with 120 ml (8 tbls) rosemary and water infusion. Pour the liquid on to 30 ml (2 tbls) powdered alum and beat in one egg yolk. Apply half the paste at a time to the hair, using it as described above.

Note: When many of these herbal remedies and beauty aids were in widespread use the herbs and flowers were freely available in gardens and the countryside; this is not now the case, but you can buy many of them in dried form from herbalists.

SKIN TONES

There was an old belief that the finest way to keep skin young and healthy was to bathe it daily in morning dew. Not just any morning dew, but the safe and gentle water gathered drop by drop from the buds and leaves of the hawthorn tree, before dawn on the first of May. Just in case your own supply of this magic moisturiser runs out before next May day, here are some more down-to-earth suggestions for your cosmetics cupboard.

There is perhaps only one 'secret' of a beautiful skin, and that is to treat it gently, and treat it regularly. An occasional blitz on a tired and under-nourished skin can be of minimal benefit, and is quite different from the relaxing, reassuring therapy of a regular routine. If cleansing, toning, nourishing and generally pampering your skin has had a low priority, make a resolution here and now to set aside a few extra minutes night and morning. It is a small enough price to pay for maintaining in good condition the delicate tissue that regulates the body temperature, wards off bacteria, helps the body eliminate harmful toxins and acts as an all-over waterproof.

CLEANSING CREAMS

Cleansing creams are quick and easy to make at home, and can be produced for a fraction of the market price. Dairy produce, purified white beeswax, vegetable oils and honey combined with flowers or floral infusions make some delightful and effective products.

ELDERFLOWER CLEANSING CREAM

In addition to their pleasant scent, elderflowers are particularly soothing to the skin, as are chamomile and lavender flowers and thyme and peppermint leaves.

2 large elderflower heads
300 ml (½ pint) plain yoghurt
45 ml (3 tbls) clear honey

These attractive pastel skin creams incorporate saffron, rose and mint for colouring.

1. Put the yoghurt and the flowers from the elderflower heads into a small pan and stir over a low heat. Simmer gently for 30 minutes, then cover and set aside for three to four hours.
2. Strain the mixture, then stir in the honey and whisk thoroughly until the mixture thickens. Pour into jars, label and store in the refrigerator.

Elderflower cleansing milk
Make this in a similar way to the cleansing cream, but substitute buttermilk for the yoghurt. The preparation does not thicken. Pour it on to cotton wool to apply to your face.

ROSE PETAL CLEANSING CREAM

This gives your skin an especially cared for feeling.

150 ml (10 tbls) grated white wax
90 ml (6 tbls) sunflower oil
75 ml (5 tbls) distilled rosewater
2.5 ml (½ tsp) cider vinegar

1. Melt the wax and then stir in the sunflower oil.
2. Carefully remove from the heat and stir in rosewater and cider vinegar. Whisk the mixture until it is light and creamy, spoon into jars, and label.

TONERS

Astringents and toners close the pores after deep cleansing and leave the skin with a fresh, tingling feeling.

For oily skins make a simple marigold infusion to use as a toner after cleansing. Pour 600 ml (1 pint) boiling distilled water on to 150 ml (¼ pint) marigold petals, stir well, cover and leave overnight. Strain, bottle, and label. For an alternative 'recipe' for greasy skins, mix 15 ml (1 tbls) herbal or floral vinegar and 150 ml (¼ pint) rainwater or distilled water.

As a toner for normal and dry skins, mix together 150 ml (¼ pint) distilled rosewater, 45 ml (3 tbls) distilled orangeflower water and 45 ml (3 tbls) of glycerine. Bottle and label. Pat the skin with the toner after cleansing.

MOISTURIZERS

The first priority here is to make sure of your skin type: milk steeped in herbs makes a gentle moisturizer for normal or oily skins, but dry skins benefit from heavier, creamy substances.

HERBAL MOISTURIZING MILK

Smooth this on to the face after cleansing and toning, or pour a cupful into a warm bath for true luxury.

300 ml (½ pint) full-fat milk
60 ml (4 tbls) chopped mint, marjoram or parsley
(this last is particularly good for oily skins)

Pour the milk on to the herbs, cover and leave in the refrigerator overnight. Strain, bottle, label, and store in the refrigerator.

COLD CREAM

Use this as a moisturizer night and morning.

150 ml (¼ pint) herbal or floral infusion of your choice
(if you use distilled water it will not be necessary to store the preparation in the refrigerator)
5 ml (1 tsp) borax
90 ml (6 tbls) purified white beeswax
300 ml (½ pint) almond oil
a few drops of essential oil or 15 ml (1 tbls) fragrant oil

1. Dissolve the borax in the herbal infusion and set to one side.
2. Melt the purified beeswax and pour in the almond oil, stirring constantly. Stir in the borax solution, remove from the heat, cool and stir until the cream thickens.
3. Add essential or fragrant oil, spoon the cream into pots, and label.

FACE MASK

Spread this mask over the face, avoiding the area around the eyes. Soak pads of cotton wool in a mild floral infusion to make eye pads (chamomile and elderflower are both good). Rest for 30 minutes, then remove the eye pads, wash off the mask, pat the skin dry and continue your usual toning and moisturizing routine.

60 ml (4 tbls) finely chopped mint
15 ml (1 tbls) clear honey
45 ml (3 tbls) milk
30 ml (2 tbls) fine oatmeal

Simmer the mint in an equal quantity of water for five minutes. Remove from the heat and stir in the honey, milk and oatmeal. When the mixture has cooled, apply evenly to the face.

BURNING BLOOMS

A room scented with perfumed candles, aromatic oil or floral incense takes on an almost mystical quality, as if the whole history of these pungent all pervading aromas is recreated in a wisp of fragrant smoke. The art of candle-making was known to the ancient people of Egypt, China, Japan and Crete. In some civilizations candles bearing marks at regular intervals were used to measure the passage of time. For thousands of years candles have been used to sweeten the air, with aromatic oils and perfume added to the basic ingredients. The 'fuel' for the candles varied according to local availability. It may have been oil from seabirds or fish, tallow or animal fat, or plant derived oils, and beeswax (considered the finest).

MAKING CANDLES

The most popular fuel used in candle craft is paraffin wax, a petroleum byproduct. It is mixed with stearin, or stearic acid, a pure form of animal fat which strengthens the wax, makes the candle opaque and slows down the burning rate.

Materials you will need
(for one candle)
135 ml (9 tbls) paraffin wax
15 ml (1 tbls) stearin
candle dye
1 wick
1 wick rod or cocktail stick
a small piece of modelling clay
3-4 drops essential oil
or 5 ml (1 tsp) fragrant oil
or special candle perfume
150 ml (¼ pint) mould

Melt the wax in a double boiler or a bowl fitted over a pan of simmering water. Cut a piece of wick 7.5 cm (3 inches) longer than the mould. You will need thin wick for a candle 2.5 cm (1 inch) thick, medium wick for a 5 cm (2 inch) candle and the thick type for a candle 7.5 cm (3 inch) or more in diameter. Dip the

Burning candles sweeten the air with their aromatic oils and perfumes.

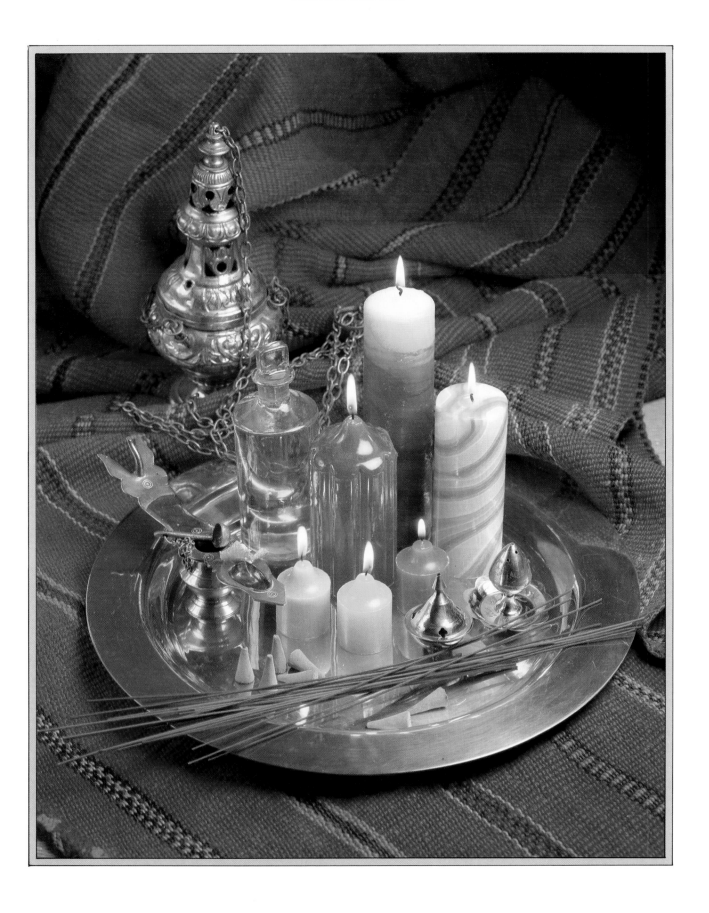

wick in the melted wax and allow it to dry. Tie it close to the middle of the wick rod, or cocktail stick. Lay the rod or stick across the top of the mould and thread the other end of the wick through a hole in the centre of the mould base. Secure it, closing the hole with modelling clay. Stand the mould upright, supporting it in a jar if necessary.

Stir the stearin and as much dye as required into the melted wax, add the fragrance and stir over low heat until well blended. Cool slightly. Pour slowly into the mould and tap it to release any trapped air. As the candle wax sets depressions will form in the top. Melt any remaining wax mixture and top up the mould as required.

Leave the candle to cool completely. Tap rigid moulds or peel back flexible ones to release the candle. Trim the wick and polish the surface of the candle with a soft, dry cloth.

You can buy flexible moulds in all shapes and sizes; flower shapes would be appropriate. Improvize by using yoghurt pots, mousse and jelly moulds, cups, or even wine glasses. (You can safely burn a candle inside a glass.)

DECORATING CANDLES

To add a finishing touch, a floral finish, to your candles, 'paint' them with pressed flowers. Melt some plain wax or the ends of white candles. Place the flowers, petals or leaves against the surface of the candle and fix them with a few quick strokes of a small paintbrush dipped in melted wax. Wild rose petals assembled in a flower shape with a daisy for the centre, a ring of fuchsia 'bells' around the top of a short, squat candle, or sprays of buttercups twining around a tall, thin candle – make each one unique.

The 'candles' burned in Biblical times consisted not of wax set hard around a vertical wick, but of a wick suspended in a dish of olive oil, which is an excellent fuel. Infuse the oil with fresh or dried herbs, flowers or crushed seeds, blended or used individually (full details are on page 133), and burn it in a traditional, boat-shaped burner or a modern glass container, for an aroma that will be as evocative as pot pourri.

INCENSE

There are two types of incense. One is a blend of powdered spices, a fixative and flowers; the other is blended with ground charcoal and gum, and shaped into cones or sticks to burn indoors.

POWDERED INCENSE

Sprinkle this incense powder on to glowing charcoal, after first making sure that the room is well ventilated so as to avoid overpowering fumes.

25 g (1 oz) sandalwood powder
15 g (½ oz) ground cardamom seeds
15 g (½ oz) ground cloves
15 g (½ oz) ground cinnamon
25 g (1 oz) powdered gum benzoin
25 g (1 oz) dried lavender flowers (or other highly aromatic flowers)
1-2 drops of essential oil

Mix the sandalwood powder, cardamon seeds, ground cinnamon and cloves together with the fixative, gum benzoin. Stir in the flowers with one or two drops of oil, and store in an airtight tin.

INCENSE CONES

This fragrance is specially appropriate for an Eastern style party. And for the following morning, or whenever a room needs a refreshing aroma, try an old herbal remedy. Rub dried herbs, such as lavender flowers, rosemary, sage, bay or lemon balm leaves to a powder, and set light to them in a fire-proof dish. This herbal incense is better than a breath of fresh air.

5 ml (1 tsp) powdered sandalwood
5 ml (1 tsp) ground cinnamon
25 g (1 oz) crushed dried bay leaves
25 g (1 oz) dried lavender or other aromatic flowers
4-5 drops of essential oil
75 ml (5 tbls) gum arabic
175 g (6 oz) quick lighting charcoal
25 g (1 oz) powdered gum benzoin

1. Crush charcoal and stir in gum benzoin, sandalwood and cinnamon.
2. Mix gum arabic to a stiff paste with water and stir into the spice mixture. Stir in bay leaves and dried lavender or other aromatic flowers, and four or five drops of essential oil.
3. Stir the mixture well and form it into shapes – cones are traditional.
4. Stand the incense shapes in a warm place for two days to dry, then wrap them in foil to retain the aroma. Unwrap the incense blocks, stand them on a dish, and light the tip to burn.

WRAPPING AND PACKING

When you create your own range of beauty and craft products – scented soaps and bath preparations, products to take good care of the hair and skin, or perfumed oils and candles which will waft their aroma into every corner of a room – you build up a selection of pleasing gifts. Perhaps you might like to give elderflower or lime cosmetics to a young girl, a rose-scented range to a friend with romantic ideals, or spice-scented products to an older person.

As soon as you start making beauty products – or even before – start collecting containers for them. For as all the expensive cosmetic houses know to their profit, attractive packaging is all part of the aura. Packaging adds a certain feeling of luxury and both complements and enhances the product.

Try to design a brand image for your range. The bottles and jars of cosmetics and creams will be received with even greater appreciation if they look decorative on a bathroom shelf or dressing table.

Collecting beautiful objects from past eras may be one of your hobbies, in which case turn this to your advantage and seek out old bottles, pots and jars for your cosmetics. Many street markets and junk shops have a stall or shelf given over to inexpensive but attractive containers dug up in someone's field or garden, often by diligent children hunting for ways to supplement their pocket money. Look out for glass bottles in deep blue, ivy-leaf green and chestnut brown. They would make attractive containers for a range of fragrant hair rinses and oils.

Old lemonade, ginger beer, and beer bottles are useful for shampoos and conditioners, and small ink bottles are ideal for oils which have a heavy concentration of herbal or floral aroma.

These lovely old bottles, made of thick glass with a hint of green or brown and with a wealth of texture in the surface, may have lost their stoppers. Except perhaps for the effect this loss has on bargain basement prices, that is not important. Buy a bag of new corks from a wine-making shop and cut them to make an airtight fit for the bottle necks.

If used containers are not your choice or you do not have the time or opportunity to seek them out, buy plain glass jars and pots or plastic screw-top bottles from chemists' suppliers.

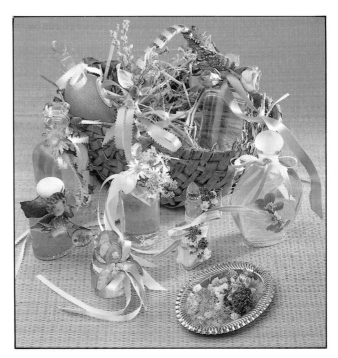

Cosmetics bottles can be 'customized' with ribbons, bows, dried and fresh flowers, seedheads and distinctive labels.

However plain or pleasing the container, you should always label all cosmetic and beauty products clearly, with the name and type of the preparation, the quantity to be used and any special instructions. Nothing is more frustrating than to receive a bottle of something that is a delightful shade of pale green and smells divine, but which is completely anonymous, and potentially a hazard.

CUSTOMIZED CONTAINERS

A label gives you another chance to stamp your personality and design preferences on your product. You can buy very attractive printed labels, edged with entwined flowers and leaves, art nouveau-style tendrils or abstract designs. Write the details clearly in indelible ink – a soapy hand groping for a bottle will obliterate anything written with ordinary inks.

The plainer the bottles or jars, the more you might like to give them a visual face-lift. Bows of narrow satin ribbon around the neck of the containers – deep pink and white striped ribbon with rose-scented products, maybe, and tiny checked gingham with pure white creams – are a simple device, and one which you could easily adopt as your cottage-industry theme.

For a handcrafted look you can wax pressed flowers on to bottles and jars, in the way suggested for decorating candles. Simply melt white wax in a pan, hold pressed flowers, buds or small leaves against the container and brush quickly over it with the hot wax. It will set on impact, holding the decoration in place, and is resistant to cold and warm water splashes.

FLOWERS AS TRIMMINGS

Fresh and dried flowers make the prettiest of parcel trimmings, adding a final flourish that is uniquely your own. It is easy to wrap a gift pack in bright blue or orange paper, tie it around and around with satin ribbon and twine the ends into tight little curls, but gathering up a posy, perhaps of small nasturtiums or pansies, to tie on to the box at the very last minute adds a special touch.

Fresh flower trimmings make a few calls on the ingenuity if they are to radiate not only charm but garden freshness too. Posies do not present many problems. You can assemble them the day before the event and keep them in water overnight. The next day, if there is to be much of a time lapse between your leaving home and handing over the gift, wrap the stems in damp tissues or cotton wool, then bind them tightly with foil to seal in the moisture. Twist a short length of ribbon, that matches the parcel, around the foil if you wish.

Single flowers or a few slender stems can have the luxury of travelling to their destination in a small plastic phial of water. Florists sell them for dress orchids, or you can improvise by using the plastic cap of a felt-tipped pen: fill it with a few drops of water,

Fresh or everlasting flowers teamed with smart ribbons and careful wrapping will make presents that much more special.

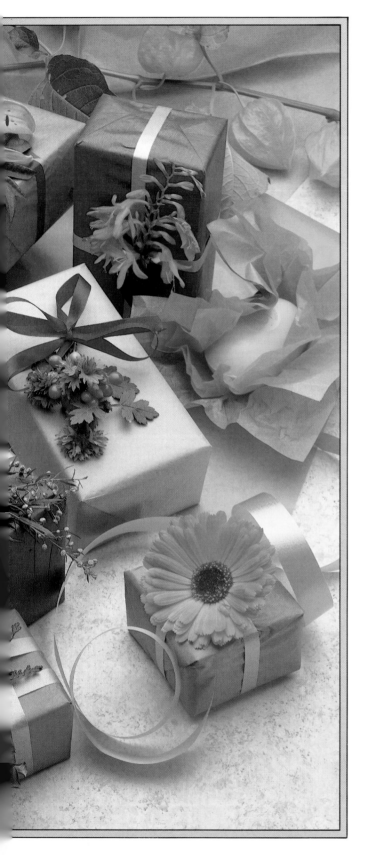

cover the opening tightly with foil pressed firmly all around it, and push in the stems. Bind the stems and the improvised stem holder with ribbon and tie a pretty bow around. This simple but effective device is a good way of keeping fashion flowers fresh. The pen top is narrow enough to push through a buttonhole or slip under a hatband.

If you are making a present which will be given almost immediately, ribbons of fresh flowers make pretty parcel trimmings. Tie a box with wide ribbon across the corners, spread the ribbon generously with glue, and press on rows of flat flower heads, touching edge-to-edge, like a living embroidery. Or dab glue at random intervals over the parcel, and press on daisies, buttercups, potentilla, celandines, or whatever you have in the garden or vase.

TIMELY PRESENTS

Presents that have a long wait ahead of them – those which will be piled under a Christmas tree or hung on its branches – are best trimmed with lasting flowers. Posies of everlasting flowers, helichrysum, statice, gypsophila and honesty make glittering trimmings.

Buy the cheapest brand of coloured tape and scatter over it dried flower heads – the perfect way to bring glory to those flowers that have come apart from their stems. Tie bows of parcel ribbon and stick dried flowers in the centre and on the trailing ends. Cut out flower shapes or 'snowflakes' from white, silver or gold paper doilies, stick dried flowers in the centres – pink and blue hydrangea or larkspur florets or small cornflowers – and scatter them over plain tissue paper wrapping.

Most important of all, keep a floral 'button box' for all the snippings and offcuts of dried flowers. A tiny spray of silver honesty, a single rosebud on a tiny stalk, a floret or two of delphinium, can all transform a simple package into a beautiful one. It's the thought, and the flowers, that count.

Chapter 5
FOOD AND FLOWERS

Flowers are delicious. That must be the verdict after browsing through old herbals and recipe books, and experimenting with new and long forgotten recipes.

To regard eating flowers and drinking in their aroma as unusual is a comparatively recent attitude. In times past it was readily recognized that flowers could contribute a combination of spiciness, sweetness, colour, shape or aesthetic appeal to dishes as varied as chrysanthemum soup and rose petal jelly. Indeed, it was only because flowers could earn their keep in the kitchen that precious space was made for them in the garden. Pansies and pinks, mallow and marigolds, primroses and roses, took their rightful place in the cottage garden alongside other practical crops like peas and parsnips.

THE CULINARY RANGE

But the practice of using flowers for culinary purposes is rooted much further back in time. The Greeks called chamomile, with its little daisy like heads, one of the most versatile flowers, the apple of the earth. The Romans made both rose and violet wines. They also made rose wine without roses, using citron and palm leaves as alternative flavourings. In the Middle Ages, hippocras, a highly-spiced wine – renowned for its supposed aphrodisiac properties – was scented with clove carnations, the sweet smelling border pinks.

In those days it was almost a case of 'marigolds with everything'. Mutton broth, 'ordinary pottage', stewed beef, crab salad, marigold bread, buns, biscuits and sandwiches, baked and boiled pudding, pickled buds, crystallized petals, conserve, cordial, wine and an after-dinner digestif, all benefited from the flavour and appearance of these spicy flowers.

Exploring the culinary opportunities that exist in the flower garden (or on a well-stocked market stall)

is as exciting as opening an imaginative and colourful cookery book for the first time. The effects you can create by using flowers as decorations and garnishes are there for all to see. But what of their flavour; how do you judge that? The answer can only be found by testing and tasting.

Pick off a petal here, nibble the corner of a leaf there, and assess the flavour. It must be stressed that you should never taste any part of any plant unless you know it is safe to eat (there is a more detailed note on page 150).

For new enthusiasts to the art of flower tasting, there are some delightful surprises in store. Chrysanthemum, nasturtium, gladiolus, lilies and marigolds are among the spiciest of blooms. In China, white chrysanthemums have been cultivated for culinary purposes for over 2000 years. The petals are used with pickling spices to preserve fish, tossed in stir-fries of beef, chicken and vegetables, floated on rice wine, and sprinkled on cooked dishes as an elegant, wax-like garnish.

Both nasturtium and gladiolus have shape as well as piquancy in their favour. The trumpet shaped flowers may be dipped in batter and deep-fried, or used as eye-catching natural containers, filled with salads, creams and sauces. The flowers may be infused in oil and vinegar to give a hot pepperiness to sauces and salad dressings, or sliced and tossed, raw, in salads. Both flowers may be added, just for flavour, to soups and stews (they emerge from simmering liquids limp and bedraggled and should then be discarded). In addition, young nasturtium leaves give a lift to green salads and the buds may be pickled and used in a similar way to capers.

In Mexico the lily, or shell flower, is the star of the kitchen. The flowers are used in great abundance to pep up sauces. In China dried or pickled lily buds – picked when they are no more than 5 cm (2 inches) long – add spice to dishes such as braised duck (with which they have a special affinity), steamed whole fish and fried rice. And in Norway lily flowers are steeped in brandy and sugar to make a liqueur.

On a still, summer evening, cool drinks made with fragrant flowers will be a welcome refreshment.

Roses take pride of place among the sweet smelling, sweet tasting flowers, and have so much to offer that it seems a crime to let their petals fade and flutter, unused, to the ground. Other flowers which have a taste for confectionery, and can be used in many of the same ways, include clove carnations, broom, honeysuckle, jasmine, lavender, mallow, pansy, primrose, acacia, violet, sweet cicely, meadowsweet and elderflower.

INFUSING IDEAS

Draw out the flavour by infusing the flowers or petals in honey for toppings, baking and tea-time spreads. Dry the flowers in sugar to carry the sweet, subtle aroma through cakes, biscuits and desserts. Steep them in milk or cream to give a hint of luxury to pancakes, waffles, ice cream, fruit mousses, crème brulée, baked custard and rice moulds. Infuse the fragrant petals in syrup to make delectable sorbets, fruit salad dressings and drinks, or give them a place of their own in the store cupboard and make a range of fragrant jams and jellies. Our recipes for rosepetal jam, honeysuckle and peach cheese and others are intended as just the tip of the inspiration iceberg.

Flower fritters for dessert were considered a great delicacy at the beginning of this century. A wisp of light batter aerated with whisked egg white enclosed clusters of acacia, sweet cicely, meadowsweet and elderflower, or single mallow and pansy flowers. Present day equipment for deep-frying, with temperature control and automatic timing, helps you to make these desserts in moments.

GARLANDS OF GARNISH

Of the many ways to prepare flowers for the table, perhaps candying is the most romantic and evocative. But there are other ways. Flowers make the most eye-catching of instant garnishes and decorations; even a couple of blooms and leaves plucked from a flower arrangement or an indoor plant will transform an everyday dish.

Lining a serving plate with leaves is a good start. Shiny variegated ivy leaves make an attractive pattern beneath a selection of cheeses, and yellow marigolds scattered on bunches of black grapes between the wedges and rounds intensify the dairy colouring – and serve as a reminder that the petals are specially good in egg and cheese dishes of all kinds.

Fresh fruit looks well with leaves. Line a plate or a pedestal cake stand with leaves – vine and hop foliage are perfect – and group polished apples, downy peaches, clusters of black cherries, fresh dates, halved kiwi fruits and tiny bunches of grapes. For a finishing touch add three or four crimson roses, echoing the colour of the grapes, or a spectacular head of deep red geranium.

Choose scented geranium leaves to line a dish of ice cream or decorate a mousse, and contrast or complement the colour of the food with flowers. A blend of pale green and scarlet tobacco flowers with pistachio cream, a stem of alstroemeria decorating an apple mousse, a spray of honeysuckle with apricot sorbet, work visual wonders.

Chopped fresh herbs and sprays of herb leaves can seem a little uninspired for garnishing vegetables and savoury dishes. If home-grown runner beans are a proud feature of the menu, give the dish a dazzle with a spray of the scarlet flowers. After all, at one time, before people realized how delicious the pods were, the plants were grown for the joy of their showy flowers. Garnish a dish of green peas or mange-tout peas with a sense of humour, and a spray of sweet peas. The flowers have a familiar flavour and there is no mistaking the family resemblance.

Scattering marigold and chrysanthemum petals on casseroles for a touch of spice certainly proves that flowers and savouries go well together. Garnish a dish of roast turkey with a single vibrant head of red geranium, a visual match for the cranberry sauce or stuffing; a chicken with flowering thyme, marjoram or rosemary to complement the filling; or a plate of cold roast beef with a deep red poppy or a single dahlia.

In Mexico there is a saying that the lily provides two feasts, one for the eye and the other to allay hunger. The same might be said of many flowers.

A word of warning

It is unwise to eat any part of any plant unless you know it is safe to do so. Some plants are poisonous. Most poisonous are the purple berries of deadly nightshade (*Atropa belladonna*). The fruits of woody nightshade (*Solanum dulcamara*), bryony, dogweed, spindle and yew are harmful. All parts of thornapple and henbane plants are poisonous. So, too, are the leaves of tomatoes, rhubarb and potatoes.

Do not be tempted by a flower's good looks. For example, foxgloves (*Digitalis purpurea*), wild and cultivated aconites, pink-flowered valerian and wormwood are all poisonous. Beware, too, of look-alikes. Several plants that look like sheep's parsley are harmful. These include hemlock, cowbane, fool's parsley and wild carrot.

SOUPS AND SALADS

Flowers can play an appealing part in the presentation of soups and salads. Often when there is no time to prepare an elaborate garnish a spray of flowers, a few blossoms or a scattering of petals, achieved in moments, is more effective anyway.

But flowers are not just pretty faces, and have a long heritage as an ingredient, not just a decoration. For centuries the Chinese have favoured white chrysanthemum petals for their spicy flavour, while in medieval Britain marigold petals had a similar appeal. Broom flowers, with their sweetness, perfectly offset any slight bitterness in salad greens, and are specially good with a honey dressing. And trumpet shaped flowers such as nasturtium and gladiolus have long been appreciated as attractive and edible containers for creamy salads and dressings.

CHRYSANTHEMUM AND BEAN SPROUT SOUP

The Chinese have a long standing liking for cooking with white chrysanthemum petals, using them in soups, stir-fries and braised dishes. This tasty soup can be made in moments.

SERVES 4.
100 g (4 oz) lean pork, cut into thin matchstick strips
5 ml (1 tsp) rock salt
15 g (½ oz) cornflour
1 litre (1¾ pints) brown stock, or chicken stock
250 g (8 oz) fresh bean sprouts, or canned ones, rinsed and drained
15 ml (1 tbls) soy sauce
45 ml (3 tbls) dry sherry
pepper
petals from 1 large white chrysanthemum

1. Toss the pork strips in the salt and cornflour. Pour the stock into a pan and bring to the boil. Add the pork, return to the boil and simmer for five minutes.
2. Add the bean sprouts and simmer for two minutes. Stir in the soy sauce and sherry, season with pepper and add the chrysanthemum petals, reserving a few for garnish.
3. Serve the soup hot, garnished with the reserved petals.

WILD LEAVES SOUP

Young wild leaves make a delicious and nutritious soup.

SERVES 4.
1 large onion, sliced
1 garlic clove, chopped
2 medium potatoes, peeled and chopped
40 g (1½ oz butter)
500 g (1 lb) mixed young wild leaves and shoots, such as stinging nettle tops, deadnettles and ground elder
1 litre (1¾ pints) chicken stock
15 ml (1 tbls) lemon juice
salt
pepper
150 ml (¼ pint) full-fat milk
small sprays of red deadnettle with flowers, to garnish

1. Fry the onion, garlic and potatoes in the butter over low heat for about seven minutes, stirring occasionally.
2. Add the leaves and shoots, stir, and pour on the stock and lemon juice.
3. Cover the pan and boil for 10 minutes, until the potatoes are tender.
4. Liquidize the soup in a blender. Return the purée to the pan, taste and season with salt and pepper. Stir in the milk and heat gently.
5. Garnish the soup with the shoots and flowers.

Note: Use any mixture of edible wild leaves and shoots, but select only very young foliage. You can include the flowers from, for example, red deadnettle and ground ivy.

CHILLED CHERRY AND BORAGE SOUP

The combination of wine-red cherries and sky-blue flowers makes this the perfect soup for a summer party.

SERVES 4.
150 g (5 oz) caster sugar
1 cinnamon stick
1 litre (1¾ pints) water
500 g (1 lb) morello cherries, stoned
175 ml (6 fl oz) dry red wine
15 ml (1 tbls) arrowroot
60 ml (4 tbls) soured cream
12-16 borage flowers, picked from stalks, to garnish

1. Put the sugar, cinnamon stick and water into a pan and dissolve the sugar over low heat. Bring to the boil and boil for five minutes.
2. Add the cherries, bring to the boil and simmer for 30 minutes. Remove the cinnamon and stir in the wine.
3. Mix the arrowroot to a paste with 30 ml (2 tbls) of the liquid. Pour on more liquid, stirring constantly, and add the arrowroot mixture to the pan. Bring to the boil, stirring, and simmer for three minutes. Remove from the heat. Stir a little of the soup into the soured cream, then stir the cream into the soup. Cool and chill.
4. Garnish the soup with the borage flowers. It looks most impressive served in bowls placed on larger ones filled with cracked ice.

RED CLOVER SALAD

Rice salad flavoured with herbs is served on a bed of red chicory leaves and garnished with red clover flowers.

SERVES 4.
75g (3 oz) brown rice
15 g (1 tbls) chopped mint
15 g (1 tbls) chopped thyme
2 spring onions, thinly sliced
45 g (3 tbls) blanched split almonds
50 g (2 oz) chopped dried apricots
red chicory leaves
about 16 red clover flowers
FOR THE DRESSING
45 ml (3 tbls) olive oil
15 ml (1 tbls) red wine vinegar
1 egg yolk
salt
pepper

1. Cook the rice in a large pan of boiling, salted water for 40 minutes. Drain the rice into a colander and refresh it under cold, running water. Drain it thoroughly.
2. Mix the dressing, pour it over the rice and toss it well. Stir in the mint, thyme, spring onions, almonds and apricots.
3. Line a serving dish with the red chicory leaves. Pile the rice salad on top. Wash and dry the clover flowers. Separate them into florets and arrange in a ring over the rice.

SALAMAGUNDY

This mixed salad was popular in England in the 18th century, when it was often arranged to resemble a posy.

SERVES 4 TO 6.
a handful of young spinach leaves, washed and dried
1 small cucumber, thinly sliced
2 dessert apples, cored and thinly sliced
15 ml (1 tbls) lemon juice
1 medium onion, thinly sliced into rings
30 ml (2 tbls) capers, drained, rinsed and drained
2 stalks celery, thinly sliced
90 ml (6 tbls) chopped red cabbage
2 hard-boiled eggs, sliced
1 bunch watercress, trimmed
1 x 40 g (1¾ oz) can anchovies, drained
4-6 nasturtium flowers
60-90 ml (4-6 tbls) mayonnaise
FOR THE DRESSING
75 ml (5 tbls) olive oil
30 ml (2 tbls) white wine vinegar
30 ml (2 tbls) chopped mint
salt
pepper

1. Mix the dressing.
2. Arrange the spinach leaves on a serving dish and place cucumber slices on top. Toss the apple slices in the lemon juice and arrange them on the leaves. Add the onion rings, capers, celery and red cabbage in rings and pour on the dressing.
3. Arrange the egg slices, watercress and anchovies on the salad. Fill the nasturtium flowers with mayonnaise and place them on top.

GLADIOLUS SALAD

Gladiolus flowers make an unusual salad.

SERVES 4.

12 gladiolus flowers, washed and dried
225 g (8 oz) full fat soft cream cheese
grated zest of 1 orange
15 ml (1 tbls) orange juice
15 ml (1 tbls) tomato purée
few drops of Tabasco sauce
freshly ground black pepper
150 ml (5 fl oz) thick cream, whipped
75 g (3 oz) peeled prawns
30 ml (2 tbls) chopped chives
1 small cucumber, thinly sliced
1 lettuce heart, shredded
15 ml (1 tbls) scented geranium leaves, chopped

1. Beat the cheese with the orange zest and juice and tomato purée. Season with Tabasco sauce and black pepper. Stir in the cream, prawns and chives. Correct seasoning if necessary. Store covered in the refrigerator until ready to serve.
2. Arrange the cucumber slices in a semi-circle on individual plates. Toss the shredded lettuce and geranium leaves together and spread them over each plate.
3. When you are ready to serve the salad, spoon the cheese, cream and prawn mixture into the trumpet-shaped gladiolus flowers and arrange them in a circle on the bed of lettuce and geranium leaves.

CAKE DECORATIONS

Real or model edible flowers make attractive decorations for cakes and desserts, and we explain both how to candy real petals and how to make decorative flowers from almond or fondant paste.

CANDIED FLOWERS

Candied (or crystallized) flowers can be made in two ways. You can paint the petals with egg white and frost them with sugar, but this method ensures the flowers will keep for only a couple of days. For longer term keeping you need to seal the petals in a solution of gum arabic crystals. Then, stored in an airtight container, they will keep for up to one year.

Small flowers or separate petals are most effective. Choose from violets, chamomile, primroses and other primula, small pansies, sweet peas, border pinks, cowslips, borage and fruit blossom, sprays of broom, heather, hyacinth and lily-of-the-valley, and separate rose and carnation petals.

Do not forget leaves as you build up a sugar-coated collection. They flatter the flowers considerably. Small sprays of young mint and lemon balm are among the most effective.

For the long keeping method, put 15 ml (1 tbls) gum arabic crystals into a jar with 45 ml (3 tbls) orangeflower water. Cover the jar, shake it vigorously and set aside for three days where you can see it so that you remember to shake the jar frequently. It is most important that the crystals are completely dissolved and form a syrupy consistency.

Wash and thoroughly dry the flowers and leaves. If they are at all damp the solution will not adhere to them. Using a very fine camel hair paint brush, paint every part of the flower or petal with the solution. Hold the flower with tweezers, sprinkle it lightly with caster sugar and shake off any excess.

Place the frosted flowers, petals and leaves on foil and dry them in a warm place such as an airing cupboard, for about 24 hours, or until they feel really firm.

Transfer the candied flowers on to sheets of foil or waxed paper in an airtight tin. Store them carefully where they will not be disturbed. They are very brittle, and break easily.

FONDANT PASTE

This is the sugar paste from which you can make realistic flowers for cake decorations.

250 g (8 oz) sugar
75 ml (3 fl oz) water
12 ml (½ fl oz) liquid glucose, or 1.5 ml (¼ tsp) cream of tartar dissolved in 5 ml (1 tsp) water
flavouring (see note, below)
2-3 drops red or yellow edible food colouring (optional)
up to 100 g (4 oz) icing sugar, sifted

1. Put the sugar and water into a large, heavy-based pan and dissolve the sugar over low heat. Bring the syrup to the boil and add the liquid glucose or cream of tartar solution. Boil the syrup for 10-15 minutes, or until it reaches 115C (240F).
2. The temperature of the sugar is important to the final consistency of the paste, which must be opaque and firm enough for modelling. If you do not have a sugar thermometer, test the syrup in this way. Drop a little into a cup of cold water. It should form a soft ball on contact with the water, and flatten when it is removed.
3. When this temperature is reached, remove the pan from the heat, wait for the bubbles to subside, then quickly beat in the flavouring and colouring. Pour the syrup slowly into a heatproof bowl. Leave it to rest for one minute and, when a skin has formed on top, stir it vigorously with a wooden spoon until it becomes opaque and firm. Dust your hands with icing sugar and knead the paste until it is smooth and free from cracks.
4. Place the fondant in a small bowl, cover with a damp cloth and set aside for one hour.
5. If you wish to make the paste in advance of modelling it into flowers, wrap it closely in waxed paper and store it in an airtight tin. It should keep for up to one year.
6. Divide the fondant into several pieces and knead each one. The warmth of your hands will make the paste malleable. Sift on to each piece just enough icing sugar to make the paste stiff enough for modelling. You will readily be able to judge when it has the right 'feel'.

Flavouring
To give moulded roses the appropriate fragrance, add two to three drops oil of roses or 5 ml (1 tsp) distilled rosewater.

ALMOND PASTE

New enthusiasts to the craft of modelling edible flowers might find almond paste easier to work than fondant paste.

100 g (4 oz) ground almonds
50 g (2 oz) caster sugar
50 g (2 oz) icing sugar, sifted, plus extra for dusting
1.5 ml (¼ tsp) almond essence
2.5 ml (½ tsp) lemon juice
1 small egg, lightly beaten
2-3 drops red or yellow edible food colouring (optional)

1. Mix together the ground almonds and the sugars. Add the almond essence, lemon juice and egg, and mix to form a paste. Add food colouring, but if you are making green leaves set aside some of the mixture before this.
2. Dust your hands with icing sugar and knead the paste until it is smooth and pliable. If you do not wish to mould the paste straight away, close-wrap it in foil and store it in the refrigerator.
3. When you are ready to mould the paste, sift a very little of the extra icing sugar on to it and knead until it is smooth.

MOULDED ROSES

Decorating a cake for a special party – perhaps a birthday or anniversary – with a nosegay of realistic moulded roses must be one of the most charming ways to 'say it with flowers'. You will soon get the knack of shaping petals and assembling them into roses. Add a few drops of oil of roses to the mixture and you can even enjoy the scent of the flowers too.

Almond paste or fondant paste
icing sugar (to dust)
one beaten egg white (optional, for use with fondant paste)

1. Roll the almond paste or fondant paste into a long roll about 10 mm (½ inch) in diameter and cut it into 10 mm (½ inch) slices. Keep the paste covered with foil while you shape each petal, to prevent it from drying out. Lightly dust a piece of greaseproof paper or foil with icing sugar and fold it in half.
2. Roll one slice of the paste into a ball, place it between the paper or foil and 'brush' it gently with the back of a spoon to make a petal shape. Press the paste so that the top of the petal, the widest part, is

furthest away from you. The paste should be very thin at this top edge, and gradually thicken towards the petal base.
3. Peel the petal from the paper or foil, and make more petals in the same way, dusting the paper or foil with more icing sugar. Petals made from almond paste may be shaped straight away; fondant petals should be left to rest for 10 minutes before shaping.
4. Using your fingers, gently roll the first petal to form the centre of the flower, then press on five or seven petals, each one slightly overlapping, to build up the flower shape. Trim the flower base neatly.
5. If fondant petals do not hold their shape well, work a little more sifted icing sugar into the mixture. If the petals do not readily stick at the base of the flower, dab on a little lightly beaten egg white.
6. Make more roses in the same way. Leave fondant flowers in a dry place for one hour to set before arranging them.
7. Arrange the flowers in a cluster in the centre of an iced cake. Stick them in place with a dab of fondant paste.
   Note: To make leaves as well as flowers from the

almond paste or fondant paste, separate a little and colour it with green edible food colouring. Roll the paste to about 6 mm (¼ inch) thick and mark the veins with a knife point.

CHOCOLATE ROSE LEAVES

Cover rose leaves with a thin layer of couverture *chocolate and you transfer all the beautiful and intricate natural markings to attractive and edible decorations. Arrange the chocolate leaves in sprays with candied or moulded flowers to decorate cakes and desserts, or serve them with coffee, as part of a selection of* petits fours.

50 g (2 oz) plain dark chocolate
12-15 well marked rose leaves

1. Melt the chocolate in the top of a double boiler or in a bowl fitted over a pan of simmering water.
2. Wash and dry rose leaves. Do not choose very young, tender ones as they tend to wilt under the strain.
3. Using a small paintbrush, coat the underside of each leaf with the melted chocolate. Place them carefully, coated side up, on a baking tray and leave them in a cool place for about two hours to harden. Store them in an airtight tin and, just before you wish to use them, peel off the rose leaves.

A CHOICE OF DESSERTS

Pansies and border pinks, chrysanthemums and carnations, deadnettles and daisies and many other garden flowers were once regularly used in cooking.

In his 16th century herbal John Gerard wrote that the tiny flowers of red deadnettle were 'baked with sugar, such as roses are'; primroses were combined with ground rice, almonds, honey and saffron to make a golden pottage; meadowsweet flowers were used as a honey substitute; pansies decorated jellies and custards; sky-blue borage flowers were baked in a custard tart, and cowslips were included in baked cream. We hope these recipes will revive the custom.

ROSE PETAL SOUFFLE

A light dessert with a subtle but unmistakable aroma.

SERVES 4.

15 ml (1 tbls) powdered gelatine
45 ml (3 tbls) warm water
3 eggs, separated
100 g (4 oz) rosepetal sugar (see page 157)
15 ml (1 tbls) distilled rosewater
2-3 drops red edible food colouring (optional)
300 ml (½ pint) thick cream, whipped
TO DECORATE
10-12 fragrant pink rose petals, washed and dried
1 egg white, lightly whisked
15 ml (1 tbls) caster sugar

1. Dissolve the gelatine in the water, stirring it frequently.
2. Whisk the egg yolks and sugar until thick and creamy. Pour in the dissolved gelatine, beating constantly. Stir in the rosewater, and colouring if you use it. Stir in the whipped cream. Leave the mixture in a cool place.
3. When the mixture begins to thicken, whisk the egg whites until they are stiff. Fold them into the mixture, using a metal spoon. Turn the dessert into a serving dish, cover and chill for two hours.
4. To make the decorations, dip the rose petals in egg white and shake off the excess. Dip them in sugar to frost them. Place them on a piece of foil and leave in a dry place for at least two hours to dry.

PANSY JELLY

In this turn-of-the-century recipe pansy flowers are set in jelly.

SERVES 4.

25 g (1 oz) powdered gelatine
45 ml (3 tbls) warm water
100 g (4 oz) sugar
thinly pared zest of 2 large lemons
150 ml (¼ pint) lemon juice
½ stick cinnamon
425 ml (¾ pint) water
whites and crushed shells of 3 eggs
90 ml (6 tbls) sweet sherry
4 pansy flowers, washed and dried
sponge-finger biscuits, to serve

1. Dissolve the gelatine in the water, stirring it frequently.

2. Put the sugar, lemon zest, lemon juice and cinnamon stick into a enamel or stainless steel saucepan, pour on the water and stir over low heat to dissolve the sugar. Remove the cinnamon stick and stir in the dissolved gelatine.

3. Beat the egg whites and shells together until they are frothy, pour them into the pan, add the sherry and whisk over the heat until the mixture boils. Remove from the heat and leave until the froth sinks.

4. Bring the mixture back to the boil and leave it to cool twice more. Line a sieve with two layers of muslin and strain the jelly. Divide the jelly between four glasses, reserving about 120 ml (8 tbls). Chill to set the jelly, place the pansies face upwards and spoon over the reserved jelly.

MARIGOLD AND APPLE TART

Bright as the summer sunshine, and absolutely delicious, this open apple flan is adapted from a recipe of the 1920s.

SERVES 6.

1 kg (2¼ lb) cooking apples
250 g (8 oz) shortcrust or sweet shortcrust pastry
juice of 1 lemon
3 large eggs
100 g (4 oz) marigold-flavoured caster sugar
(see below)
150 ml (¼ pint) thick cream
petals of 2 orange marigolds, washed and patted dry
3 marigold flowers and 3 small marigold leaves, to decorate

1. Peel, core and quarter the apples and drop them at once into a bowl of water containing lemon juice. Heat the oven to 200C (400F) gas 6. Grease a 23 cm (9 inch) flan ring and a baking sheet.

2. Roll out the pastry and use it to line the flan ring. Trim the edges and prick the base.

3. Drain and dry the apples and make slits close together on the rounded side. Arrange the apples, rounded sides up, in the flan case. Bake, uncovered, in the oven for 20 minutes.

4. Beat the eggs and sugar until pale and frothy. Stir in the cream and marigold petals.

5. Remove the flan from the oven, pour on the custard and bake for a further 20-25 minutes, until the custard is set.

6. Leave the flan to cool, transfer it to a serving plate and decorate with the marigold flowers and leaves.

Marigold-flavoured sugar

Mix washed and dried petals with twice their volume of sugar, spread the mixture on baking trays and place in the oven at the lowest setting for one and a half to two hours, turning frequently, until the sugar has absorbed the moisture from the petals and dried. Cool and store, sieving the sugar before using. (This recipe and method can be used for any flower-scented sugar).

A Victorian recipe for a glistening jelly decorated with pansy heads makes a special tea-time treat.

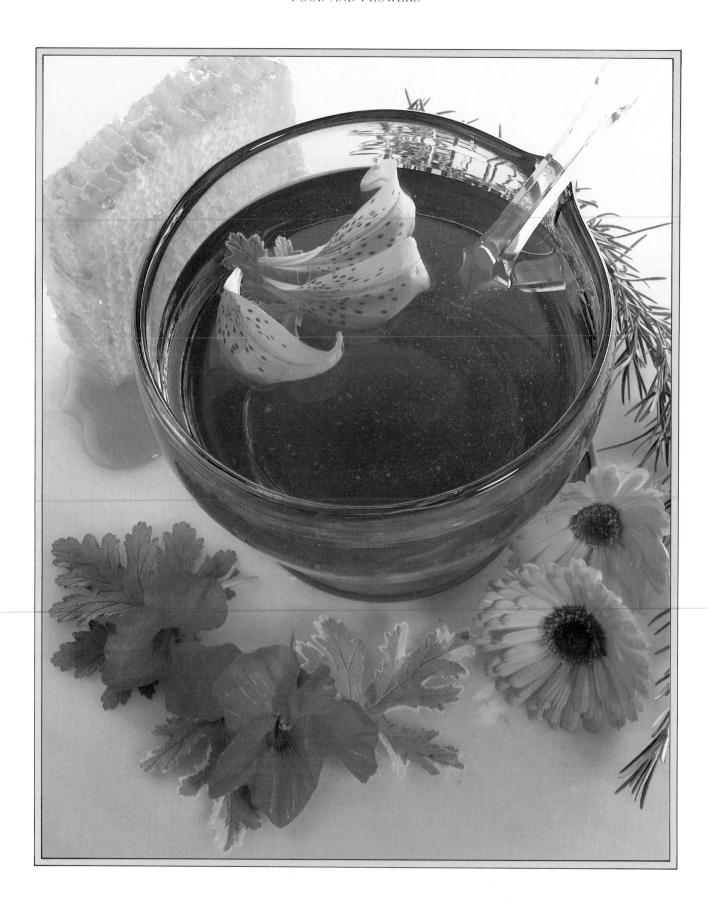

FLOWERS IN THE LARDER

For generations there have been few tasks more satisfying than stocking up the larder shelves with jams, jellies, chutneys, cheeses and butters made from the fruits of the orchard. It is only in recent times that a line has been drawn between produce that is edible and that which is supposed to be purely decorative. In these recipes – for rose petal jam, honeysuckle and peach cheese, pickled gillyflowers, and others – we have fudged this line; if a flower is edible and has a pleasant fragrance, experiment with ways to capture it now, and enjoy it later.

ELDERFLOWER AND GOOSEBERRY JELLY

Elderflowers and gooseberries go together well. Wrap a few of the flower heads in muslin when you make gooseberry jam, bake or poach the fruit, and liquidize it for fruit fool.

MAKES ABOUT 1.5 KG (3¼ LB).
2 kg (4½ lb) gooseberries
1 litre (1¾ pints) water
4-6 large heads elderflower
sugar (see method)

1. Put the gooseberries, water and elderflowers into a large pan, bring to the boil and simmer gently until the fruit is cooked. Mash the fruit occasionally with a wooden spoon.
2. Strain it for several hours through a jelly bag hanging over a bowl. Do not squeeze the bag to hasten the dripping process as that will cloud the jelly.
3. Measure the fruit juice and weigh 500 g (1 lb) sugar to each 600 ml (1 pint) juice.
4. Put the fruit juice and sugar into a large pan, heat gently until the sugar has dissolved. Then bring to the boil, stirring occasionally. Boil rapidly for 15 minutes, or until the jelly reaches setting point.
5. Pour the jelly into warm jars, cover, cool and label. Store in a cool, dry, dark place.

Honey will be enhanced with an infusion of flowers or herbs.

ROSE PETAL JAM

Use this preserve sparingly, as a spread on toast, a filling for sponge cakes or spooned over ice cream.

MAKES ABOUT 1.2 KG (2¾ LB) JAM.
500 g (1 lb) fragrant rose petals
6-8 rose-scented geranium leaves
700 g (1½ lb) sugar
300 ml (½ pint) water
45 ml (3 tbls) lemon juice

1. Pick off the white bases from the rose petals. Discard any damaged or discoloured ones. Wash and dry the petals and geranium leaves and place them in a bowl. Pour on half the sugar, stir well, cover and leave for two days, stirring occasionally. Discard the geranium leaves.
2. Put the remaining sugar into a pan with the water and lemon juice and heat gently until the sugar has dissolved.
3. Add the rose petal mixture, stir well and heat gently. When the sugar has dissolved, bring to the boil and boil rapidly for 20 minutes, stirring occasionally, until the jam reaches setting point.
4. Pour the jam into warm jars, cover, cool and label. Store in a cool, dry, dark place.

FLOWER HONEY

You can infuse inexpensive blended honey with the flowers of your choice and create a unique tea-time spread.

500 g (1 lb) honey
1 cup fragrant petals or leaves
water to boil

1. Divide the honey between two jars. Wash and dry petals such as rose, violet, honeysuckle, lavender, jasmine, broom, carnation and lime flowers, or scented geranium or other fragrant leaves, and share them between the jars. Stir well, cover the jars and stand them on a trivet or folded cloth in a pan.
2. Pour in cold water to come to the neck of the jars, bring to the boil and simmer for 30 minutes. Remove the jars from the pan, leave to cool and set aside for 24 hours.
3. Heat the jars again and strain off the petals. Pour the honey into small, clean jars.

   This extra special honey is good for baking, stirred into plain yoghurt, spooned over ice cream or spread on toast.

FLOWER SYRUP

Fragrant syrup is a delicious standby. You can use it as a dressing for fruit salad, for poaching fruit, in baked puddings, to make sorbet and as a basis for wine cups.

500 g (1 lb) sugar
300 ml (½ pint) water
1 cup fragrant petals or leaves

1. Place the sugar in a pan with the water. Add fragrant petals or leaves – as suggested for flower honey – and stir well. Heat gently until the sugar has dissolved, bring to the boil and simmer for 10 minutes. Cool the syrup, then strain and bottle.
2. Store the syrup for up to two weeks in a refrigerator. For longer keeping, sterilize the bottled syrup by bringing it to the boil in a pan of water and boiling for 10 minutes. Cool, label and store in a cool, dark place. Or freeze the syrup in a container with a lid.

HONEYSUCKLE AND PEACH CHEESE

The term 'cheese' denotes the texture of this preserve, which is set in decorative moulds and cut in slices to accompany cold meats, poultry and game, or as a sweetmeat to serve after dinner, with coffee. Honeysuckle and peach cheese is specially good with ham.

MAKES ABOUT 1 KG (2 LB) PRESERVE.
1 kg (2 lb) peaches
300 ml (½ pint) water
1 cup honeysuckle flowers, washed and drained
juice of 1 lemon
sugar (see method)

1. Halve and slice the peaches, but do not peel them. Crack and discard a few of the stones. Put the peaches and the kernels in a pan with the water, honeysuckle flowers and lemon juice. Bring to the boil and simmer for 30 minutes, until the fruit is tender.
2. Press the fruit through a nylon sieve and weigh the pulp. Add an equal weight of sugar and cook over low heat, stirring frequently, until the paste is thick and dry, and a spoon drawn through it leaves a trail. This may take 45-60 minutes.
3. Spoon the preserve into lightly greased decorative moulds such as trifle and mousse cases. Cover the surface closely with waxed paper, then cover the moulds with transparent 'jam pot' paper covers. Label and store in a cool, dry, dark place.

'ORANGE FLOWER' BUTTER

Highly scented flowers such as orange blossoms and Philadelphus make a delightful tea-time spread which has the consistency of soft butter.

MAKES ABOUT 1 KG (2 LB).
1 kg (2 lb) cooking apples, chopped
300 ml (½ pint) water
1 cup orange or Philadelphus blossom, washed and drained
sugar (see method)
30 ml (2 tbls) orangeflower water

1. Put the apples, water and blossoms into a pan, bring to the boil and simmer for about 30 minutes, until the apples are soft. Press them against the sides of the pan occasionally.
2. Press through a nylon sieve and weigh the pulp.
3. Weigh 350 g (12 oz) sugar to each 500 g (1 lb) pulp. Put the sugar, fruit purée and orangeflower water into a pan and heat slowly until the sugar dissolves. Simmer over low heat, stirring frequently, until the preserve is like thickly whipped cream.
4. Spoon it into warmed jars, cover, label and store in a cool, dry, dark place.

PICKLED GILLYFLOWERS

This recipe, inspired by an 18th century notebook, gives a method for preserving clove carnations. You can pickle rosebuds in a similar way, substituting thinly pared lemon zest for the cinnamon.

FILLS 4 × 100 G (4 OZ) JARS.
1 cup clove carnations
350 ml (12 fl oz) white wine vinegar
100 g (4 oz) sugar
½ stick cinnamon
2 blades mace

1. Cut off the calyx and the white base of the petals. Thoroughly wash the flowers and toss them on kitchen paper to dry.
2. Put the sugar, vinegar, cinnamon and mace into a pan, heat slowly until the sugar dissolves, then bring to the boil, stirring occasionally. Boil for three minutes, then cool.
3. Pack the flowers into small, sterilized jars and pour over the vinegar to cover them. Close the jars with lids that seal, label and store in a cool, dry, dark place.

AROMATIC DRINKS

There is more to sipping a cup of herbal or flower tea than meets the palate. Tisanes were well authenticated by herbalists two and three centuries ago, and were the main form of medicine made at home.

Chamomile tea was considered a gentle and soothing sedative; lime flower tea was recommended for its effect on the nervous and digestive systems; elderflower, yarrow and lungwort tisanes were all thought to relieve bronchitis and colds; marigold tea was taken in the morning to relieve melancholy and lavender flower tea was said to be a sure remedy for nervous headaches – some claims were made for its properties as an aphrodisiac, too.

Cool refreshing drinks, made with flowers from the garden, are a summertime bonus.

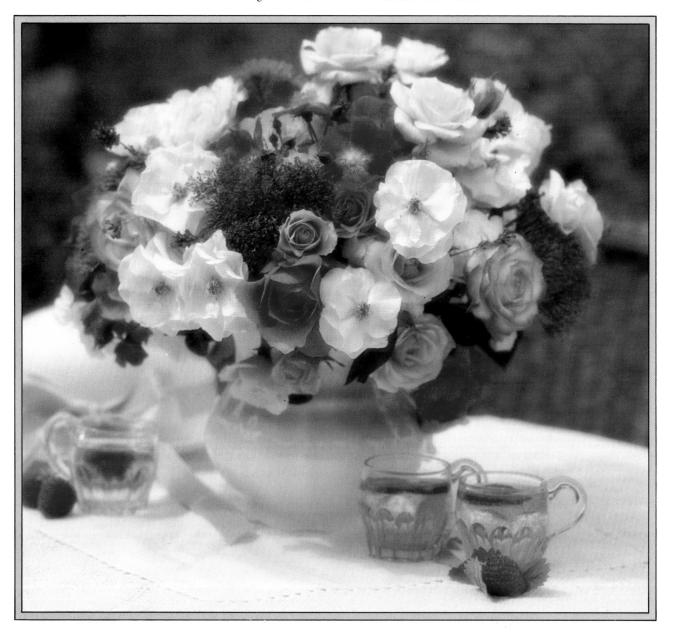

TISANES

With so many credentials to their name, it is no wonder that herbal and flower teas are popular again. You do not necessarily need to search for materials in the garden. First your herb and spice rack may offer possibilities. Dried mint, thyme, rosemary and marjoram leaves, and fennel and fenugreek seeds all make tasty teas. Buy other dried leaves, flowers and seeds from herbalists or health food shops, for convenience sake in tea-bags if they are available.

If you use a teapot keep one specially for tisanes, otherwise the tannin in 'ordinary' tea might spoil the delicate flavours. For each cup of tisane allow about 10 ml (2 tsp) lightly bruised fresh leaves or flowers, and 5 ml (1 tsp) if the materials are dried. Trial and tasting will tell you whether you prefer to use more or fewer leaves in future.

Pour on 225 ml (8 fl oz) boiling water, stir well and cover the pot to prevent too much of the volatile oil being lost in evaporation. Stand the pot in a warm place, leave it to infuse for 8-10 minutes, and then strain it. Tisanes may be sweetened with honey and decorated with a thin slice of lemon, orange or lime.

LINDEN TEA

Surely home-based medicine at its most delicious! If you do not have the chance to gather the sweet smelling lime flowers in midsummer, the tea will be just as good if you make it with dried flowers. The tisane is calming, relaxing and helps to induce sleep.

MAKES ONE CUP.
10 ml (2 tsp) fresh or 5 ml (1 tsp) dried lime flowers, lightly crushed
225 ml (8 fl oz) boiling water
honey, to sweeten (optional)
1 thin slice lemon

1. Put the flowers into a pot reserved for the tisanes, pour on the boiling water, stir well, cover the pot and set it aside in a warm place for 8-10 minutes.
2. Strain the tea and taste it. Sweeten it with honey if you wish, and decorate it with a slice of lemon.

CLOVE CARNATION TEA

If ever you have the chance, look at a catalogue of speciality teas and gather ideas for your own blends, adding fragrant flowers and leaves to scent leaf tea. Rose petals, red clover flowers, nasturtium flowers, lemon-scented geranium leaves, all make interesting teas with a difference. For this sample recipe, which makes three cups, our choice was clove carnation, or clove-scented pink, a highly perfumed flower which in Elizabethan times was thought to have the power 'to comfort the heart'.

MAKES 3 CUPS.
15-20 ml (3-4 tsp) Earl Grey tea
a handful of clove carnations
600 ml (1 pint) boiling water
sugar or honey, to sweeten (optional)
3 thin slices orange

1. Put the tea and carnations into a pot, pour on the boiling water, stir well and cover the pot. Leave it in a warm place for 10 minutes.
2. Sweeten the tea with sugar or honey to taste, and serve with a slice of orange.

ELDERFLOWER 'CHAMPAGNE'

Serve this delicately flavoured, non-alcoholic drink well chilled and with a slice of lemon.

MAKES 5 LITRES (8 PINTS).
6 large heads elderflower
700 g (1½ lb) sugar
30 ml (2 tbls) white wine vinegar
5 litres (8 pints) water
3 lemons

1. Put the elderflowers, sugar, vinegar and water into a large jar or bowl. Squeeze the juice from the lemons, cut the peel into thick strips and add to the container. Stir well, cover and leave for 24 hours. Stir or shake occasionally to dissolve the sugar.
2. Strain into sterilized bottles, leaving about 5 cm (2 inches) space, and screw on the caps. Store in a cool, dry, dark place.

Fresh and aromatic borage and mint make a decorative garnish on elderflower champagne.

ELDERFLOWER MILK SHAKE

A 'vitality' drink full of protein, vitamins – and flavour.

SERVES 4.
600 ml (1 pint) buttermilk
3 large heads elderflower
30 ml (2 tbls) honey
2 eggs, separated
60 ml (4 tbls) plain yoghurt
ground cinnamon
scented geranium leaves, to decorate

1. Heat the buttermilk with the elderflowers and honey to just below boiling point. Cool and strain – a coffee filter deals efficiently with the minute flowers.
2. Pour the flavoured buttermilk over the egg yolks, beating constantly, or mix them in a blender.
3. Whisk the egg whites until stiff, then fold them into the buttermilk.
4. Pour the drink into four tumblers, top each one with a spoonful of yoghurt and sprinkle it with cinnamon. Decorate with geranium leaves. Serve chilled with a wide 'fun' straw.

ROSE GERANIUM BOWL

A non-alcoholic 'punch' in which the apple juice is transformed.

MAKES ABOUT 1 LITRE (1¾ PINTS).
700 ml (1¼ pints) unsweetened apple juice, chilled
75 g (3 oz) sugar
3 lemons
8-12 rose-scented geranium leaves, plus extra to decorate
45 ml (3tbls) lemon syrup
ice cubes
300 ml (½ pint) carbonated mineral water

1. Put the apple juice and sugar into a pan. Squeeze the juice of two lemons. Cut up the peel and add it to the pan with the geranium leaves. Heat gently until the sugar dissolves, then bring to the boil, stirring occasionally. Boil for five minutes, then set aside to cool.
2. Pour the syrup and lemon juice over ice cubes in a jug, strain on the apple juice and pour on the mineral water. Mix well and decorate with thin slices of lemon and geranium leaves.

MARIGOLD COOLER

A non-alcoholic punch, chilled tea spiced with marigold petals, makes a refreshing drink.

MAKES 850 ML (1½ PINTS).
20 ml (4 tsp) Earl Grey tea
20 ml (4 tsp) marigold petals
2 strips thinly-pared orange zest
450 ml (¾ pint) boiling water
juice of 2 oranges
about 120 ml (8 tbls) crushed ice
10 ml (2 tsp) grenadine syrup
300 ml (½ pint) carbonated mineral water, chilled
4 marigold flowers
4 sprigs lemon balm or mint

1. Put the tea, marigold petals and orange zest into a pot, pour on the boiling water, stir well, cover the pot and leave to infuse for one hour.
2. Put the crushed ice into a jug, pour on the orange juice and syrup, and strain on the tea. Cover and chill for one hour. Pour on the mineral water and stir well. Decorate the jug with the marigolds and herb sprigs.

MINT AND BORAGE CUP

You can make this tingling-fresh herb lemonade with other aromatic leaves such as lemon balm or golden marjoram.

MAKES ABOUT 850 ML (1½ PINTS).
1 handful fresh mint leaves
60 ml (4 tbls) water
juice of 2 lemons
25 g (1 oz) sugar
425 ml (¾ pint) carbonated mineral water, chilled
borage flowers, to decorate
ice cubes, to serve
FOR THE SYRUP
25 g (1 oz) sugar
225 ml (8 fl oz) water

1. To make the syrup, put the sugar and water into a pan, heat gently until the sugar dissolves, then bring to the boil, stirring occasionally. Boil for five minutes, cool and chill.
2. Put the mint in a blender or food processor and liquidize with the water and juice of one lemon.
3. Stir together the syrup, mint mixture and juice of the other lemon. Cover and chill for one hour.
4. Stir in the mineral water, decorate with the borage flowers and serve with ice cubes.

INDEX

Numbers in italics refer to illustrations

A

achillea, 68, 89
aconite, *6*, 150
agapanthus (lily of the Nile), 80
air drying, 66, 68-9, 76-8
Alchemilla mollis, *6*, 12, 33, 68, 74, 89
Allium aflatunense, 69
allspice, 93
almond oil, 138, 139
Almond Paste (recipe), 155
alstroemeria, 14, 33, *49*, 61, *63*, 150
anemones, 10, 12, 14, *15*, 16, 26, *30*, 31, *44*, *49*; artificial, 100, 111-12, *113*
angelica, 80, 136
antirrhinums, 48, 56, 65, 66, 70
apple blossom, 30
apple mint, 39
aquilegia, *54*, 81, 89
aromatic (scented plants), 7, *36*, 36-9, 52, 56; flowering shrubs, 38; herbs, 36, *38*, 39, *39*; preserving and holding fragrance, 90-7; roses, 36, 38, 39
artificial flowers, 7, 22, 45, 100-29; anemones 111-12, *113*; bluebells, 111-12, *113*; Christmas, 122-3, *123*; daffodils, *106*, 107-8; fabrics used, 100; fuchsias, 111-12, *113*, *114*, 115; grapes, 116-17, *117*; Mexican poppies, 104-5, *105*; nylon, 100, *124*, 125; paper, 100, *101*, 102-16; poinsettia, 122, *123*; ready-made, 126-7; ribbon roses, 118-20; roses (paper), 109-10, *110*; spider chrysanthemums, 111-12, 115-16; sunflowers, 120-1, *121*; tulips, *101*, 102-3
asparagus fern, 46
asters, 48
avocado oil, 138, 139

B

balconies, flower arrangements for, 45, 46
basil, 93
baths: beauty in the, 136-8; dispersing and floating oils, 136-8; drying effect on skin, 136; petal and spice, 131-2; vinegar, 138
bay leaves, *38*, 39, 52, 56, 69, 82, 84, 132
beech leaves, 52, 66, 82, 84, 127
bells of Ireland, 14, 23, 55, 74, 82
berberis, *54*
bergenias, 26, 84
blackberries, *40*, 66, 84
bluebells, 41; artificial, 100, 111-12, *113*, 126
borage, 39, *39*, 88, 156, 163; Chilled Cherry and Borage Soup, 152; Mint and Borage Cup, 164
borax (drying agent), 70
bouquets, floral, 56; bridal, *60*, 61, 64
broom, 26, 41, 69, 73, 84; culinary use of, 150, 151, 153, 154

Broom Flower Salad, 153
bryony, 150
bulb flowers, 10-11, 37
busy Lizzie (Impatiens), 65
buttercups, 19, 41, 42, 48, 59, 66, 69, 72, 86, 88, 89, 144
buttonholes, floral, 56, *62*

C

cake decorations, 154-5; almond paste, 155; candied flowers, 154; chocolate rose leaves, 155; fondant paste, 154; moulded roses, 154, 155
Californian poppies, 58, 65
camellia, 33, 48, 55, *62*, 73, 74, 100
campanulas, 34, 51, 61, 100
candied (or crystallised) flowers, 150, 154
candles, perfumed, 142-4, *143*, 145; decorating 144; how to make, 142, 144; olive oil, 144
candytuft, 59, 81
Canterbury bells, *6*
caraway, 39, 52, 80
cardamom, 93, 144
carnation oil, 138
carnations, *6*, 14, 17, 19, 37, 45, 47, 48, *49*, *50*, 51, 61, *63*, 88, 90, 92, *92*, 154; clove, 39, 93, 148, 150, 160, 162
carrot leaves, 69, 80
chamomile, 39, 48, 74, 96, 136, 139, 148, 154; tea, 138, 161
chervil, 80
Chinese lanterns, *40*, 66, 81
Christmas decorations, 55; artificial flowers, 122-3, *123*; trimmings for presents, 147
chrysanthemums, 12, *15*, 16, *16*, 17, 19, 33, 45, 47, 48, 56, *57*, 65, 88; artificial spider, 100, 111-12, 115-16; culinary use of, 148, 150, 151
Chrysanthemum and Bean Sprout Soup, 151
cinnamon, 39, 93, 144
clarkia, 10, 19, 23, 48, 58, 74, 80
clary, *59*
cleansing creams, 130-1, *131*, 141
clematis, 28, 47, 86, 93
clove apples, *94*, 94-5
Clove Carnation Tea, 162
clove carnations, 39, 93, 148, 150, 160
clove oranges, *94*, 94
clover, 41, 89, 152
cloves, 39, 94, 144
colour(s), 10, 12-20; adjacent, 16; complementary, 10, 14, *14*; matching moods, 17-19; neutral, 17, 19; primary and secondary, 12; retention in flower pressing, 88-9; shades, tones and tints, 14; wheel, 12, *12*, 14, 16
comfrey leaves, 139
containers, 10, 11, *13*, 28-35; artificial flowers, 126, 127, *127*; beauty products, 145-6; dried flowers, 74; flower floats, 33-4; garden, 47; glass and marbles, 33; grouping for design, 33; and holding material, 30, 31; jugs, 31, 33; pot pourri, 96-7; vases, 30, 34; wooden, 34
coriander, 93

cornflowers, *6*, 14, 19, 41, 48, 51, 58, 61, 65, 68, 93
cosmetic bottles, 'customized', *145*
cosmetics *see* health and beauty
cosmos, 58, *59*, 89
cotinus, *54*
cowbane, 150
cow parsley, 19
cow parsnip, 80
cowslips, 42, *43*, 88, 154, 156
crab apples, *40*
cupressus, 12, 45, *45*, 55, 123
curry plant, *38*
customized containers for beauty products, 145-6

D

daffodils, 14, 19, *22*, 88; artificial (paper), *106*, 107-8
dahlias, 12, 19, 69, 72, 150
daisies, 19, 58, *59*, 66, 69, 72, 88, 89, 100
daisy chains, 56, 58
dandelion leaves, 136
deadly nightshade (*Atropa belladonna*), 150
deadnettles, 42, 156
delphiniums, 11, 19, 23, 26, 34, 48, 55, 61, 66, 68, 73, 80, 88, 93
desiccants for drying flowers, 66, 69-73, *73*, 79
desserts, 156-7; Marigold and Apple Tart, 157; Pansy Jelly, 156-7, *157*; Rose Petal Souffle, 156
dill, 36, 39
dip-dyeing, *81*, 82
dock, 80, 82
dogweed, 150
doronicum, 34, 48, 65
dress sprays or corsages, 61, 64, 65
dried flowers, 7, 22, 37, 66-99; air drying, 66, 68-9, 76-8; desiccants, 66, 69-73, 79; designs, 74; dying and spraying, *81*, 82, 84; glycerine technique, 66, 82-5; harvest of seeds, 80-1; holding the scents, 94-7; parcel trimmings, 146, 147; pot pourri, 7, 37, *71*, 90-3; preserving techniques, 66, 68-73, *73*; preserving the fragrance, 90-3; pressing flowers, 66, 86-9
drinks, aromatic, *149*, 161-4; Clove Carnation Tea, 162; Elderflower 'Champagne', 162, *163*; Elderflower Milk Shake, 164; Linden Tea, 162; Marigold Cooler, 164; Mint and Borage Cup, 164; Rose Geranium Bowl, 164; tisanes, 42, 138, 161-2

E

elderberries, *40*
elderflowers, 136, 137, 139, 145, 150, 161
Elderflower and Gooseberry Jelly, 159
Elderflower 'Champagne', 162, *163*
Elderflower Milk Shake, 164
eschscholzia (Californian poppies), 58, 65
essential oil, 136, 138, 139, 144
euphorbia (spurge), 11, 28, 51, 55
evergreen leaves, 55, 56, 83-4, 89

F

face masks, 142

fashion and flowers, 7, 56-65, 147; headgear, 58-9; summertime, 65; tussie-mussies and nosegays, 56; Victorian posies, 56, 60-1; wedding day flowers, 60, 61-5, 63
Fatsia japonica, 55, 84
fennel, 36, 39, 52, 68, 80, 89, 93, 133, 139, 162
fenugreek, 132, 162
festivals of flowers, 56
feverfew, 39, 39, 50
fig leaves, 55, 84
flag irises, 19, 81
floating flowers, 33-34, 47
floral crowns, 56, 58, 64
floral oils, 133, 136-8
floral ring, 25
floral sashes, 65
florists' tape (gutta percha), 61, 65, 73
flower-ball trees, 46
flower fritters, 150
Flower Honey, 158, 159
flower jewellery, 65
Flower Loaf, 100, 128, 129
flower patchwork, 34
flower press, 86, 87, 88
flower-shaped bread rolls, 128, 129
Flower Syrup, 160
flowers: aromatic, 36-9; artificial, 22, 45, 100-29; bulbs, 10-11, 37; dried, 7, 22, 37, 66-99; and drinks, 161-4; and fashion, 7, 56-65; and food, 148-60; for health and beauty, 130-47; fresh (cut), 8-51; wild, 14, 41-2, 43
foam, foam blocks, 10, 22, 24, 24, 25, 26, 30, 33, 34, 42, 44, 74, 84
Fondant Paste (recipe), 154
food, 7, 148-60; cake decorations, 154-5; candied flowers, 154; desserts, 156-7; garnishing with flowers, 150; infusion of flowers, 148, 150; poisonous plants, 150; preserves, 159-60; soups and salads, 151-3; *see also* drinks
fool's parsley, 150
forget-me-nots, 19, 26, 93
forsythia, 23, 96
foxgloves *(Digitalis purpurea)*, 28, 80, 150
freesias, 21, 31, 39, 47, 50, 61, 63, 65, 126
fresh (cut) flowers, 8-51; aromatic, 36-9; basket display, 6, 8-9; colour sense, 10, 12-20; containers, 28-35, 47; cutting stems, 10, 11; in the open air, 45-7; on the table, 48-51; parcel trimmings, preserving life, 11; 146, 146-7; ribbons, swags and posies, 51; shapes, 20, 22-8; wild flowers, 41-2, 43
fruit: artificial grapes, 116-17, 117; and flowers in wooden containers, 34, 35
fuchsias, 14, 44, 88, 144; artificial (paper), 100, 111-12, 113, 114, 115

G
gaillardias, 19, 81
garlands of flowers, 56, 57
garnishes of flowers, 150, 163
gazania, 34, 65
Geranium ibericum, 88
geraniums, 26, 48, 56, 93, 132, 150; Rose Geranium Bowl, 164

gerberas, 18, 19
geum, 34, 59
gillyflowers (clove carnations) 39, 93, 148, 150, 162; Pickled, 160
ginger, powdered, 93
gladiolus, 20; culinary use of, 148, 151, 153, 153
Gladiolus Salad, 153, 153
glycerine technique of preserving flowers and leaves, 66, 82-5, 127
godetia, 59, 73
golden rod, 66, 74, 93
grape hyacinths, 19, 30, 80, 82
grapes, artificial, 116-17, 117
grasses, 58-9, 59; dried, 69, 74, 80, 81
Greek spiny spurge, 81
gum arabic crystals, 154
gypsophila, 6, 19, 66, 147

H
hair, 7, 138-9, 140; colour change, 139; floral adornment of, 56, 58, 59, 65; home-made shampoos, 138; rinsing and conditioning, 139
hanging basket, 44
hats, floral decoration of, 56, 58-9, 64
hazel leaves, 4
head-dresses, floral, 10, 58-9, 59; bridal, 61, 62
health and beauty (cosmetics), 7, 130-47; beauty in the bath, 136-8; floral and herbal oils, 133, 136-8; hair care, 138-9, 140; lavender, 132, 133, 136; packaging beauty products, 145-7; petal and spice baths, 131-2; skin tones, 141-2; soaps, 132-3, 134-6
heather, 69, 154
helichrysum, 31, 48, 68, 74, 147
hellebores, 26
hemlock, 150
hemp agrimony, 42
henbane, 150
henna, 131
herb ring, 38
herb Robert, 89
herbal oils, 131, 133, 136-8
herbal tisanes, 42, 138, 161-2
herbals, 7, 148
herbs, 9, 36, 39, 39, 52, 56, 80, 150; for baths, 132, 136, 137; for pot pourri, 93
hippocras (spiced wine), 148
Hogarth curve, 26
holding material, 11, 30; crumpled wire mesh, 10, 30, 33, 34, 84; foam, 10, 22, 24, 24, 25, 26, 30, 33, 34, 42, 44, 74, 84; pin-holders, 10, 30, 34, 84, 126
holly, 52, 55, 84, 89, 123
hollyhocks, 28, 66, 80
honesty, 40, 54, 66, 74, 80, 82, 147
honeysuckle, 28, 45, 55, 56, 93, 132, 150
Honeysuckle and Peach Cheese, 160
hostas, 28, 52, 55
houseleek, 136
hyacinth, 14, 37, 39, 56, 69, 72, 73, 80, 82, 93, 154
hydrangea, 11, 33, 48, 69, 74, 82, 88
hypericum, 84
hyssop, 136

I
Iceland poppies, 88
incense, 142; cones or sticks, 144, 145; powdered, 144
incense candles, 143
iris, 14, 19, 52, 62, 100
ivy leaves, 6, 45, 46, 51, 52, 55, 56, 89, 123

J
jams and jellies *see* preserves
japonica, 45, 84
jasmine, 93, 150
jasmine oil, 138
Jerusalem sage, 81, 82
jugs, 31, 33, 36-7
juniper, 55, 132

K
Kerria japonica, 65
knapweed, 81, 82

L
labelling beauty products, 145
lady's mantle, 7
lamium, 28, 51
language of flowers, 98-9
lapel flowers, 10, 62
larkspur, 7, 10, 19, 23, 58, 65, 69, 72, 74, 93
laurel, 55, 56, 84, 89
lavender, 12, 38, 39, 52, 55, 74, 89, 93, 94, 132, 133, 136, 137, 144, 145, 150
lavender bottles, 95-6
Lavender Flower Tea, 161
Lavender Vinegar, 139
Lavender Water, 133
leaves: culinary use of, 150, 151; deciduous, 82-3; designing with, 52-5, 61; evergreens, 55, 83-4, 89; fragrant, 93; as highlights, 55; preserved in glycerine, 82-4, 127; pressing, 86, 89; retaining colour (when pressing), 89; skeletonising, 89; tending foliage, 52, 55; water treatment, 55
lemon balm, 39, 39, 93, 96, 132, 133, 154
lemon thyme, 93
lemon verbena, 93, 96
lilac, 19, 38, 69
lilies, 14, 19, 38, 47, 48, 56, 63, 132; artificial, 127, 127; culinary use of, 148
lilies-of-the-valley, 31, 65, 69, 72, 74, 93, 154
Lime Flower Tea, 161, 162
lime leaves, 52, 66, 84, 127, 145
Linden Tea, 162
loofah soap, 136
lovage, 39, 52, 69, 80, 136
love-in-a-mist, 54, 59, 61, 81
L-shaped composition, 24, 26
lungwort tisane, 161
lupins, 11, 55, 80, 82

M
mace, 93
magnolia, 55, 89
mahonia, 40
mallow, 42, 45, 58, 59, 65, 80, 148, 150
maple leaves, 54
marbles, 10, 126, 127

marguerites, 34, 41, 45, 48, 56
marigold, 12, 14, 19, 34, 45, 48, 51, 56, 65, 66, 88, 93, 96, 132, 133, 136, 139, 141; African, 72; culinary use of, 148, 150, 151, 157, 161
Marigold and Apple Tart, 157
Marigold Cooler, 164
marjoram, 7, 36, 39, *39*, 52, 93, 150, 162
matricaria, 59, 66, 69
meadowsweet, 150, 156
melilot, 41
Mexican orange blossom *(Choisya ternata)*, 38, 78
Mexican poppies, artificial, 100, 104-5, *105*
mint, 36, 39, 52, 93, 132, 133, 136, 154, 162, 163
Mint and Borage Cup, 164
mock orange blossom (philadelphus), 38, 160
mullein, 68, 80

N
narcissus, 61, 66, 88; artificial, 100, *106*, 107-8
nasturtiums, 26, 34; culinary use of, 148, 151, 152
necklaces of flowers, 65
nettles, 41, 136, 139
nicotiana, 14, 36
night-scented stocks, 36, 69, 93
nosegays, 56, 69
nylon flowers, 100, *124*, 125

O
oak leaves, 52, 56, 84, 127
oatmeal soap, 136
oats, *59*
oils: aromatic burning, 142, 144, 145; bath (dispersing and floating), 136-8, 139; essential, 136, 138, 139, 144
orange blossom, 93, 160; Mexican, 73; mock (philadelphus), 38, 160
'Orange Flower' Butter, 160
orchids, 41, *62, 63*, 66, 70
oregano, 93

P
packaging of beauty products, 145-7, *146*
paeonies, 14, 33, 69; artificial, 127, *127*
pansies, 14, 66, 72, 88, 93; culinary use of, 148, 150, 154, 156
Pansy Jelly, 156, *156*
paper flowers, 100, *101*, 102-16
paraffin wax, 142
parsley, 39
patios, flower arrangements for, 46, 47
pedestals, 23, 26, 30, 37, *45*
pelargoniums, *38*, 39, 55, *60*
peppermint leaves, 133, 139
perfumed baths, 131-2
periwinkles, 19, 28, 51, 55
petal and spice baths, 131-2
pin-holders, 10, 30, 34, 84, 126
pinks, 17, *27*, 39, 45, 48, *59, 60*, 69, 148, 154
poinsettias, 11; artificial, 100, 122-3, *123*
poisonous plants, 150
pomanders, *94*, 94-5, 97

poppies, 11, 12, *13*, 14, 17, 41, 42, 55, 74, 81, 88, 150; artificial Mexican, 100, 104-5, *105;* Californian, 58, 65; Iceland, 88; ready-made, 127, *127*
posies, 10, 51, 146, 147; bath, 131-2; bridal, *60*, 61, 64; dried flower, 74; 'shower', *50*, 51; Victorian, 56, 60-1
potato leaves, 150
pot pourri, 7, 37, *71*, 90-3, 94, 95, 96-7, 133; additives, 93; display of, 97; dry, 92, 96, *97;* floral ingredients, 92-3; herbal ingredients, 93; lemon-scented golden, 96, *97;* moist, 90, 96; rose, 96
preserves, 159-60; Elderflower and Gooseberry Jelly, 159; Flower Honey, *158*, 159; Flower Syrup, 160; Honeysuckle and Peach Cheese, 160; 'Orange Flower' Butter, 160; Pickled Gillyflowers, 160; Rose Petal Jam, 159
preserving and holding the fragrance, 90-7; lavender bottles, 95-6; pomanders, 94-5, 97; pot pourri, 90-3, 96-7; scented pillows, 96
preserving flowers and leaves, 66, 68-73; air drying, 66, 68-9, 76-8; drying in desiccants, 66, 69-73, 79; glycerine technique, 66, 82-5, 127
pressing flowers, 66, 82, 86-9, *88;* designing on the flat, 89; equipment, 86, *87;* keeping the colour, 88-9
primroses, 14, 41, 42, 58, *60*, 88, 148, 150, 154, 156
pussy-willow catkins, 84

Q
Queen-of-Hungary water, 131

R
ranunculus, 31, 34, 47, 65
Red Clover Salad, 152
rhubarb leaves, 150
ribbons of flowers, 51, 55, *64*, 65, 147
rosebuds, 17, 48, 51, 58, *60*, 61, *62*, 65; artificial (paper), 110; dried, 7, 66, 68, 69, *71*, 73, 74, 93, 96
rose-hips, 84; wild, *40*
rosemary, 39, 51, 52, 93, 131, 132, 133, 136, 137, 139, *139*, 150, 162
Rose Petal Jam, 159
Rose Petal Soufflé, 156
rose petals, *4-5*, 48, 56, *71*, 88, *132*, 144, 148; baths, 131, 132; candied, 154; pot pourri, 90-3, 96-7
roses, *6*, 7, *9*, 11, 14, 17, *32*, 33, 34, 38, 59, 65, 90, 126, 133; artificial paper, 100, 109-10, *110;* artificial ribbon, 118-20; bush, *40*; Chocolate Rose Leaves, 155; culinary use of, 148, 150, 154, 155; damask, 36, 38; dog, *32;* Moulded, 154, 155; perfumed, 36, 37, 38, 39, 90; wild, *64*, 65
rosewater, 130, *137*, 141
rue, 66, 80
Russian vine, 47, 55

S
sage, *38*, 39, *39*, 52, *54*, 80, 89, 139
saintpaulias, 12
Salads, 151, 152-3; Broom Flower, 153;

Gladiolus, 153; Red Clover, 152; Salamagundy, 152
Salamagundy (mixed salad), 152
sand as drying agent, 70, *72*
savory, 39
scabious, 41, 48, 56, 81
scarification, 42
scent bottles, 145, *145*
scented pillows, 96
sea lavender, 74
seed art, 80-1
seeds, seedheads, seed pods, 55, 84; dip-dyeing, *81*, 82; dried, 66, 68, 69, 74, *75*, 80-1; preserved in glycerine, *83;* wild-flower, 42, *43*
senecio, 68, 89
sesame oil, 136
shades of colour, 14
shampoos, home-made, *131*, 138
shapes (in flower arrangement), 20, 22-8; beauty rules, 26; cardinal points, 23-6; Hogarth curve, 26; 'L-shape' composition, *24*, 26; natural, 22-3; traditional, 22-3; triangular, 23-6, 74
sheep's parsley, *18*, 19, 41, 89, 150
'shower' posy, *50*, 51
silica gel crystals, 70
skin creams, 131, *131*, *140*, 141
skin moisturisers, *131*, 141; dry, 142
skin toners, *131*, 138, 141
snowberries, 84
soaps, scented, 132-3, 145; home-made, *131*, 134-6, *135;* loofah, 136; oatmeal, 136
Solomon's seal, 45
sorrel, 66, 82
Soups, 151-2; Chilled Cherry and Borage, 152; Chrysanthemum and Bean Sprout, 151; Wild Leaves, 151
speedwell, 19, 88
spice and petal baths, 131-2
spices, 93, 95, 144
spindle, 150
spray painting, 82, 84
starch, powdered (as drying agent), 70
stearin, 142, 144
stefani (hoop of flowers), 56
stems, 23-4; artificial flowers, 100, 126; cutting, 10, 11; dried flowers, 72, 73, 74; pressed flowers, 86, 89; treating, 11, *11*
stinging nettles, 41
stocks, 133; night-scented, 36, 69, 93
stratifying, 42
summertime fashions, *64*, 65
sunflower oil, 136
sunflowers, 7, 22, 81; artificial, 120-1, *121*
swags, 46, *46*, 51, 55
sweet cicely, 93, 133, 150
sweet peas, *6*, 14, *31*, 58, 61, 69, 93, 126, 150, 154
sweet Williams, 47

T
tables, flower arrangements on, 48-51
tarragon, 39, 93
teasels, 41, 81, 82, 84
thistles, 19, 68
thornapple, 150

thyme, 36, 39, 132, 133, 150, 162
tints, 14
tisanes, flower or herbal, 42, 138, 161-2; Clove Carnation Tea, 162; Linden Tea, 162
toadflax, 41
tobacco flowers/plant, 61, 89, 93, 150
tomato leaves, 150
tones, 14
triangular shapes: asymmetrical, 25-6; equal, 23-5, 74
tulips, 10, 11, 12, *26*, 56; artificial, 100, *101*, 102-3
Turkey red oil, 138
tussie-mussies, 56

V
valerian, 136, 150
verbena, 93
vetch, 41
vine leaves, *45*, 48
vinegar infusion, 138, 139
violets, 12, 14, 41, 42, 69, 148, 150; candied, 154

W
wallflowers, 19, 89
walnut skins (for deepening brown hair), 139
wedding day flowers, *60*, 61-5
wild carrot, 150

wild flowers/plants, *14*, 41-2, 43, *43*
willow, 45, *57*, 68, 69
winter jasmine, 23
wiring flowers, *64*, 64-5
wooden containers, 34
woody nightshade, 150
wormwood, 150

Y
yarrow, 68, 80, 139
yarrow tisane, 161
yew, 12, 55, 56, 123, 150

Z
zinnias, 11, 12, 45, 48, 66, 93

Picture Credits

Alan Duns: endpapers, half title, 8/9, 68, 72/3, 90, 91, 92, 97, 132.
Ray Duns: 29, 66, 87, 101, 105, 106, 110/1, 113, 117, 119, 123, 124, 130/1, 135, 137, 146/7, 158.
Laurie Evans: 4/5, 156/7.
Nelson Hargreaves: 13, 14, 16, 16/7, 18, 22, 24 (t, b), 26, 27, 30, 31, 32, 39, 43, 81, 83, 163.
James Jackson: 153.
Di Lewis: 149, 161.
Peter Reilly: 2, 6, 15, 21, 25, 36/7, 38, 40, 44, 45, 49, 50, 53, 54, 57, 58/9, 60, 62, 63, 64, 67, 71, 75, 121, 126/7, 129, 139, 140, 143, 145

Acknowledgments

The publishers would like to thank Joan Green and Micky Scammell for making the artificial flowers on pages 105, 119, 123, 124; Clive Ross for making the small roses on page 119; Dorothy Ross for making the flowers on pages 101, 106, 110/11; and Sue Trenchard for making the flowers on page 113.

The publishers would also like to thank Ronnie's Fresh Flower Stall, Berwick Street Market, London, for supplying most of the flowers photographed in this book, and Albert Weaver, Master Baker, of Wethersfield, Braintree, Essex, for making the flower loaf and rolls.